'Frank, exacting and poignant … Jonathan Jansen's account is an odyssey into South Africa's colour-separated private spaces and serves as a bridge and glimmer of possibility. A must read!'
— *Professor Thuli Madonsela*

'What a powerfully South African story Jonathan Jansen shares with us here. He writes with a combination of elegance, empathy, compassion and insight such as few others can. Our deep thanks to him.'
— *Professor Crain Soudien*

'For those who admire Jonathan Jansen for his flaming courage in confrontational truth-telling, this engrossing memoir is a treat – heart-tugging, richly crammed with Jansen's quirks and humour and griefs. It is more than an account of how a vulnerable, impassioned young man gained the stature and authority Jansen now wields: it is an account of our country's history, the grievous failings of the past, and, perhaps more sadly, even, those of the present, but also of the hope that hard work, principled action, commitment to justice, and above all, education, given boldly but humbly to the younger generation, offer to us all.'
— *Judge Edwin Cameron*

'Jonathan's faith helped him to navigate his life, his loves and his stellar career. This memoir shows beautifully how his faith underpinned his commitment to reconciliation and the things that unite us in the face of angry opposition and despite the strain it caused him.'
— *Archbishop Thabo Makgoba*

'This book is both intellectual blockbuster and emotional roller coaster, a journey into the razor-sharp mind of South Africa's best-known educationist as well as the warmth and passion of one of our nation's most generous hearts – I was challenged to think and moved to tears.'
— *Reverend Professor Peter Storey*

Breaking Bread

A memoir

JONATHAN JANSEN

Jonathan Ball Publishers
JOHANNESBURG & CAPE TOWN

All rights reserved.
No part of this publication may be reproduced or transmitted, in any form or by any means, without the prior written permission of the publisher or copyright holder.

Text © Jonathan Jansen (2024)
Cover image © Jonathan Ball Publishers photographed by Brenda Veldtman (2024)
Published edition © Jonathan Ball Publishers (2024)

Published in South Africa in 2024 by
JONATHAN BALL PUBLISHERS
A division of Media24 (Pty) Ltd
PO Box 33977
Jeppestown
2043

ISBN 978-1-77619-358-5
ebook ISBN 978-1-77619-359-2
audiobook ISBN 978-1-77619-447-6

James Matthews' poem (chapter 3) is used with permission. Every effort has been made to trace copyright holders and to obtain their permission for the use of copyright material. The publishers apologise for any errors or omissions and would be grateful to be notified of any corrections that should be incorporated in future editions of this book.

* To protect the privacy of certain individuals, names have been changed.

jonathanball.co.za
x.com/JonathanBallPub
facebook.com/JonathanBallPublishers

Cover by Rudi Louw
Design and typesetting by Melanie Kriel
Set in Adobe Garamond Pro

To my mother, who taught me to stand up for something
and
To my father, who taught me to stand up when I fall

Contents

Author's note	ix
Introduction	1
1. Unlikely union	5
2. Seeing the light	34
3. An inspiring teacher	59
4. Undergraduate struggles	83
5. Back in the classroom	109
6. New horizons	136
7. University leader	162
8. Reconciliation broker	191
9. Development activist	221
10. Learning lessons	247
Coda	261
Index	263
About the author	270

Author's note

I use the word coloured with great reservation. It is a political classification that gained legal status and social import as an everyday separator between whites and Africans. The consequences have been devastating for relationships across these stigmatising categories. That said, I recognise that 'race is an enduring fiction that draws real blood'* and that as a writer, to ignore its operations in society without further commentary is to sustain its value for those invested in difference.

All quoted references from scripture (in italics) come from the King James version of the Bible, the one on which I was raised, whose prose still beguiles, and which remains more familiar to me than other translations.

* Words of Robin Kelley (2016) reflecting on the book of Jeff Chang, *We Gon' Be Alright: Notes on Race and Resegregation*, Picador

Introduction

Like most memoirists, I started this project with two hesitations. One, who could possibly be interested in reading about a life that was in long parts ordinary? And two, what should I leave out?

The first was resolved when Gill Moodie, a superb editor from Jonathan Ball Publishers, persuaded me that a personal memoir would enjoy broad public interest. I had been asked before to pen a memoir but kept putting it off because I did not think there was much to say. I also felt that this is something you do in your 70s and 80s. But then I was confronted with the problem of memory, something that creeps up on you in your 60s. I was forgetting things about my past. This was not good. I wanted to write from memory as much as possible. That was the deciding factor.

The second hesitation will never be resolved. I have included many of the critical incidents in my life but omitted some for various reasons. I do not want to embarrass friends and family. Vague or contested memories did not make the cut. Things that were important to me but not necessarily as significant for a reading audience were also left out; resonance with your readership is an ever-present consideration for a writer.

There was an added problem with what to include, since my life is an open book. In many of my writings I have already told parts of my story, from a tribute to my mother in *Song for Sarah* to ten insights shared with youth in the book *Learning Lessons*. Nor can one write a weekly newspaper column for more than a decade without sharing much of oneself. 'You'd better say something new,' said my publishing editor when I told her of this dilemma. Readers of my other writings will indeed find much that is new in that I share content not made public before but also because this first book-length account of my life puts together the story in a different way than the snippets shared in other writings.

In the months of writing first drafts of the manuscript, I asked friends and colleagues (and one or two strangers who work in bookshops) about what they would like to see in a memoir of this kind. The most common request was that I write about how I became the person I am today. I wrote mainly with that in mind and hope the forces and fortunes that shaped me thread through the ten chapters.

I do not plan in any detail the writing of a book, whether a memoir or a curriculum theory text. I make the plan by writing. This means the first version is a rough draft which will be rewritten 10–15 times until I feel satisfied that the story holds together. It is something I now do comfortably since I come from the school of writing which insists that you 'get it down before you get it right'.

Because of memory challenges, I have tested individual sections with friends who were part of that chapter of my life. I do not, for example, remember what I was really like at school – at least to others – so friends from high school offered invaluable feedback during the writing months. Nor do I remember finer details from my University of the Western Cape experience. Once again, fellow students provided the plaster that filled the cracks. Family input was critical, especially for the more sensitive parts of our history that include incest and land theft.

I should have anticipated that thinking back to difficult moments would loosen some scar tissue. I found myself emotional at times remembering difficult things like the disappearance of my father. I had buried those feelings deep in my soul and had to grapple with them to tell this story faithfully. Other challenging moments are recorded here and I leave it to the reader to trace these inflection points in my life's journey.

An important goal of this memoir was to give readers a sense of time and place with respect to my upbringing. My personal story would be bland without understanding the social, educational, political, cultural and religious milieus in which I was formed. Put differently, this is not simply the straightforward story of a grateful life but one of a resilient community on the Cape Flats.

In this context I tried not to be overly judgemental of the conservative, evangelical church community which gave me my founding values. I happily point out the positive influences from my church life but also the harm caused by things like missionary racism and religious exclusivism. Readers will no doubt see that I left this church but that in many ways it never left me.

There is little value in using a memoir to go after your enemies. I have read too many such books. For the most part, I speak positively of the people who made me possible with the necessary gratitude. There are two exceptions, though, and they are violent teachers and racist lecturers; to ignore their influence in shaping me would leave gaping holes in the memoir. I am grateful to them too, if only for teaching me how not to be in the journey of life.

I spent much time thinking about how to incorporate the influences of my immediate family on my life and learning. It is an issue because throughout my career we have had a tacit agreement that I would not drag the family into the fray when it came to the everyday challenges of a campus leader who was also something of a public nuisance for taking contrarian positions on education and politics.

But a memoir is different, and I wish it to be known that nothing I have achieved would have been possible without the bonds of family, by which I mean Grace, my wife, and Mikhail and Sara-Jane, our children. I dealt with our intertwined stories in two ways – through inclusion in the general text where appropriate and as discrete sections in different chapters.

The best memoirs, I read somewhere, tell a story about a life that is bigger than oneself. I like that very much and try to draw from the minutiae of my life the kinds of lessons that I hope fill in that bigger story which, as the title indicates, is about 'breaking bread'.

Enjoy.

1
Unlikely union

*'Don't worry that children never listen to you;
worry that they are always watching you.'*
Robert Fulghum

And God said to Abraham, Sarah thy wife shall bear thee a son and thou shalt call his name Isaac. That's my parents and the name of my younger brother. Except they were not characters from Genesis 17. These were the members of a Cape Flats family headed by an improbable couple.

For years I wondered about the statistical chances that an Abraham and a Sarah would even cross paths somewhere in this vast land. They were different in every way. Abraham Christian Frederick Jansen was English-speaking, Sarah Susan Johnson was Afrikaans. He was from Denver Road, Lansdowne, in the bustling city of Cape Town. She was from Mark Straat in the rural, picturesque town of Montagu. Dad was Anglican while Mom belonged to the Dutch Reformed Mission Church, the segregated one for coloured people.

The tall Abraham was shy and reticent among strangers while the shorter Sarah was mostly at ease with people regardless of station. Abraham came from a working-class family, raised in a wood-and-iron home by an alcoholic father (his mother died when he was a little boy) whose children became chars and factory workers.

Sarah, on the other hand, was comfortably middle class with respectable parents whose children went to work as nurses and teachers from the large home they lived in before it was cleared out for whites. It was not only the 180 km from Montagu to Cape Town that made theirs an unlikely union.

Then as now, people from upcountry areas moved to the Cape for jobs. Sarah (and later her relatives) made that trip to work as a nurse at

Brooklyn Chest Hospital, which served patients with tuberculosis. There she met another nurse and future lifelong friend, Rosalind Flanders (later Moore), who belonged to a fervent community of evangelical Christians called The Brethren. They gathered in churches called assemblies, and Rosalind took Sarah to a gospel service at the Athlone assembly where she became born-again (converted, in common parlance) and, in time, a devout believer. She left the Dutch Reformed Church for good because there you could smoke, dance and drink and still enjoy church membership without having to repent. Not that Sarah did such things; the Johnsons were not those kinds of people.

Abraham also came under the influence of the Athlone assembly through one of its outreach programmes and was saved from his sins. Gone were his debauching days in clubs where Abraham and his sister Edith were known as accomplished dancers. Redeemed, Abraham entered the ascetic world of the Brethren.

Abraham and Sarah were married by Sam Moore, an Irish missionary who 'laboured' among the coloured people, 'planting churches' across Cape Town. The couple's task now was to give their children biblical names. I am Jonathan David, the eldest, named after two men who expressed deep love for each other in the Old Testament. David says of Jonathan, 'thy love to me was wonderful, passing the love of women'. No, I'm not going there.

My brother who arrived after me carries the name of Jesus' disciple, Peter, though there is no possible parallel between the two unless the disciple was into squash. Naomi, the Old Testament woman followed faithfully by her daughter-in-law Ruth, came between the two boy pairs in more ways than one, often the cause of fights between us. Isaac followed, as if required of parents named Abraham and Sarah. Teasing, I would sometimes tell my audiences that I wished my parents, too, would offer up our Isaac as a sacrifice.

And then the deviation. My youngest sibling was Denzil, named after the son of the English madam for whom Abraham worked as a domestic (Dad had many jobs over the years) in Rondebosch; I never got to ask my father what he was thinking in naming this cute baby brother after a white madam's boy.

The act of naming your children after biblical figures was not uncommon among Brethren parents. Sometimes I felt it was to prove your holiness: 'hey look, their kids have Bible names', though I figured out early in life that the naughtiest children were often the ones with the holiest names, like my friend Peter de Vries and my cousin Phoebe Rademeyer. 'Think carefully before you give your children Bible names,' said someone on social media. 'Last night I was robbed by Moses.'

I would not be able to compose this memoir without recognising how the faith of my parents shaped my life, learning and leadership in deep and enduring ways. It was a faith that taught me good values that abide to this day. It was a faith that taught me bad values that I have spent a lifetime trying to overcome.

Abraham and Sarah's early life together was not easy, a story my family could knit together from a treasure trove of handwritten letters shared between the young couple from courtship through the first years of marriage. The content of those yellowed notes written on Croxley stationery swung like a pendulum between love and business. Affection the one moment, practicalities the next: I will be coming to Montagu by train to visit you my love, writes Abraham. When are you coming, I need you here, says Sarah.

The first years of marriage were tumultuous as the newly married Jansens tried to figure out where to settle down. The urgency would be resolved if Abraham could find permanent, well-paying work. He left Cape Town to work in Port Elizabeth (PE) while Sarah stayed in Montagu with first-born Jonathan. The letters reveal a strain in the relationship because of the distance between them.

Early photographs show the couple with the little boy in Kleinskool, the residence of Brethren friends such as the Benjamin and Hendricks families. There was a Brethren assembly at the entrance to this small settlement on the outskirts of PE, marked to this day by a little petrol station. Things did not work out there so the couple moved to the southern areas of the Cape Flats, 750 km from PE, setting up home in a council house in Steenberg near the schools my siblings and I would attend. Years later, Abraham and

Sarah moved to the area next door called Retreat because the house there had one more bedroom to accommodate the revolving door of Montagu relatives looking for work in Cape Town.

You never owned a council home (that became a possibility only near the end of apartheid). You paid rent to the city for decades while remaining landless tenants. The irony was that many council dwellers had their own homes stripped from them to make way for whites. With a stroke of a bureaucrat's pen an area would be declared white, followed by forced removals to the wastelands of the Cape Flats. Only years later would I understand the full social and economic impacts of dispossession, the most important being the inability of black people to transfer property from one generation to the next – resulting in the enduring racial inequalities so visible in South Africa today.

To fit a family of seven and upcountry relatives into a council house meant sharing beds into the teenage years. Naomi and one or other aunt shared her bed, something my sister deeply resented as she entered her teens. For the boys, the obligatory double bunk that made spatial sense in those small rooms. There was a small kitchen, one toilet and another small space promisingly called 'the dining room' which you entered through the front door off the street.

Somehow, the plasticity of the mind helped make this council house a livable space. It did not seem small to us as children, in part because such confined spaces were 'normal' and in part because there were many ways to move furniture around to accommodate family and friends.

How visitors from the church and relatives from elsewhere fitted into that dining room remains a mystery. But we were happy around the table. There was lots of laughter, jokes, reminiscences, teasing and much more, but not before a solemn prayer by Abraham. At least it was only one prayer; Grandpa Johnson in Montagu would pray before and after a meal in Dutch: '*Segen vader, geven eten, laat ons nimmer u vergeten. Amen.*'

Christmases were the best because Abraham shared a birthday with baby Jesus. That is, if you believe Jesus was born on 25 December. There was a dilemma, of course. Abraham expected two sets of gifts, one for Christmas and one for his birthday. One year, I bought a pair of socks and split them into separately wrapped packages, one for each commemoration. The birthday boy was only mildly amused. Still, there are routines around the table of working homes that build family, friendships and fortitude despite the lack of things.

Birthdays meant a cake, singing and a gift. Those gifts were predictable though. In your early years, a colouring book and crayons; as you grew older, a small Bible or concordance. Sarah would come into your room very early, sing a song and read an exhortatory text about a young man or woman from the Bible. Before you were saved, a crisp message of the need to repent was intertwined with 'happy birthday'. After you were saved, there was another biblical text about keeping your eyes on the Lord. But no birthday passed without some admonition from on high.

Abraham had his own rituals of birthday greetings, such as when he wrote this text inside a card for his beloved Sarah, a praise song of patriarchal bliss from the Old Testament book of Proverbs:

> Who can find a virtuous woman? For her price is far above rubies
> The heart of her husband doth safely trust in her, so that he shall have no need of spoil
>
> She looketh to the ways of her household, and eateth not the bread of idleness
>
> Her children shall rise up and call her blessed, her husband also, and he praiseth her
>
> Favour is deceitful, and beauty is vain; but a woman that feareth the Lord, she shall be praised

Back around the dinner table at 51 Tenth Avenue, Retreat, the drama was endless: the cat had disappeared. Spotty the dog had been run over by a car. A relative in Pacaltsdorp, the home of the Jansen clan near George in the Southern Cape, had died. In more hushed tones, an unmarried sister in the church had fallen pregnant; it was the end of the world when this happened. There was also unspoken drama when the police came looking for Isaac, my activist brother who slept on the upper bunk near the window in the back room so that when the banging on the door happened at 2 am he could slip easily into the dark. The swine never caught him.

The drama that did the most personal damage to my childhood psyche involved a young nurse who burst into our home and sat quietly in one of the chairs that flanked the little half-moon table with its jar of fading flowers. Because No 51 was a corner house, all the travails and turmoil of the avenues descended on our home. Behind the house were majestic white dunes through which people had trampled a path that ran directly past the northern fence of Crestway High School all the way to Retreat train station. You saved a good 20–30 minutes with this direct route through the dunes, but it could cost you. Behind the minor dunes and in the bush alongside were all kinds of hoodlums who could ambush you for hard-earned money or violent sex.

I still remember the image of that woman, possibly in her mid to late 20s. She had a round, beautiful face with hair slightly out of place for a nurse. Her exterior was calm but those big wide eyes told me she had been through some brutish hell. I scanned her face for a clue and then I saw it, halfway down her white, starched nurse's uniform: a trace of blood. Even in my mid-teens in the closeted environs of our home, the horror started to register. This woman had been raped in the dunes.

This disturbing event told a much larger story about Sarah's house. Outside it there was trouble – from alcoholic fathers and violent gangsters to drug lords and deadbeats. Inside there was calm. I became aware that I was living in a bubble in which hardworking, sober parents applied a no-nonsense regimen of values that upheld truth and shunned turpitude. And nobody was more of a target than the eldest son.

I was told this repeatedly: you are the eldest, set the example. The weight of moral expectation fell on my shoulders. I could not, for example, attend my matric ball, the event that marks the end of your school years and where you say goodbye to close friends from five years of high school – even longer if you attended the same primary school.

I was emotional when as a 17-year-old I tearily asked my mother in the kitchen: 'But Mommy, why can't I go to my matric ball?' Those who grew up in English-speaking homes on the Cape Flats would know that when your mother switched to Afrikaans, a powerful, non-negotiable message was about to hit your senses. Her response? '*Meng jou met die semels dan eet die varke jou op!*' I did not think of my friends as pigs (*varke*) or matric functions as littered with pig food (*semels*, broken husks). But the metaphor did its job. In this Christian home you would not risk your faithfulness to the Lord with a night of sinful partying. Deviate, and the punishment was swift.

Of course, like any other child, I tested the rules. So, when my primary school announced that we were all going to the Quibell family's Princess Bioscope on Retreat Road to watch the recorded 1968 Olympics, I decided to go despite the enormous risk. I rationalised that this was, after all, the Olympics, not one of those romantic movies with kissing and stuff. So off we marched in straight, teacher-managed lines, my face part-covered with my school jersey in case one of the Brethren aunties reported me to the domestic authorities.

I thoroughly enjoyed the Olympics and the novelty of watching athletics on a big screen in the dark. I still remember the shock and excitement of seeing Bob Beamon breaking the world long jump record. But there was an unease. I would hear later of a Brethren friend whose mother marched down the dark aisles of a makeshift movie venue calling after her daughter.

Conscience is a horrible thing, and you were always threatened with the ultimate judgment: what if the Lord came while you were sitting in this den of iniquity? The 'rapture' of believers was standard doctrine in the Brethren. The second coming of Jesus while relaxing at Quibell would have been poor timing for sure, but my main task now was not to be seen on the way home from the bioscope.

By the time I got back home to 51 Tenth Avenue, Sarah had already plucked a leafy branch from the Port Jackson tree hanging menacingly over the front gate. Somebody must have run home and told the family matriarch. That evening, I did all the disciplines of the Olympics in my parents' bedroom. I jumped onto the bed. Under the bed. Onto the lower cupboard. Around the chair. Top bunk. Bottom bunk.

Sarah did not just beat you. She took you through the hiding in a one-way conversation delivered in staccato rhythm. '*Laat. Dit. Vir. Jou. 'n. Les. Wees.*' It was the language switch again, which meant she was angry. Let. This. Be. A. Lesson. To. You. Every thrash of the twig was a single word. I tried to explain that it was the Olympics, not the wrong kind of movie. The retort was swift. '*Moet. Nie. Vir. My. Sê. Bokdrolletjies. Is. Rosyntjies. Nie.*' It was worse when Sarah went metaphorical. Do. Not. Tell. Me. That. Buck. Droppings. Are. Raisins. So much for playing the Olympics card.

All my friends in Tenth Avenue had a slightly different version of their beatings. 'Wait till your father comes home.' Their deferred beatings were reserved for the more menacing and muscular of the two parents. The man of the house would return from work to be informed by the wife of some transgression, then dispense punishment. That would not work at No 51 because Abraham was the softie, the good cop. He found it difficult to inflict pain on anyone, let alone his children. Sarah was the enforcer, and I knew from tense whispers through their bedroom wall that she would have loved him to 'put his foot down' with the kids.

That did not mean Abraham never became angry. He got hold of me once at a point when he was very upset. I remember the moment clearly. The boys in the street were playing soccer under the light of the lamppost in the early evening just in front of the house. Abraham shouted to me to bring in the empty dirtbin on a day when the council rubbish truck would have collected the domestic waste.

I heard my dad, but every time I was about to fetch the bin the soccer ball came tantalisingly close to my feet. This went on for a while as I drifted towards and away from the bin, ignoring Abraham's entreaties. Then, out of the blue, I felt myself rising from the earth. It was Abraham lifting me by the scruff of the neck. He threw me through the air in a perfect parabola so that I landed head-first in the empty bin. My soccer buddies howled with laughter. Abraham, in the colloquial language of the Cape Flats, had snapped. He never touched me again.

Punishment was central to Brethren teachings. *Train up a child in the way he should go and when he is old, he will not depart from it.* Since both Abraham and Sarah worked, there was always one or other auntie to keep an eye on us after school or during the holidays. I was convinced they were psychopaths. For the slightest infringement they would launch into us.

Not greeting quickly enough. Not coming indoors fast enough. Not making your bed neatly enough. Not responding to an instruction appropriately enough. Yes, Auntie Margie. No, Auntie Edie (the one from Kalbaskraal near Malmesbury). Yes, Tietie Omi. Whack. A shoe, a slipper or a belt. Sometimes the Jansen boys and a visiting cousin were locked in a room and Auntie Margie would climb into us with one of her *sloffies* (soft shoes). These aunties were energetic. No need for yoga or Pilates in those days. Thwacking children was their stretching regime.

For these beatings they had cover. You dare not complain to your parents, for there was an unshakeable assumption that governed adult discipline: there must have been a reason that Auntie X gave you a hiding.

This logic extended to another disciplining institution: school. Teachers would beat you with a cane for the slightest infringement. Coming late. Not doing homework. Getting a sum wrong. Forgetting to return a library book. Any reason whatsoever, and you knew that complaining at home would almost certainly lead to another hiding; there must have been a reason. So, you simply said nothing.

Of course, those were the days before human rights, children's rights or any rights at all. Today, parents bring lawyers to school. Corporal punishment is banned, at least in policy. Hitting a child is a serious offence that can get a teacher fired. Older teachers explain the increase in school violence and the bad behaviour of learners in relation to the new disciplinary regime.

For Abraham and Sarah, punishment was locked into their belief system as fundamentalist Christians. *The wages of sin is death*. I had memorised that verse from Paul's letter to the Roman church among many others threatening pain and even extinction. *It is a fearful thing to fall into the hands of a living God*. Shudder. Evil must be admonished.

Sarah's strict regime of truth and punishment was not, however, restricted to her own children. She was known to apply the law to anyone within her circle of friends who trespassed in plain sight. The Dawson boys, in their middle to late 20s, regularly encountered her wrath.

One day I witnessed a miracle. One of the Dawson boys had made his way over the dunes then turned sharp right at No 51 to proceed about 150 metres down the road to the home of their mother, a kind and respectable woman whom Sarah held in high regard. As usual, the Dawson boy was drunk when he turned the corner. The brothers hoped to make that turn when Sarah was on duty at the hospital.

I watched the fearful chap navigate the corner and, thinking the coast was clear, stagger gleefully homewards while holding our little fence for balance. Then, horror of horrors, he saw Sarah bent down doing her gardening. I watched as their eyes met, then all hell broke loose. Sarah stood up slowly, balancing herself with one hand on her knee and the other pressing down on a sharp garden shovel. The poor man was immobilised, partly due to shock and partly because Mrs Dawson had taught her boys to be respectful to other adults.

Sarah was now facing the drunk Dawson boy over the flimsy wooden fence. 'You are a disgrace to your mother. She is a decent person who taught you right from wrong and yet you come past my house drunk and without any shame.' This went on for a few minutes. Immobilised, he stared straight ahead with unblinking eyes.

Then the miracle. The Dawson boy thanked my mother for the reprimand, composed himself and began the short journey home. I swear to this day that the young man who moments earlier was swaying all over the place walked in an upright position, leaning only slightly backwards while executing goosesteps that would have made a Russian soldier proud.

As I peered over the fence, I was convinced my mind was playing tricks on me. The Dawson boy had been miraculously cured and, in biblical terms, walked away *clothed and in his right mind*. There is nothing funnier than a drunk man trying to convince the law (the cops, Sarah) that he is sober by trying to walk upright.

That rigid application of Sarah's law caught my friends off-guard as well. Because No 51 was alongside the dunes, there were always children playing with slides made from paraffin cans. You cut open the can, bent the sharp sides inwards so as not to cut yourself, made sure the smoother inner part of the can was facing down and applied a liberal coat of candle wax for speed. Then you made your way to the top of the dunes and slid down in one of two ways. You could sit and have some control over the speed of descent. Or you could lie on your stomach and fly through the air as you hit the inevitable bumps in the dunes, usually caused by a submerged tree stump, all the way to the bottom.

After a couple of hours of this, you were thirsty and tired, and what better place to find refreshment than the house right there on the corner – especially if you did not know better. I remember a boy coming to the door covered in sand and with hints of a runny nose.

'Water please, Mrs Jansen.'

'Just wait a minute.'

Sarah disappeared into the bathroom and started running a cold bath as she prepared the necessary equipment. Then she returned to the front door, led the unsuspecting youngster to the bathroom, and scrubbed him with Sunlight soap until he was spotless. Shivering and covered in a towel, the poor kid downed the glass of water with audible gulps, never to return to the corner house. The word got around.

I often wondered why adults were so committed to inflicting pain on children. Gradually it became clear that this was all they knew as parents. It was, in fact, how they were disciplined and a lot of this became clear as I listened to Abraham sharing memories with his sisters, especially Auntie Edie from Port Elizabeth and Auntie Doris from Bishop Lavis, the more regular visitors to No 51.

One of the stories they reminded each other of was the day my grandfather decided to punish one of his little girls for an act of wrongdoing. He took her hand and pressed it onto the fiery stove plate. They bellowed with laughter as they recalled this cruel and inhumane act of their father. '*Wie nie wil hoor nie moet voel*' (those who will not listen must feel pain) was one of Sarah's favourite sayings.

This strange relationship with one's parents in those days was not only defined by constant punishment; it was also noteworthy for the absence of demonstrable love. These were the days before Oprah and giveaway hugs. Your parents did not say 'I love you' the way we do routinely these days with our children and grandchildren. I do not remember being hugged by either of my parents. It certainly did not mean you were unloved; they just did not show it through words or PDAs (public displays of affection). You understood you were loved and that was enough. More than that, the fact that they worked so hard for you was supposed to be sufficient evidence that your parents loved you.

Sarah was the hardest-working person I have known. She would toil for a full day at the hospital, come home to make dinner, go to church, return and prepare meals for school the next day, corral the children to ensure chores and homework were done, then prepare us for bed. Afterwards, she would take out the Singer sewing machine and repair a torn pair of school trousers or knit jerseys for the Brethren to take to the poor in small upcountry areas over the weekend. By the time she dropped into bed, she had time for only a few hours' sleep before returning to work.

The stress would sometimes show, especially when Sarah worked the night shift, a 7 pm to 7 am stint, at the nearby orthopaedic hospital. She would arrive home just in time to prepare us for school and clean the house. The few hours' sleep would often be interrupted by knocks on the door, a persistent hawker or a sister from the church 'popping in'. Sarah was unfailingly gracious and would rise from her bed to entertain the visitor. Soon she had to get ready for work again. After the third night or so, Sarah would be edgy and you would hear her saying things in Afrikaans with deep emotion: 'I work my hands to the bone and you cannot even make up your bed.' At that moment we knew our mother was struggling.

Abraham saw little value in hard work (I have learnt from the English how to duck the truth with language, so I will not use the word 'lazy' because he was my father, after all). He was the happy-go-lucky guy everybody loved. He changed jobs often, from domestic worker to stationery clerk to driver for a laundry firm to fruit-and-veg hawker to general driver to full-time missionary. I recognised early on that my dad could not hold down a job because he did not apply himself fully.

This became even more obvious when Abraham was a driver for Nannucci Dry Cleaners. The job entailed picking up dirty laundry and dropping off the pressed clothing when it was done. It was hard work, so Abraham hired 'boys' who went from door to door delivering suits and dresses on hangers, with plastic covers protecting the clothes.

These young men were characters. One became a pop star in the Cape while another is said to have run into trouble with the police for trying to kick out the back window of a City Tramways double-decker bus. His defence? The bold print on the window read: '*Stamp die ruit uit!*' Apparently he did not see the fine print: 'in case of emergencies'. It was the same boy who, in an attempt to show my father he was literate, proudly read him a bold headline in the *Cape Times*: Cape to Ten Rand. It was actually CAPE TO RIO, the annual yacht race to Brazil.

It was hard, sweaty work but Abraham sat in his car doing little else other than driving, writing receipts and collecting the money.

After school and during the holidays, my brother Peter and I would be the boys doing that job. This was where I saw what was really happening. Abraham had a route which took him by the houses of Brethren families in suburbs such as Gleemoor and Rondebosch East. He would leave us in the laundry van then stop at a favourite home and spend an hour or two drinking coffee and eating snacks. We could hear the laughter coming down the passage. Abraham returned without any laundry before doing the same at the next home of believers. Eats, laughter, no laundry. Here was the problem: he was paid on commission. No laundry, no money. I was not in the least surprised that my father eventually moved on to another job.

Now he could be his own boss, hawking fruit and veg. Abraham could wake up late, take as many breaks as he wanted and close early. Once again, I would watch him as the bakkie filled with produce from the Maitland market made its way down the avenues. Then it happened: 'Ag, Mr Jansen, I'm a bit short this month. Can I get some potatoes and carrots and I will sort you out on Friday.' Unbelievably, Abraham would grab a healthy portion of what was asked for and give it to the beggar. 'Don't worry about it. Sort me out when you can.' Needless to say, the business went bang.

It was at this point that Abraham made desperate plans. After another job as a messenger/driver for a shipping firm on the Foreshore, my dad decided to become a full-time missionary to Rietbron, a small town in the Karoo. There was no consultation. Abraham came home one day and announced his decision. To say there was consternation in the family would be an understatement; his income, however small, helped keep us afloat even though we all knew it was the predictable and more substantial salary of Sarah that made the difference.

Sarah made a decision that day that defied Brethren norms. She would not be the obedient sister following her husband to a godforsaken Karoo town. For this she paid a price, not the least being one of the senior elders 'throwing *skimp*' (sarcasm) from the preacher's platform about women who refuse to accompany their husbands into full-time ministry. Sarah was no flaming feminist but this thing about men making decisions for women that throw the entire family into disarray was simply not on.

Abraham took a small caravan and lived among the people of Rietbron, preaching the gospel, making converts and planting a church. He spent much of his time writing to Brethren churches asking for money. At least he no longer needed to work fixed hours for a boss.

Then tragedy struck. The details are unclear but it appears Abraham was making doughnuts in the little caravan, a process that used boiling oil. He might have fallen asleep but somehow the oil fell all over his body, leaving deep holes and scars on his back and, for some reason, leading to memory loss and severe mental disorientation.

Abraham was treated for his burns then placed in a mental hospital back in Cape Town, where he remained for all intents and purposes what the locals call 'a vegetable'. One day, nurse Sarah decided this was enough. She brought her husband home and healed him. Before long, he was back to his regular self, entertaining drop-ins and making his '*flou* jokes' (weak or dad jokes), as they were called on the Cape Flats. Abraham was happy at home but we were still a salary short.

Sarah soldiered on as the sole breadwinner until retirement. There was the customary celebration party at the hospital, then she left for good. Except the next morning I found my mother all dressed up in her starched white uniform with nurse's cap and red name badge. Sarah was ready to go to work as she had for decades. But work was no longer there. Tears were running down her face.

When friends and strangers ask about my 18-hour workdays, I know this comes from watching my mother Sarah work.

Abraham had other qualities. He loved people, especially those on the lower rungs of the ladder of life. This is where he felt more comfortable. As a result, Uncle Abie, as he was called, was the person to consult when you were in trouble. There was the young brother who was constantly castigated by his father-in-law, a senior elder in the Brethren, because he did not meet the standard for his daughter; the chap was now homeless. Another young man wanted to know how to stay faithful; 'the best time to pray', Abraham advised, 'is when you don't want to pray.' And there were any number of young mentees who wanted clarity on one scripture or another.

A free spirit, Abraham took risks all his life. He could not afford a car but he bought one anyway. What this meant was that the cheap, second-hand vehicle would break down all the time, much to the irritation of the more sober-minded Sarah. It became a joke among the cousins that Abraham would drive us in a car from Cape Town to Port Elizabeth then return in another one or need to have the jalopy fixed by his best friend, Uncle Gollie (Goliath), who was his brother-in-law. The risk of walking away from a salaried job to become a missionary, or any other dubious venture for that matter, was easily justifiable because 'the Lord will provide'.

Abraham's faith was sincere. When he prayed at home or in church he dropped to his knees. It was not proper to stand before the living God. To humble yourself in this way was to recognise the might of God and the weakness of the supplicant. When he prayed or preached, I felt moved by my father's sense of the divine – and by this humble hawker (or whatever job he was doing at the time) who regarded others as more important than himself. He was one of the best preachers I could listen to because of his skill at making complex ideas simple; this was one of his favourites as he taught the distinction between the biblical concepts of grace and mercy:

> 'Grace is God giving you what you do not deserve
> Mercy is God withholding from you what you do deserve.'

The humility with which Abraham lived his life came at a cost to a self-conscious young teenager. One Saturday, he took me on a trip to minister to a family of poor farmworkers in the rural areas outside Cape Town. I might have been 12 or 13 but still remember the strong and unpleasant smell from the floor of the spartan outhouse where the labourers lived; I believe the floor was made from horse manure. It was early morning and therefore breakfast time.

The family placed enamel bowls of stiff porridge on the table; there did not seem to be much else in the house to eat. Then, to my horror, I saw a thick collection of flies on the plate of porridge in front of me sucking up the sugar that covered the meal. There was no way I could eat this *pap* and I looked at Abraham to confirm my decision.

My dad looked back with an unspoken message in his determined eyes: 'This is all they have; the family is watching us; you will eat the porridge.' With a lump in my throat, I slowly made my way through the porridge with a giant spoon while swishing away flies with my free hand. It was a lesson about humility that remains with me.

These were the kinds of experiences that made me aware of class gradations. The people serving porridge were poor, living off *papsak* (cheap wine) payments to farm labourers and small amounts of cash. They were completely dependent on the white farmer and did not own the basic brick building in which they lived. Abraham also grew up poor, but in the urban areas of Cape Town. Alcohol ruined his father and his only brother, Uncle Alfie, meaning there was no income apart from what the children brought in by doing menial work as chars, delivery 'boys' or factory workers. Work was precarious and workers dispensable, which meant Abraham's family was always between jobs.

Sarah's salary kept us hovering at the lower end of the lower middle class. We did not own our council home but there was the occasional car. We struggled to pay off lay-bys but there was always something to eat. We all had school uniforms even if they were handed down from the older boys to the younger ones, with elbow patches covering the wear and tear on a blazer. We paid small amounts monthly to Flanders for Funerals so that when a family member died the coffin and graveyard plot would be affordable. We sold syrupy doughnuts on a Sunday to cover emergencies. These were the fragile threads that kept the Jansens afloat.

Many families living in the avenues during my childhood hung on precariously to their lower middle-class status. You did not notice class differences on the Cape Flats as clearly as when apartheid ended. At that point, most middle-class families moved from council houses to the *koephuise* (fancier houses in the suburbs which you could buy) and their children to the former white schools. Families from even more derelict flats moved in. Fine lines of class and culture meant you could easily backslide into relative deprivation.

I also gained consciousness of those class gradations when I first ventured into the world of teenage romance. In the senior years of high school, I became aware of a beautiful young woman called Patience, the daughter of my mother's best friend, Rosalind Moore. We had met each other at family and church get-togethers but now I saw her differently. Nothing romantic was said but we met regularly at Grassy Park library, which had a selection of classical music records. Patience studied piano at Livingstone High School and I pretended to know my Bach from my Brahms. After, listening to favourites on headphones, I would walk her home.

This went on for a while until one fateful afternoon. Her father, Uncle Walter, was working under the bonnet of his car. As we approached Patience's house, he looked up and I could see from the frown on his face that he smelt a rat (me). Coming over to me, he saw a needleworked patch covering a hole in my corduroy trousers and put his finger in there to open up the tear that my mother had tried so hard to conceal. His smirk was the message: you're not my daughter's class. My pride kicked in and I decided not to pop the lingering question to Patience. Years later, she married Dr Dreyer and they were the perfect match.

What kept the Jansens on the respectable side of the class line was an exceptionally strong sense of values inspired by their brand of evangelical faith. Chores were part and parcel of a strict code of discipline. We trampled blankets in baths of water. We slid on thick cloths to shine the floor in the small living room. We took turns washing, drying or packing away the dishes. We polished shoes, washed windows, made beds and, as we got older, helped to prepare meals.

Being the eldest, and with the corresponding burden of 'setting an example', I did more than my four siblings. I had to prepare their school lunches, make breakfasts that vacillated between Jungle Oats and mealie meal, and boil the rice for dinner when Sarah returned from her day shift. One of those eldest-boy routines was doing the Saturday morning 'shopping for the week', which meant going down Retreat Road to buy vegetables from a greengrocer, meat from the butcher and other odds-and-ends as far as a nurse's money would stretch.

Respectability was a big issue for barely middle-class families. It was what distinguished you from homes in the area whether the father was a drunk, the mother swore, the house was always untidy, the teenage daughter was pregnant, the children fought in the streets, everybody smoked and nobody went to church except at Easter and Christmas.

The symbols of respectability were on display in the decent council homes. A Bible was prominent on a side table. Immaculate doilies were neatly positioned in the dining room. There was always a beautiful picture of a green landscape or children learning around a globe. Often, the picture depicted a giant eye of God hovering over a path that splits into a broad road 'leading to destruction' (hellfire) and a narrow road to the gates of heaven. It is broad for a reason: most humans are going to hell. It was the chosen few, like the Jansens, who did the right thing in raising God-fearing children.

To maintain this image of respectability, the family was determined to communicate the fact that they were doing well, thanks to God's grace. One of those routines amused me then and now. Close friends of Abraham and Sarah would often come for dinner after the gospel meeting on a Sunday evening. I enjoyed witnessing the love and respect these church friends showed each other, the warmth as they told stories about their children and, with lowered voices, the gossip about a brother struggling with smoking (a demon) or a sister who secretly danced at a local nightclub from time to time (a serious demon).

Amid the banter and good humour, Sarah would call me or one of my siblings. 'Listen, run to the shop and get me Romany creams, Eet-Sum-Mor biscuits and cream crackers with a chunk of cheese.' Then the redirection. 'But go and come back through the back door.' The fellow believers were to think that these goodies were in the cupboard all the time, as behooved respectable people.

It was freshly baked doughnuts, however, that made Abraham and Sarah particularly popular among the Brethren and the broader community. Abraham was the maestro behind this Cape Flats delicacy; Sarah got into the business much later. He would rise early on a Sunday and make the dough before cooking it in hot oil, dousing the doughnuts in syrup and sprinkling them lavishly with coconut. Knocks on the door started early: 'half-a-dozen doughnuts please.' The margins were small but these sales made a difference. After church, the believers would arrive for their portion at a discounted rate or, if Abraham was selling, 'sort me out when you can.'

It was a happy childhood in which food played a central role. Family and friends came all the time. At Christmas, Auntie Doris could be relied on to bring her famous chicken pie for her older brother. But she also brought her favourite stories that would have Abraham roaring with laughter as if he was hearing them for the first time. One of those tales was about how Auntie Doris confronted one of her growing well-built sons. Terrence had reached the age where he would stand his ground with a posture that appeared to challenge his rather petite mother. 'I stood back and lifted my leg and showed him a karate kick to the chin.' Abie was sitting, eyes closed as he laughed, one leg kicking furiously back and forth, as was his habit when having a good time.

There were patterns to the food. On Sundays there was a pudding, normally jelly and custard in summer and sweet potato or sago pudding – again with custard – in winter. There were no puddings during the week unless one of us had a birthday. On Thursdays, Abraham would come home early from his work as a laundry driver and join us on the field alongside the house to kick the soccer ball into the distance before returning indoors to prepare dinner – always a strong curry that only he and I could eat.

It was also not unusual in those days for Monday's leftovers to appear inside Tuesday's school sandwiches. It worked well with meats, less so with stews, though cabbage or beans kept overnight was tasty with chutney, even if it did soak through the bread a bit. But it was the Sunday roast with one or two slices of beetroot that made the best school sandwiches on Mondays; on such days, you did not share your lunch with a fellow student who had conveniently left his at home.

Perhaps the most important lesson I learnt from my parents about generosity with food and friends is this: when you give freely to others, you never lack anything. Not once did I go to bed hungry even though the little we had was shared with all and sundry. It is a mystery that remains with me to this day. The blessed couple had a verse for this: *Be not forgetful to entertain strangers for thereby some have entertained angels unawares.* Those angels coming through our home must have put on a hell of a disguise.

I learnt that the family table was about much more than food. We were breaking bread together. It was how community was built. Bringing together their friends from church around a table guaranteed that their children would in turn become our friends. To this day, most of my friendship circles are the children of our parents' friends; sometimes you even married them. Such close-knit communities built enduring bonds of companionship and solidarity over generations.

I grew up in this bubble that created an unreal world. Outside lurked great danger. Gangsters were everywhere. Young men my age circulated in and out of prison. Others ended up in one of the two nearby cemeteries in Grassy Park and Muizenberg. I was aware of the perils but also the seductions. Fortunately, I had the compelling example of my parents.

I noticed that they never fought with each other; yes, whispered arguments came through the thin walls of the council house but nothing serious. Abraham never raised his hands against his wife, though this was not uncommon up and down the avenues. In a disagreement, Abraham was usually the one to back down even though there was a scripture hanging over their heads giving direction: *Wives, obey your husbands.*

One day the bubble burst.

Abraham disappeared. I was in my first year of university and fell into deep despair. Sarah said nothing. As so often in a personal crisis, she became even busier and tears flowed down her cheeks as she pummelled dirty dishcloths in the little sink. I sensed that this disappearance had nothing to do with getting lost somewhere or even a separation between them. But I could not put my finger on the problem because Sarah said nothing.

Weeks passed. One day, Uncle Willem, a dear old man in our church, gave me a letter and asked me to pass it on to my father. He was cheery and happy to see me, so at first I suspected nothing. But as I walked home, something told me this letter might explain our father's strange absence. So, I did something I had never done before – I opened a letter addressed to one of my parents.

The bottom fell out of my life. A woman was demanding to see my father. He had spent time with her, she had a lot of bleeding afterwards and she might need to see a doctor. Could he come by and assist her.

No, not my father. He was an elder in the church. Nothing he ever did suggested he did not love my mother or care for us. Maybe he was set up? As I sat on the dunes above the house, I knew one thing: I could never let my mother see this letter. It would break her heart a million times over.

I looked up at the wire fence running around the perimeter of Crestway high school on the other side of the dunes. For the first and only time in my life, I contemplated suicide. I felt empty inside like never before, drained of all joy. All kinds of calculations went through my mind. How high up the fence would I have to string the rope to hang myself? I sat there for hours. Eventually I got up and went to see one of the senior elders in the church so he could deal with the matter. I gave him the letter and made it clear that my mother was not to see its contents.

Not long afterwards, Abraham returned home. I have no idea what he and Sarah talked about but she appeared from the bedroom with a moist but determined face to make sure we all understood that things were to continue as normal. I wanted to hug my mother but that was not what we did. I was angry with my father and avoided him as much as I could. It was difficult even to greet him, and I sulked around the man who was my hero.

One day, my father had had enough. As I walked past him in the little council house on my way to campus, he lashed out. His basic message as he shouted was that I respected my lecturers more than I respected him.

I hardly greeted. That was not how they had raised me. I needed to stop this behaviour and start respecting him. I was shocked; not by what he said but that this gentle man could say it at all.

What I could not tell him in response was how he had broken my heart. I could not tell him how I had boasted to my friends about my dad's amazing memory. What was hard to say in that moment is how I used to look forward to him coming home early on a Thursday and, without fail, coming onto the makeshift field alongside the house and kicking the ball much further than Sammy's father next door, who actually played amateur soccer. Given the chance again, I would have told him how proud I was of my father's passionate preaching – with eyes closed – as he warned of sin and destruction. Most of all, what I could not tell him was that I loved him more than ever and that I was so glad my daddy was back home.

I listened and absorbed his anger, frustration and pain. In that moment, I had no words.

During the years that followed, a lot of mending of relationships took place. Mom and Dad seemed reconciled; for that generation, big people's problems were not their children's business. Gradually, I engaged my father again on all kinds of subjects and pretended to find his dad jokes funny.

'Man goes for an operation. Afterwards, doctor tells him there is good news and bad news. "The bad news is I amputated the wrong leg. The good news is the other one is getting better." ' I actually did think that was funny (if horrific), but after ten tellings it became a bit much. We patched things up without actually talking about patching things up. It was the way things were in those days. My father was back and things seemed normal again except for one unspoken hurt.

In the Brethren, if you commit a terrible sin you are 'put out of fellowship'. Other churches call this excommunication. It means you no longer sit with the true believers in the inner circle on a Sunday morning for the breaking of bread. Other churches call this communion. You sit at the back. It is the ultimate humiliation. Abraham really struggled with this, though I think he simply stayed home on Sunday mornings while working on his return to 'full fellowship'. What hurt even more is that he could never again be an elder. It was how the Brethren rolled.

He did, however, become active in preaching again and threw himself into evangelical work that eventually became a full-time commitment. Things felt normal and the family of Abraham and Sarah moved forward.

My parents did fairly well in school by the standards of the time. Both got what was called the 'JC', or Junior Certificate, which meant they completed Standard 8 (now Grade 10) and were therefore qualified for a reasonably good job as a clerk or a nurse. Few black people did matric in those days. Abraham went to a somewhat prestigious black school, Livingstone High, which became known for the quality of its teachers and the eloquence of their politics. Giants such as Neville Alexander and RO Dudley became household names in the Cape and Livingstone students carried themselves with a bit of an air.

Sarah, on the other hand, finished primary school in Montagu. But in rural black towns, the high school was for the few white children. Blacks became boarding students in larger towns like Paarl or Worcester. Sarah did her JC at Noorder Paarl High School, where she did well enough to qualify to become a nurse.

Abraham was the smart one. He could memorise Bible verses with remarkable fluency. Memorising random things was his gift. There was the standard joke at family get-togethers that his cousin Martin Marks called him one day when his car had been stolen because the police needed the registration number. Abraham obliged.

On trips to PE, he would take us through our paces as other cars whizzed by. One car would pass the other way with CBS as the starting letters on the number plate. 'Yes?' he would ask. None of us knew. Mossel Bay. CX? Knysna, he would inform us. CZ? Beaufort West. This could go on for a long time. He revelled, too, in his remarkable memory of historical events big and small.

Because of their church, neither Abraham nor Sarah was into politics. *Your citizenship is in heaven.* But they had a keen sense of injustice. You remember into adulthood your parents' emotional states as much as anything they might have said, and I recall Abraham's sadness when Martin Luther King Jr was shot and killed. I remember the heaviness in his emotion when he spoke of the six million Jews murdered by the Nazis. Those memories stay with me not because of the facts of those tragic events but because of the emotions with which such knowledge was transmitted from father to son.

Having been achievers in education by the standards of the day, it was important to Abraham and Sarah that all five of us matriculated. At the time, that was rare for a large family. The more common story on the Cape Flats is of one child being yanked from school to go to work and lighten the family's economic burden. There were two candidates for removal: the older child or the less promising one academically. There was usually some resentment on the part of the child sent to work which went something like this: 'I had to go to work so that you could study.'

Not the children of Abraham and Sarah. All of us were shepherded through matric (today's Grade 12), even our youngest brother, Denzil. He was the nicest kid, a high jump champion at school and popular among his friends. Denzil, however, found academics a much less interesting pursuit. I loved having a kind, generous and playful baby brother. Whenever I returned home from studies abroad he was the first to hug me and grab my bags. Small things one remembers.

Then tragedy struck.

On his 21st birthday, Denzil was driving home one or more of the church youth after a celebration along dark farm roads in an area called Philippi, not far from the family home. A horse ran headlong into the car, instantly killing this wonderful human being. I received the news while celebrating Christmas on the Stanford University campus in the Bay Area of California. Our South African friends had travelled to the west coast that December from Duke, Harvard and Chicago so we could be together for the holidays. I had to leave them and find money for a ticket home. The Stanford alumni office gave me what amounted to an advance for a book and I flew back to Cape Town.

It was the death of their child that gave me new insights into Abraham and Sarah. I heard that when my father got the terrible news in a telephone call around midnight, he did not scream or question. No performance. He woke the family, called them into the dining room, told them Denzil had died and fell on his knees to thank God for his baby boy's life. Inside, he was torn apart. Outside, he was the calm leader of the household. It was perhaps the greatest gift of a father to a son: impulse control, the ability to manage your emotions in a crisis.

Sarah was a little different. She, too, did not perform her emotions for everyone to see at events such as funerals where loved ones would wail their very public grief. But you would know she was hurting when her eyes teared up and filled her beautiful, olive-skinned face. This happened when Denzil died but also when she received news from doctors at Groote Schuur Hospital that the cancer in her bowels had spread too far and there was nothing more they could do. The family should make her feel comfortable in these last stages. The usual messaging, in other words.

I happened to be travelling for work from Pretoria through Cape Town on my way to Oudtshoorn and decided to sleep at the family home. 'I have something to tell you,' said Sarah as she guided me to the living room. It sounded serious. She never talked to me like this. We sat down together. Sarah told me of the bad news and then, without warning, cried intensely for about 15 seconds as I watched in horror and heartbreak as the one who had carried me into life told me hers was almost over. Then, as suddenly as she had started, she stopped, looked up at me, and asked: 'Tea?'

On my way to the ostrich town the next morning, I had to pass through Montagu, where my mother and I were born. There is an intriguing 'entry' into the town, a little archway of rocks 'built by the Italian prisoners of war during World War 2', Sarah used to tell us. I parked my car to the side of this structure near one of the riverbanks that complete this beautiful area of the Boland. Then I sat down outside the car to have a good cry as I imagined the hundreds of times my mother must have passed under this archway to go to high school, seek work, find love and return home.

That journey was not always easy, I discovered. The young Sarah did not only move from Montagu to Cape Town, she left the Dutch Reformed Church for something very different: an evangelical church. That break with the family church in which her eldest brother, Johnny, was the choirmaster and her brother-in-law a deacon could not have gone down well. Sarah also made a decisive culture shift – she would raise her children in English. Since I first gained some kind of family awareness as a child, I knew the Jansen children were looked at differently by our cousins.

Every weekend visit, every school holiday, going to Montagu meant feeling a certain kind of strangeness among cousins, a visible aloofness. They did not even try to speak to the Jansen children in the only language we spoke well enough. You had to work to fit in, which we did. And yet at the back of my mind I knew this burden was felt even more strongly by my mother who had, in her Montagu family's estimation, given up important cultural bonds of faith, language and culture.

Still, I felt out of place in the Montagu family. There were no hugs from our grandparents, no squeals of joy and delight when we came through the door after a long trip from Cape Town. Pa Johnson was a nice man; he had a round face like his daughter Sarah and I only knew him as blind. His roots were Jamaican. But he did not 'see' us and could not do much apart from being pleasant with all who came through his grand home in the *dorp* and, after the forced removals, his small township home.

Ma, on the other hand, was ice cold, almost angry. Her name was Kulsum, a descendant of Malay slaves. '*Basta*' was her favourite word, meaning, in a child's ear, 'stop that nonsense'. Even when she visited us in Cape Town, she was removed, staring for hours through the council house window and not saying much to her grandchildren. It was weird.

Over the years, I tried to figure out that casual aloofness from the Montagu grandparents and most aunts and uncles. Was it because children in general were not taken seriously in those days? Was it because there were too many other grandchildren with their own children who lived in the area for us younger ones from the Cape to even be noticed? Or was it because these were Sally's (Sarah's given name by her family) children?

Being accepted by Abraham's family was different and the same. My Jansen grandfather was often drunk the few times I saw him as a little boy. I don't think he had any sense of us as grandchildren. From a few available letter exchanges between Pa Jansen and my father, there is not a single reference to the new baby or toddler Jonathan. Most of the content has my grandfather asking and thanking my father for money sent. It feels strange reading those letters in today's culture of doting grandparents. Pa Jansen's second wife was pleasant enough but we were not her own grandchildren and, again, there was no warmth, let alone whoops of joy when we visited the Lansdowne home.

And yet in each family there was at least one aunt who was overjoyed to see us, spent time talking to us and made special cookies for us. On Sarah's side there was Auntie Emmie (Emelia) in Montagu, who took great delight in Sally's children. I adored her. She looked so much like my mother it was scary, and they were similar in their mannerisms, both warm and generous. On Abraham's side, there was his sister in PE, Auntie Eddie (Edith), who was the one I could confide in, especially during my teenage years. She spent hours with me, talking about 'the things of the Lord' and offering practical advice about everything from girlfriends to life goals. Unsurprisingly, it is her children who are our closest cousin friends today. From those early childhood experiences, I learnt a vital lesson: that just one caring adult in the extended family can make a lasting impact on the children.

Most of the adults around us were not like Emmie or Eddie, so you did not really know them. You could not ask deep questions about family origins or strange relatives. Nothing like that until we became much older. Suddenly, older family were willing to talk to you and share buried secrets about things you could only wonder about as a child. Questions like where do the Jansens come from and, more ominously, where does Auntie Violet fit in?

The Jansen clan has its roots in the Outeniqua area and especially Pacaltsdorp in the southern Cape, a segregated coloured township outside the white city of George. My dad's oldest surviving uncle at the time was Uncle Hans, the younger brother of my grandfather, David Jansen, from whom my second name comes.

Uncle Hans would sit outside the family house in Pacaltsdorp, opposite Londt's garage, and watch the world go by. On our way from Cape Town to PE and back, Pacaltsdorp was the halfway house for tea or something more substantial. Years later, I stopped by the old house. Now a teacher and later a professor, I was warmly welcomed by Uncle Hans with a loud pronouncement of the clan name, 'Jansen!'

After a few such visits, I started to piece together a story. One day he was sitting in the same area when a couple of white men marched towards him and threw some plans in his direction. 'These are yours,' the rude men said. They turned out to be plans for the fairly fertile strip of land on which Uncle Hans lived. The visitors, by his account, were the white Jansens who must have experienced a tinge of conscience and decided to give back what was not theirs. It fell to Uncle Hans to share this news with the family and make plans to divvy up the extensive property. But there was a snag.

Uncle Hans had already built a big family home on the land, and several smaller homes, as if it was his alone. Now, he divided up the rest of the property with a fatal mistake that forever soured relationships with one part of the family.

His parents had eight children altogether including a daughter, called Eva, who died in childbirth. Eva had married a white man whose surname was Marks. But when Eva died her mother was also pregnant, so here was my grandmother feeding her own child on one breast and her daughter's child on the other. This arrangement led to a deep schism between the children of the Markses and those of the Jansens.

When Uncle Hans divided the land among his nieces and nephews, including my dad, he left out the Marks family, the children of his late sister. The reason for this ridiculous decision I will never understand, but the bitterness it unleashed spanned generations. Some Marks will still not talk to me or my siblings. One of them, after a hearty dinner I organised, told me this injustice was why God punished the Jansens by killing my youngest brother in that horrific car accident. I was furious at his absurd reasoning but at the same time became aware of the deep hurt that lingered on that side of the family. None of the Jansens got rich with this scheme and I later found that Abraham sold his small plot because he could not afford the rates.

Another puzzle about the Jansens would also shortly be resolved. Where did Auntie Violet fit in? She was always off to the side during visits to the

Pacaltsdorp house, quite reserved and more or less pleasant. But there could be little doubt that Auntie 'Vi' was not mentally 100 per cent.

In my early teens, I could not fit her into the family structure. She was clearly not my dad's cousin in any straightforward sense. She had a child, but that did not help in placing her. When I asked the question as a young boy it was slapped down with such ferocity that I knew never to ask again.

Years later, I was able to piece together the story from snippets here and there extracted from older cousins, half of a concession from my father, and some common sense. It was perhaps the Jansen family's deepest shame.

My great-grandfather had slept with his daughter, this act of incest producing Auntie Violet. A shadow at all family gatherings, Auntie Violet was there physically but was hardly acknowledged socially, emotionally, intellectually and spiritually. The sin could not be named, the sinner even less so. This was, after all, the ultimate scandal and it must have lain heavily on the mind and body of this quiet human being who could not be talked about. My great-grandfather was arrested, tried in court, found guilty and dispatched to do years of hard labour in prison for his grievous crime.

To conclude, I was formed by the unlikely union of Abraham and Sarah who carried into their marriage family histories of sin, shame and segregation. Both of their families were uprooted from their homes, losing not only property but dignity, security and self-confidence. Their joint commitment was to give their five children a fighting chance in a wicked world. For this to happen they anchored their lives in an evangelical church where your sins could be washed away. In fact, you could reboot your life because inside you, as a born-again Christian, *old things have passed away; behold, all things have become new.*

They tried hard. They believed fervently. And they raised five children by the precepts of scripture. Their discipline was harsh. Their love was measured. And sometimes they faltered.

But in their union, Abraham and Sarah never gave up.

2
Seeing the light

'Let it be known: I did not fall from grace. I leapt to freedom.'
Ansel Elkins, *Autobiography of Eve*

I preached on trains. The early morning commuter train ran from Retreat to Mowbray, from where I would take the bus to the University of the Western Cape for undergraduate studies. There were about a dozen stops on an 'all stations' train, giving us preachers enough time to sow the seed.

There was stiff competition from the Pentecostal preachers also seeking the opportunity to preach the gospel to a captive audience. They were even more fiery and entertaining than those of us from the mainstream evangelical churches like the Brethren who did not speak in tongues or swing from the chandeliers. The pattern, though, was familiar. We would wait to board the train at Retreat and as soon as the doors closed, the first brother to jump up and command the crowd would have the slot on this suburban line. '*Ek groet julle in die wonderlike naam van Jesus!*' That was pretty much code for, 'I'm on' (and not you other contenders).

Afrikaans worked much better here in the packed third-class carriage. English was more appropriate in the first-class carriage where the more *sturvy* (uppity, pretentious) people sat with their newspapers and fancy clothes. On the other hand, you would be silly to preach in that section of the train because you would almost certainly be chased off to third-class where you could take your chances.

Nobody asked the third-class passengers for permission to shout in their ears that early in the morning. Some responded respectfully. Men would take off caps or hats. Women would bow in silent prayer, putting their hands together. Believers would share an 'amen' when a juicy statement was made or a potent verse recited. Others just stared at the ceiling or through the train's thick windows. I often wondered what the Muslim passengers thought, especially since Christians living near mosques would sometimes complain about the call to prayer waking them up in the early morning.

After an initial disappointment that a Pentecostal brother had jumped up first, I quite enjoyed some of their preaching. It was a mix of gospel promise, deadly threat and high entertainment. Promise: *whosoever believeth in Him shall have eternal life.* Threat: the Bible says that when you go to hell there will be weeping, wailing and gnashing of teeth. Entertainment: and for those of you who do not have teeth, teeth will be provided (that the prophecy might be fulfilled, I suppose).

No such extravagance when I or the Brethren brothers preached. Just straight down the line gospel messages which alternated between the citation of a biblical verse and a pointed exposition thereof. One hand waved the Bible, the other held onto the overhead handgrip or the upright pole as the train swayed from side to side.

A fine line separated the mainstream evangelical churches from the Pentecostals all around us. Their faith was much more exuberant. They would run, jump, weep and wail, unencumbered by the formalities of faith. Someone giving a testimony would speak openly about their sin or their salvation. Bodies quivered under the influence of the Holy Spirit and there were 'catchers' for those who fell over under the spell of a pastor's prayer. Drums, keyboards, guitars and tambourines all made a joyful noise unto the Lord. The first time I attended a Pentecostal church, I got a splitting headache.

The Brethren tolerated the Pentecostals and the less buoyant versions of evangelicals, such as the Baptists and the Docks Mission believers. At least they were going to heaven, like us, even if they were the victims of poor doctrine. The Anglicans, Catholics and Dutch Reformed people, on the other hand, were headed straight to hell because they did not believe in salvation by faith, performed child baptism and did not preach the gospel. These people also permitted all kinds of sins that should have disqualified them from breaking bread. The Muslims and Hindus were so far out, they did not stand the slightest chance of entering the pearly gates. My role as a preacher was to be crystal clear about the dividing line between the redeemed and the condemned, and what better place to convey that message than the suburban train line?

My journey to becoming a train preacher was somewhat predictable. If I had to pinpoint a moment that started my journey of faith it would be a moment outside my aunt's home in PE at 51 Sayster Street in Bethelsdorp Extension. They, too, had been forcefully relocated to this house on the outskirts of the city from their large and lovely residence in the now-white suburb of Fairview.

I was playing soccer with my brother Peter and cousin Epaphras on the street outside Auntie Edie and Uncle Gollie's home. Suddenly, the door opened and out came a group of Brethren women who had been at a sisters' prayer meeting. One of them came straight towards me: 'Johnny, I want to tell you that even before you were born, we were praying for you.' Then, and as the years passed, I was bowled over by this enormous act of grace. These adults cared about me while I was still in the womb. Put differently, I was bound to this community even before I opened my eyes.

The track towards salvation from there on followed a clear path. Years of Sunday school as a child. Conversion in my early youth. Conviction that I should be baptised. Then sharing my public testimony and, in time, a platform to preach the gospel with an older brother before venturing out alone as a train preacher. You were, of course, under pressure from the moment you gained consciousness of the world around you that in the Brethren you are expected to be born again. Like many in the church, I was born into the Brethren without having a clue about how this immersion in the faith would become for me a life-altering experience.

Though established in Ireland early in the 19th century, the church was more commonly known as Plymouth Brethren because of a powerful movement in the UK city of that name. It was a group that broke away from the establishment Church of England. Shortly after the new church was formed, there was a more radical breakaway called the Exclusive Brethren, as opposed to the one which Abraham and Sarah called home, the Open Brethren. The Exclusives were even stricter on membership.

Much later, the Open Brethren experienced another kind of breakaway called Chapels. They were less doctrinaire than the Brethren though still fashioned on the same basic teachings and the preaching of the gospel. But they could bring in a band and open the platform to men who were not necessarily from the Brethren assemblies but known to be solid teachers of the Word. Most of the Chapels were found among the white assemblies.

You knew you were in a traditional Brethren church when you heard people pray in old English. To this day, the faithful churches address God in words like 'thee', 'thou' and 'thine'. It became increasingly awkward for young believers, especially those who went to university. When you switched to 'you' and 'your' in community prayers, there was no resounding 'amen' at the end. You knew you had drifted from the truth.

Regardless of form, what these new believers sought was a simplicity of worship. There was no elaborate liturgy or ordained ministers. They did not regard themselves as a denomination and were proud that their church did not have a name. One day we were travelling to the beach in our little car with the neighbour, Auntie Lilly Fredericks and her children, packed inside. 'There's Mrs Jansen's church,' blurted Auntie Lilly as we raced down the M5. 'No', said my mother, 'the church is the body of believers; that's just a building.'

The Brethren took the literal Bible as their sole authority on matters of doctrine. Only men could preach and women had to cover their heads. Adult baptism was reserved for those who became saved (born again). They prided themselves as fundamentalists on teaching the Word to edify believers and they believed in the second coming of Christ, something that could happen at any moment. If you died before this event, the rapture, you went straight to heaven as a born-again Christian: *absent from the body means present with the Lord.*

On that basis the believer would come into fellowship, which meant sitting around a small table on a Sunday morning where, after some preliminaries (praying, singing and perhaps a short Word from one of the men), the bread and wine were passed around. Those sitting at the back could only observe and a visitor without a letter of commendation from another assembly, regardless of their Christian status, would have to sit at the back as well.

Any sign of exuberance was out, and this showed up most clearly in the role of instrumental music. At the breaking of bread on Sunday mornings, all singing was a capella. One's mind was to be devoted wholly to the Lord and an organ or a piano could detract from that task. An accordion accompanied us at open-air gospel meetings, presumably to keep us all singing in tune and to attract the attention of passersby.

In the gospel meeting a piano or an organ was allowed, and the more permissive assemblies allowed both. Those of us who played these instruments knew you were not to attract attention to yourself, whether you could read music from the hymnbooks (*Sacred Songs and Solos* or the *Believers Hymn Book*, depending on the service) or whether you played by ear.

I loved playing the piano but in the Steenberg assembly where I started, my best friend was more accomplished. Archie Dick (we called him Lennie so as not to confuse the son with his father of the same name) was trained in piano by the white music teacher on the other side of the Retreat railway line. He played the Western classics with ease and the gospel hymns with the necessary reserve. Another friend, a guitarist, was frogmarched out of the Lansdowne assembly with his guitar by an elder called Peacock. It was regarded in some places as the instrument of the devil, which you could understand when you saw how those rock 'n' rollers twisted it around their bodies.

To this day, many assemblies do not have a band or a worship group leading the singing, formulae for highly successful and more charismatic mega-churches as far as attendance is concerned. Even with the limited instruments available, it was also important how you played. Nothing ostentatious, or you would be rapped over the spiritual knuckles.

We all felt sorry for an older brother, Bill de Jager, who was an accomplished jazz pianist before he met the Lord. I used to watch him closely and memorise his incredible chords for my own rendition of *Love Lifted Me* or *I Come to the Garden Alone*. But we all knew Uncle Bill was consciously censoring himself, even though every now and then he was tempted to do 'the roll', that playing out of a tune so that your fingers rolled from left to right across the keyboard. When he did that, he would look at me with a twinkle in his eye. But that was at a home gathering, not in the church.

Good music could, of course, lead to dancing, and you were on the edge of hell if you moved your body, a serious restriction on the saints. The more liberal churches had no such restraint and I remember their retort to us traditionalists, 'Why should the devil have all the good music?' as they danced to the gospel tunes.

To this day I can't dance. I feel self-conscious when I move. When my daughter insisted on the father-daughter dance at her wedding I was terrified but dared not show it. So, I did the dance and my friends assured me that the video went viral; what they did not add was 'for all the wrong reasons'. It is hard to explain how a prohibition from your growing-up years can still affect your body movements decades later.

There was one more evil that was prohibited in Brethren homes and that was the accursed television set. As houses around us started to get small, affordable TVs, we were left stranded. I stole out of the house to watch a neighbour's black-and-white set from the fence outside. At the beginning, some believers' homes did have TVs but then a European missionary told a well-circulated story from Brethren platforms. He had ordered a TV for his household but when it arrived, the large box carried a caption: 'Bring the world into your home!'

This was clearly a sign from God, so the brother packed up the TV and sent it back. After all, it is standard teaching in the Brethren that *you are in the world but not of the world.* The world, in Brethren teaching, is a reference to all the evil out there, and while we might live in this world as Christians, we cannot be part of it.

Of course, there were Brethren who allowed a TV into their homes with sometimes hilarious consequences. Uncle Jack was overruled by the teenagers in his home, so when he came in from a Brethren meeting he would walk holding the Bible against his face to shield him from the abomination in the corner. My Uncle Gollie referred to the two antennae springing from the TV as the horns of the devil. And a great-aunt of my wife asked me to help her fetch a box from the cupboard in her bedroom. Entering, I saw a television set. 'Don't worry, my boy,' she explained, 'I only use it to watch the epilogue.' In those days, the apartheid government started and ended the limited hours of programming with some dominee doing a Bible reading and a prayer.

This was the fundamentalist faith in which I was raised, and which shaped in powerful ways the person, parent and professional I am today. Until my mid-20s, I threw myself fully into the work of the church as a youth leader and a gospel preacher to the point of exhaustion, for this happened at the same time as I was studying at university and starting a family.

The routine of activities was energy-sapping. The high point of the week was the 'breaking of bread' on a Sunday morning. Then Sunday school in the afternoon followed by the open-air meeting where you preached to people with a loudhailer or simply the exertion of your voice. In the evening was the gospel meeting, followed by an informal get-together at a believer's home. Monday was the prayer meeting and Tuesday the cottage meeting, where you preached the gospel at someone's home. The elders might have a midweek business meeting but Thursday was the Bible study. Friday was an off night, Saturday was the youth meeting.

Then the Sunday routine all over again. Those were only the official meetings, for any number of informal events could be arranged, like a youth trip up the mountain or visiting those who were ill or suspected of backsliding. It was tiring but also fulfilling.

There was so much about growing up in this church that I enjoyed and appreciated. I was drawn to the simplicity of worship. Nothing extravagant, just bread and wine *to remember the Lord's death until He comes*. I loved the clear and simple message of the gospel, nothing complicated: *Repent and be converted that your sins might be blotted out*. I found comfort in the certainty of the teachings of scripture: *The Lord is my Shepherd; I shall not want*. I found the promise of a new life something to look forward to amid the struggles of everyday living on the Cape Flats. *In the twinkling of an eye*, we would be gone when Christ returned to fetch the church.

No doubt my fundamentalist faith made life easy here on earth. For every question there was an answer, for every anxiety a comfort, for every problem a solution. And I was convinced of the truth of the gospel, not only because of the claims of scripture but because of the witness of lives.

I saw first-hand the transformation of the lives of men and women who were gangsters, alcoholics and drug dealers. Something happened to ordinary people that changed them in deep and enduring ways. Like Tony

Cooper, who had been a feared gangster across the Cape Flats. Anxious mothers would hastily pull their children into the safety of the house when he came down the road with his troops. Short, dark-skinned and with piercing eyes, it was hard to believe this warm, generous and captivating soul was once a figure of fear in the avenues. I could not argue with the evidence before me about the transforming power of grace.

But I also saw people in the middle classes without the more obvious afflictions of the avenues testify to lives that were more meaningful and joyful after their born-again experiences. Like one of my best friends, Neal Dreyer, a dentist, whose life was hollow before salvation at a gospel meeting in the City Hall transformed him into one of the most visible testimonies of decency and devotion that I have seen.

Though not talked about, that transformative power of the church was also evident in the lives of members without much formal education or social standing. Men and women who were barely literate would, over time, learn to read the Bible, memorise key verses, understand complex stories and communicate through preaching and teaching. The Brethren, with its tradition of lay ministry and its focus on the literal Word, would make generations of working-class and poor men and women literate in apartheid society.

As impressive were the ways in which the church would take a lowly council worker or toiling artisan and elevate him to high leadership as an elder or a deacon. Some made that transition from being followers in the week to leaders at the weekend with difficulty. How do black people disempowered for so long suddenly know how to lead without expressing the worst imitative behaviours of their bosses during the week? One person who struggled was elder Luck, who struggled with the concept of meeting decorum and would on occasion find himself carried out of the church horizontally after a disagreement at a business meeting.

Others, like Uncle Japie James, were born for leadership. His strong democratic instincts and leadership common sense were evident. This humble man had a good grasp of scripture but also an understanding of the human condition. I would often seek his counsel with another university student in the church even though our mentor had little by way of formal education. From Uncle Japie I learnt early on the difference between knowledge (what to know) and wisdom (how to know), even though the great leader of our church had not progressed beyond primary school.

The church therefore offered ample opportunities for leadership development, even if that was denied in the apartheid workplace of the times.

For me, one of the most enduring benefits of being raised in the Brethren was learning how to speak in public. Because of the lay-preaching tradition, those with the gift of preaching would be identified early on. I still remember the first time. The white brother could not make it from the fancy suburbs to be our gospel preacher on a particular Sunday night either because he was ill or protesters' tyres were burning on the roads into the area. One of the older brethren said: 'Brother Johnny, the speaker cancelled. We will sing a few choruses and then you're on.'

The first time this happened, I almost collapsed. What? Me? What on earth was I going to say? The next time, you wished the booked speaker would *not* show up so you could have another opportunity. You learnt to speak by observing others, and I had powerful role models. Ernest de Vries was a fearless speaker who would say things nobody else would dare say, like, 'How can you backslide when you did not slide forward in the first place?' Tony Cooper could speak with a passion that would move you in your innermost being. When the former gangster uttered these words from the gospel platform, you knew they were real, genuine and personal:

> I came to Jesus as I was
> Weary, worn and sad
> I found in Him a resting place
> And He has made me glad

And then there was my closed-eyed preacher father every now and again inserting a slice of humour into his message: 'The fact that you were born into a Christian home does not make you a Christian; no more than sleeping in the garage makes you a motor car.' That point was for many of us unconverted children of Brethren parents.

Watching these men closely since childhood meant I learnt which verses quoted while preaching made an impact on the audience. I found that a short, pointed message was much more effective in keeping people's attention (to this day I use three, seven or ten points to structure a speech). I knew there had to be a balance between instilling fear (hell) and offering hope (heaven). And I realised that the ending was everything: the call to action, which in this case was salvation.

You learnt by imitation because the Brethren did not like Bible schools or any form of further education, as I would soon find out as I prepared for university. There was always the threat that a Bible school could steer believers away from their fundamentalist moorings. After all, the Brethren had Bible studies every Wednesday or Thursday night, and they were more than adequate for learning the scriptures and 'rightly dividing the Word of truth'. Any enterprising brother who showed some initiative by referencing a Greek (New Testament) or Hebrew word (Old Testament) to clarify a passage of scripture would be frowned on. *'Genoeg exegesis'*, a preacher friend was admonished in rhyming prose, *'praat liewers van die Here Jesus.'*

And then my eyes started to open.

I gradually became uncomfortable with the exclusivism of the Brethren. Things were black or white, right or wrong. Grey is not a colour in any fundamentalist faith. When one of us brought devout Christians from another evangelical church to break bread on a Sunday morning, that person would be forced to sit at the back. There was no letter of commendation from another Brethren church. That mean-spiritedness I knew was wrong.

When a lively brother took some youth to a weekend beach outing and decided to do communion at the camp, he was severely reprimanded because 'the Lord's table does not move'. A silly attempt at reason but devastating for one generation of youth leaders after another. The breaking of bread, meant to signify the joyful communion of believers around such a sacred remembrance, was now a set of manmade laws about who was in, who was out, and where exactly the Lord's supper could be had. Even as a youngster, I knew this was petty.

When you were 'in fellowship', things were comfortable and you enjoyed the warm embrace of brothers and sisters. When you were 'out of fellowship', you instantly felt the cold and the distance from those who were once your most treasured friends and mentors. It was an unforgiving space that policed the boundaries of inclusion with the fierceness of a sect. I knew this was wrong.

Even before feminism gained a foothold in secular politics, I could not explain the treatment of women in the Brethren. There was a male chauvinism that was scary in its meanness. By this I refer not only to the interpretation of scripture: *let your women be silent in the church for it is not permitted to them to speak but they are commanded to be under obedience as also saith the law*. Men thrived on the literal interpretation of Paul the Apostle's missive with no space for deliberation on culture, history, time and place. Of course, literalism was applied selectively (none of them stoned adulterers) because it aligned with a conservative culture brought to the Cape by 19th-century European missionaries.

It was more than the silencing of women. There was a rigid and unrelenting policing of women's bodies. The length of the dress you wore to church; you would take or be given a cloth to cover your legs when seated so as not to distract the men. You had to wear a hat when in prayer; otherwise there was shame on your head. Lipstick and nail polish could get you put out of fellowship. And you dared not cut your hair, for long hair is your honour and cutting it is tantamount to disgrace and dishonour. Women wore dresses so as not to confuse their identities with those of men. And so it went, an endless number of transgressions that women could fall foul of.

My sister experienced the effect of these regulations. Naomi had joined the American group Campus Crusade for Christ, which had a lively ministry at universities. Being American, everyone wore jeans. So, she came home with these offending garments and one night put them in the washing machine, never to be found again. Our mother had made the jeans disappear and, by later accounts, they were cut into pieces.

Grace Hendricks, my future wife, also fell foul of the rules when she slightly trimmed her long hair. Her father noticed and, passing by his daughter, gave her an almighty slap across the body followed by a ban from church for some time. There were countless other aggressions.

What was at once ridiculous could take on forms of pettiness that I found disturbing even in the world of the 1970s and 1980s. A woman in some assemblies could not sing a solo unless accompanied by a man; a duet was more legitimate. There was a women's meeting where they could speak and pray among themselves, but then I discovered there was a brother sitting at the back. I could never quite figure out his role as 'the brother responsible for the sisters' meeting'. Was it to ensure that these women, infantilised by men, stuck to the fundamentalist script? Or was it to have a male report on the content of the sisters' meeting to the AGM where women were not allowed to speak? Or both?

All of this was counterintuitive when it came to real life. Everybody knew that some of these women were outstanding students of the Word and would be able to deliver much more powerful ministries than most men in the church. Women like Auntie Josie Flanders, Auntie Barbara James or Sister Joy Oliphant. We also knew as children that often the final authority in the home was a powerful Brethren sister who was reduced to silence and obedience during those few hours in church.

If women were dressed up like European ladies and men were required to wear suits (or unmatched trousers and jackets) and ties, where exactly did all of this come from? The colonials, of course, and herein lies one of the most fascinating of observations about the Brethren in South Africa. While assemblies were planted throughout South Africa, it was in Cape Town that the number of churches exploded in the coloured community – not among Africans and modestly among whites, most of whose assemblies dissolved over time.

Why did coloured people embrace the white missionaries with their European values, Western dress and dogmatic faith? Simple, said an old Brethren stalwart: '*Hulle is mos wit verskrik*' (they are enamoured by whiteness). Crude but correct. Most coloured people, caught between European culture and their indigenous African/Khoisan/Malay roots, found themselves beholden to whiteness, its values, mores and beliefs. They desired upwards not downwards, not only in their social ambitions but in their religious aspirations as well.

The white missionaries who came through our homes and churches knew this and Cape Town became a happy destination for visiting Europeans. They could live white privileged lifestyles in apartheid South Africa, all the while professing concern for the souls of the natives. They lived in white suburbs, their children went to white schools, they had shorter, separate lines at the post office, separate compartments on the train and, when they qualified to vote, they kept the apartheid machinery running while non-whites were denied the vote. A comfortable life they would never enjoy with modest means in Ireland or England.

It was left to my Uncle Joey Marks, my Dad's cousin, to teach me the basics of politics. He was a huge man with an ill-kept salt-and-pepper beard, always smiling but with the muscular frame of a man who lifted heavy trays of fish at I&J in town. Long before he became a leading light in the United Democratic Front, a mass-based anti-apartheid organisation, Uncle Joey was my mentor on race, politics and the ways of the Brethren.

He told me with thinly veiled anger about an incident involving a white South African brother from the assemblies who worked in one of the trades. Their van stopped at a missionary home and the white brother went inside for tea while Uncle Joey was left in the car as 'the boy'. He was brought tea in a dirty mug and never forgot the racial insult. One moment they were worshipping together, the next they were separated and he was reduced to the help. He told many of these stories with such emotion that a steady anger built within me about these white missionaries.

Slowly things started to fall into place in my mid-teens so that by the time I reached the end of high school and prepared to go to university, I was still devoted to my faith but uneasy about the relationships with the whites in our church. What made matters worse was seeing how the coloured believers bowed and scraped in front of these whites. When brother Anderson or brother Logan came home for tea and cake after the gospel meeting, coloured couples fell over their feet to ensure they felt at home. The best cutlery and tea sets were brought out and we were all very polite. There was much less fanfare when the black brother Oliphant came home after preaching the gospel on a different Sunday night. I was beginning to make up my mind about race, racism and the Brethren simply by observation.

It was time to challenge this hypocrisy and what better moment than the Wynberg Conference, one of the mega-activities of the different assemblies where we came together three or four times a year for Bible preaching and the communion of the saints. A stocky man at the door, the brother of my future father-in-law, welcomed believers. With my political eyes now open, for the first time I understood what he was doing. As people came in, he waved the coloured believers to the back of the hall and, with a much brighter smile, accompanied the white believers to reserved rows of seats in the front like an usher at a fancy theatre.

I had had enough of this charade, and as soon as he pointed me to the back I shot past him to the right and planted myself between the white brothers in the front row. Fred Hendricks came running after me but it was too late. I had taken my seat and he knew it would be risky to try to uproot me without making a scene. The poor man was fuming through his make-believe smile but I was determined not to move.

After that day, I was a marked man.

My problem was that I took the gospel seriously. I really did believe that Christ came to break down the artificial barriers that separated us, such as the racial classifications of the apartheid state. What does the cross of Christ mean if not only our upward, redeeming relationship with God but also our sideways, reconciling relationship with each other? Racial separation was more than wrong – it defied the central message of the cross.

There was no shortage of efforts on our part to begin to bridge these divides between ourselves and the white youth of the assemblies. One of our key initiatives was organised around a lovely camp called Wattle Park in Sun Valley near Fish Hoek, or what locals amusingly call 'the deep south' of the Cape Peninsula. The camp wardens were a progressive white couple called Duncan and Morag who I am almost sure were hippies in their former lives. A welcome escape from the narrow quarters of the council houses and the suffocating atmosphere of the church, here at Wattle Park we could talk more freely about difficult issues, including the church, race and politics.

It was a liberating experience and a small group of whites, the children of missionaries, were in attendance. Whether they were there willingly or under compulsion I cannot say, but I remember two young women in their early 20s, one of them a missionary's daughter, sitting huddled in a corner as if something terrifying was about to happen to them. They did not participate throughout the weekend despite the lightness of the event and the invitation to talk openly. We pretty much ended up talking to ourselves and to the two liberal wardens.

Back in church, the Brethren had a convenient set of laws behind which to hide and maintain white privilege and coloured subordination. The Reservation of Separate Amenities Act prevented us eating together; the Prohibition of Mixed Marriages Act from marrying each other; the Group Areas Act from living together. And so, the opportunity to worship together was a concession granted on condition that there was no common table in public spaces around which black and white believers enjoyed a meal. The racial segregation within the Wynberg hall was therefore simply another way of complying with legislation. In my mind, God's law was higher than these manmade laws so I was going to defy them.

The Maitland conference was the last straw. The usual pre-conference invitation from the hosting church said that 'tea will be provided but will friends please bring their own refreshments'. In that deceptively innocent phrase from a letter read out on a Sunday across Brethren churches lay a multitude of sins. The foundation of my Christian faith was about to be shaken to its core.

The first session of the conference was inspiring, the hymns uplifting, the prayers moving, the message motivating. Then came the lunch break, and all the black believers went outside onto the grass. They brought their cake tins (with triangular sandwiches) onto the lawn or ate from their car boots. Tea was provided, as promised.

There was just one question: where were all the white brethren and sisters with whom we had just shared a warm first session of uplifting praise and passionate preaching? I went back inside the hall and looked around. The whites were nowhere to be found. Strange. So, I walked to a door at the side of the hall.

I opened it and could not believe what I saw. There, on a long, polished table, was a feast of meat, fruit and desserts that could feed the nation. Around the lavish table sat the white believers having the time of their lives. I stared in horror, hoping against hope that what I saw was not true, a mirage. They did not even seem to notice, these European missionaries mixed with local whites, living their best lives while playing church-church in the main auditorium. My heart sank.

As the lunch break ended, everyone gathered inside the main hall as if nothing had happened. I walked out of the door of the church that day, boarded the train home and felt as if someone had punched me hard in the stomach. I had no desire to do any train preaching that afternoon. It was the beginning of the end as far as my attachment to the Brethren was concerned.

Nobody just walks away from their faith. I never did. But this organised form of the evangelical church with its rank hypocrisy on race and fellowship was too much. I lingered on, and the longer I did so, the more trouble I walked into.

I had to swallow hard as I listened to a brother preach the gospel at my home assembly in Retreat one Sunday evening. 'To whom shall I compare Barabas?' the young preacher asked. Barabas was a common criminal about to be executed for his crimes when the Jewish people demanded that he be freed in exchange for Jesus, who would then be crucified. The Roman governor, Pontius Pilate, obliged. I remember the shock registering in my emotions at the height of the liberation struggle: 'Barabas reminds me of an ANC terrorist.' While it might not jar that much today if the preacher compared the ANC to a thieving, common criminal, at the time it was deeply offensive. One misguided soul could be forgiven for such a silly comparison but I soon faced a much larger problem.

Our core group of friends were mostly first-generation professionals with degrees and diplomas in the assembly I now attended in Carrington Avenue, Athlone. Among our friends were teachers, dentists, doctors, nurses, librarians, civil servants and university academics. One of them started a youth singing group that presented a beautiful cantata. They would sing at one of the assemblies, then somebody would preach a short sermon to cap things off. All very pleasant.

One Sunday evening, the group was to sing at a white Brethren church in the northern suburbs of Cape Town; this was rare at the time. They made the mistake of asking me to do the after-singing sermon. I decided to speak on one of the most fascinating passages in the Bible that has been so thoroughly misinterpreted by the mainstream churches. It is the story of the Good Samaritan (though that descriptor does not appear in scripture) and its basic contours are as follows: a presumably Jewish man takes a trip from Jerusalem to Jericho. A bunch of thugs beats him up and robs him. There he lies in a ditch.

As Jesus tells the story, a priest comes upon the scene and walks by on the other side of the road. In the same way, a Levite (religious order) also walks by. Then, says Jesus, a Samaritan sees the poor fellow and his heart goes out to the man. He bends down, bandages him up, puts him on his donkey and delivers him to a nearby hotel. 'And if there is an overrun on the bill,' says the Samaritan, 'let me know and I'll sort you out.' Something like that.

Here is what is intriguing about this story. Jesus told it in response to a question from a smart-alec lawyer about his preaching that we should love our neighbour. 'And who is my neighbour?' asked the legal man. The priest and the Levite were clearly religious figures who were so hung up on their formulaic faith that they could not see the practical needs of those in despair right before their eyes. So far, so good, as mainstream interpretation goes.

But I believe Jesus was telling another story, I told the horrified congregation of white brethren and sisters with two rows of scared coloured singers with wide eyes in front of me. This was a story of racial reconciliation, of defying the norms of society, of stepping out of our racialised comfort zones. Here was the punchline: why, after all, would Jesus take the time to point out the religious and indeed racial identities of the priest and the Levite to contrast their behaviour with the Samaritan?

Jews and Samaritans hated each other and avoided contact. There were, in contemporary language, two different races and *that* is what Jesus was teaching us. How to cross the racial divide, reach out to each other and begin the process of healing and caring for those presumed to be different from us. Which one of the three men did the right thing, Jesus asked the smarting lawyer: the Samaritan, of course. Now, go and do likewise.

As I sat down after that short sermon I could feel the heaviness in the air. There was no polite let alone thundering 'Amen!' Nobody came to greet me as I left the building, a most unusual reaction to a speaker. I knew this was not the end of the matter, but I also knew delivering that sermon was the right thing to do. Outside the assembly there were protests in the streets and upheaval in society as the apartheid monster was coming to its ignoble end in the late 1980s. How could I preach as if we were on another planet?

More than the whites, my coloured brothers who invited me were angry. I was summoned to a meeting the Monday evening after the prayer service. They seemed mesmerised but what they mumbled was a fairly clear discontent. I was being political and should have stuck to the narrow meanings of the gospel. Here was a small opening to begin communion with the white assembly; why would I mess it up with politics?

I was mildly amused because I could see on their faces the real reason for their Anglophile anguish: I had embarrassed them in front of white people.

If you grew up in the Brethren, you would sooner or later encounter a carefully threaded together set of selective scriptures that kept you out of politics. *The powers that be are ordained of God.* I often wondered how that could possibly be true of the Nazi regime that dispatched millions of Jews and 'misfits' to the gas chambers. *For our citizenship is in heaven.* The preferred interpretation is that you should strive for a higher politics, the ultimate prize. *You are in the world but not of the world.* In other words, you are simply passing through so do what you must along the way, but you don't belong here. *Submit yourself to the governing authorities.* Auntie Rose (Rosalind), my mother's best friend, would keep chirping whenever she saw me to douse my activism: *the poor always ye have with you.* I tried in vain to give context to that statement of Jesus or his radical words in the Sermon on the Mount: *to preach the gospel to the poor, to preach deliverance to the captives, to set at liberty them that are bruised.*

But when the submissive terms of the gospel are drummed into your head from Sunday school through youth and adulthood, you begin to believe the government can torture you but, as a Christian, you must submit to the authorities. Fortunately, as I started my university life I enjoyed exposure to a much richer literature on the Christian in an evil world. I sat on the floor in one of those political safe houses in Observatory where Steve de Gruchy delivered a memorable lecture on the Christian and politics. I was exposed to the life of Dietrich Bonhoeffer, who stood up to Hitler and paid the ultimate price for his unwavering Christian commitment. And I was transformed by the incomparable oratory of Allan Boesak as he stood on a cafeteria table at the University of the Western Cape and gave me my first sense of black theology.

This is what the Brethren feared: these nice young believers going off to university and being exposed to a godless communism. But, to be honest, while this was a period of enlightenment, it was also one of fear. What happens if I have to readjust everything I believe to fit these new frames of thinking? Is it possible to be a fervent evangelical Christian and a social activist at the same time? I felt deep unease in my heart and decided to read everything I could on the social gospel. The writings of John Stott were helpful, charging evangelicals to serve in the secular world.

But there were no easy answers. The Boesaks and the De Gruchys were intellectually superb but none of them conveyed a conviction about sin, a love for the Lord and a passion for saving souls. I never sensed in their talks the kind of deep devotion that drew me to the evangelical church to begin with. Is the Bible for them nothing more than an activist script that you draw on when convenient for your politics? I wrestled for months on end with what seemed to be incompatible views about the gospel.

It did not help that back at my church in Steenberg there was more than enough preaching to discourage the few of us making our way to university, the first in a generation. *Much learning doth make thee mad.* You felt targeted. Perhaps the most traumatic of those encounters happened one Monday night after the prayer meeting. As was our practice in those days, the youth would hang around on the stoep outside the hall to chat.

Then, half-running out of the hall came Reggie Bynes, an elder who always conveyed the sense of a bumbling funnyman. He made his way straight through the group of youth, stopped in front of me and announced: 'I have also been to college. St Mary's College – at the feet of Jesus.' In other words, why waste your time at university when there is a superior institution for learning, as demonstrated by Mary when she sat at the feet of her Lord?

The encounter was simultaneously embarrassing and frustrating. I was exhausted and had worked hard to get back to church that night still smelling of formaldehyde from my late-afternoon classes in the biological sciences building at UWC on the other side of the city. What I needed more than anything else was encouragement to stay the course. Instead, an elder felt this was his opportunity to tell me I was wasting my time.

There were many other ways to remind you of the fundamentalist tract: 'God said it, I believe it, and that's good enough for me.' Billy Graham caught my attention early on when he said something like, 'People doubt whether the whale swallowed Jonah; well, if God told me that Jonah swallowed the whale, I'd believe it.' This kind of fundamentalist commitment requires that you suspend disbelief and follow the literal word wherever it might lead. My dear mother-in-law, a kind lady, loved to sing or hum hymns while doing her work at home. I often felt she reserved this one for me just as I was passing her:

> Enough for me that Jesus saves
> This ends my fear and doubt …
>
> I need no other argument
> I need no other plea
> It is enough that Jesus died
> And that he died for me

Read carefully and you get the emphatic refrain, 'it is enough', and the dismissal of any reasoning or contention that might stir fear or doubt since 'I need no other argument'. This is not very biblical, because the apostle Peter enjoins believers *to give an answer to every man that asketh you a reason for the hope that is in you with meekness and fear.* That sounds to me like an invitation to dialogue, not the shutting off of reason.

Still, I was drifting towards some middle ground between the fundamentalist faith of my church and the freewheeling political gospel of my campus. Nothing, however, would unmoor me from my founding church more than what happened next.

As a lay preacher, I was a popular choice at many of the assemblies to preach the gospel on a Sunday evening. Someone who booked me regularly was an elder at the Welcome Estate assembly. He was a mild-mannered and respectful person and I appreciated having the confidence of one of the senior believers in the Brethren churches.

Until I met his daughter.

Marrying a fellow church member would otherwise have been a natural progression for Brethren youth. You were, after all, encouraged to find your life mate within the assemblies, presumably to minimise doctrinal differences that might strain a marriage. A husband or wife from another denomination was not a good idea and marrying an unbeliever was a very bad idea, for then you would be 'unequally yoked' (like cattle, yes) and promptly 'put out of fellowship'.

A standard story was shared with Brethren youth down the ages to signal the perils of being unequally yoked. Imagine you are the believer standing on a table with your partner, the unbeliever, on the floor below you. Now, which is easier? You, the believer, pulling your partner up, or the unbeliever on the ground pulling you down? Correct. Downwards is easier. So, beware of becoming like your unbelieving partner. The physics of this two-way motion is relatively easy to explain. The spiritual lesson still eludes me.

Yet for all intents and purposes, I was the ideal candidate to marry the beautiful and charming Grace Hendricks. I did not smoke or drink, cardinal sins in the Brethren. I had completed a university science degree and was earning a decent salary. My family was respectable and the Jansens and the Hendrickses knew each other well. Grace's maternal grandparents were in fact spiritual mentors to Abraham and Sarah.

So, we fell in love and started to plan for a future together. At that point there was still the expectation that out of respect you would go to see the parents and ask whether you could 'go out' together. It was a fairly senseless gesture in my estimation, but I was not immune to following custom and respecting what the parents might expect. Even so, in my head this was a done deal. I ticked all the boxes and confidently went to see the parents on the appointed night, though with the inevitable butterflies in the stomach of a young man.

What happened next I did not see coming. Grace and I sat on one side of the living room, her parents on the other. They looked sombre. The man who booked me regularly as his gospel speaker appeared grave. I started explaining with faltering voice that we had been 'going out' for a while and would like their blessing to continue doing so since we were now at a serious stage of the relationship.

Then the bombshell. We do not approve, they said. You have not been going out long enough. This is unacceptable. And by the way, the father tells his daughter, we are going to the prayer meeting now and by the time we get back you must be out of this house. The mother said nothing, so I had no idea how she felt except to suspect that this was a joint decision delivered by the head of the household.

I felt sick and for the first time in my life I had something of an emotional breakdown. Our friend Chris Abels, a physician, provided medication to stop me hyperventilating. At unexpected moments, I found myself struggling to breathe, especially at night. This was a strange experience because I had never been ill up to that point.

What bothered me was the reason. How could a year of courtship not be enough? We were not going to get married tomorrow. Slowly the truth dawned on me: I was dark-skinned and their daughter was light-skinned. Here was a coloured family for whom a mixed marriage was not one between whites and blacks; their mortal fear was one between light-skin coloured and dark-skin coloured couples. Mrs Arendse, an elder's wife at Grace's church, made things even clearer, telling her 'you should think about what your children will look like'.

Everything else in that moment was irrelevant – my formal education, my spiritual devotion, my steady job. I could deal with white racism but this was something else for which I had no defences at the time – coloured racism. While Grace and I were courting, we were regularly stopped by police who thought they had caught a couple in contravention of the Immorality Act; with a related piece of legislation, the Prohibition of Mixed Marriages Act, it governed intimate relationships between black and white couples. I will never forget the elation of the coloured policemen when they thought they had a catch. Where do you live, they would ask each of us. Then their faces dropped because Retreat and Athlone were coloured residential areas.

Soon it became clear to me that the racism in this family ran deep. I could not (and later would not) enter the coloured homes of some of my future in-laws' relatives; I had to wait in the car outside if Grace wanted to drop off something or meet a visiting cousin from Canada. Much of her extended family gave me the cold shoulder. And they were all believers in the same church.

Grace then made a decision that I long admired, for it meant breaking ties with her closest family. She packed her earthly belongings (we were on a deadline, 'before we get back from prayer meeting'), I climbed into the roof to gather the trousseau and off we went into the night with a big problem on our hands. Where would she stay? My parents would welcome us into their small council house but your girlfriend staying in the same space would raise eyebrows. So, we called around and found friends who had a spare room available until we made more permanent arrangements.

I was angry. How could an elder in the Brethren embrace me as his preacher only to deny me as his daughter's suitor? Could the cross of Christ mean so little to these Bible-professing believers when they were radioactive racists? What does church even mean to these hypocrites?

So, I wrote an angry letter asking those questions and making the accusation that the behaviour of her parents was anti-Christian in every sense. I drove by and slid the letter under the door but never heard a word back on the matter from my future in-laws.

Many months passed and we married. Grace's grandfather (and his wife) broke ranks with their daughter and her husband. They cared for us and counselled us during the difficult days before the wedding. Pa would take Grace down the aisle because on this special day, the most important in her life, her father had let it be known that he was working that Saturday. That he would have made alternative arrangements for his older daughter's wedding made it both painful and all too obvious that my he was still seething. His wife, however, did show up.

As our married life continued and children were born, the relationship became normal again. It was as if nothing had happened. Nobody talked about the rejection of our request to court, the daughter being thrown out of the house or half the family not attending the wedding. Then I noticed something interesting. My father-in-law made obvious efforts to reach out to us. We could not leave town after a visit from where we lived in another province without swinging by for his deliciously baked biscuits. He was warm, gracious and genuinely happy to see us and, of course, the grandchildren. It was how the older people asked forgiveness in those days: through their actions. You never apologised to children.

By this time, however, I had already moved away from the Brethren church, deeply grateful for the foundational values that it had taught me such as the simplicity of faith, the gifts of grace and the value of community. What I could not deal with was the normalised racism, the spiritual exclusivism and the pettiness that made rigid rules out of cultural preferences. I also learnt from my interactions with large parts of the Brethren that fundamentalism rejects you just as passionately as it first embraces you.

I discovered in the process of breaking away from my parents' church that it was possible to be a committed Christian without consigning everybody else to hell. Wherever we lived in the world, we would enjoy Shabbat with our Jewish friends on a Friday night and break the fast with our Muslim friends during Ramadan. I discovered, too, that it was possible to live an anxiety-free spiritual life by being comfortable with uncertainty. This is tough for a fundamentalist. Experience had taught me that rushing around trying to convert every soul 'before it was too late' was much less effective than simply leading a life of sacrifice and commitment as a testimony to others.

And I had learnt the hard way that so many of those I love in the church live comfortably with 'hearts full of hate and mouths full of scripture'.

I decided to live church rather than go to church and make sure that my example rather than my words would influence people.

One day, a group of Muslim men came to see me in my office at Stellenbosch University. I was happy to have their company and to learn of their work in bringing different religious communities together. Towards the end of their visit, they asked whether on the coming Friday I would break the fast with them during their holy month of Ramadan. I was thrilled to receive the invitation.

As they left, I realised that the men had not given me the address of the mosque. Cape Town has many. I ran after the brothers and said: 'Wait, you did not tell me where we will be breaking fast.'

'Oh,' said one of the Muslim men, 'at the Wynberg Shul.' Wait. What? At the synagogue?

And so it came to pass that on that Friday night, Jonathan, the son of evangelical Christians Abraham and Sarah, celebrated Shabbat with the Jewish community before breaking fast with the Muslim brothers and sisters. As I delivered my talk that evening, I looked around with teary eyes and asked my mixed audience where in the world this communion of believers could happen so easily without anyone giving up their religious identities but everyone committing to their common humanity.

I was breaking bread again, but this time with the broader faith community. And everyone was welcome around the table.

3
An inspiring teacher

'The only interruption to my education was my schooling.'
George Bernard Shaw (paraphrased)

It was the 50th anniversary of Sullivan Primary and its accomplished principal, Ernest Moore, had invited me as an old boy to the celebrations. The school opened in the first year of my formal education, 1963, so I was delighted to fly down from my job as vice-chancellor at the University of the Free State to be part of the ceremony. There was just one problem. With no school hall, we were seated outside in the howling wind with the canvas top threatening to blow away and people scurrying to keep the plates and spoons from following suit. It was not unusual for the south-easter to ruin an outdoor party, or in this case the half-century anniversary of my primary school.

I called over the principal and said to him, 'Meneer, it has been 50 years. We need to solve this problem.' Thanks to Mr Moore's energy and imagination, we quickly made plans for a new hall and inside a year the building was completed through a public–private partnership. For the first time in decades, the school could now have assemblies in all kinds of weather. I was overjoyed to be part of the project and even more excited to see parents involved, if only by purchasing one or two chairs for the new hall. Most importantly, the children could do music, drama and physical education in this state-of-the-art facility and carry those memories with them long after they leave school.

I do not myself have pleasant memories of my primary schooling. In fact, the only recollection I have of the founding principal, Mr Stober, is of him clobbering me with a cane for coming to school late in my first year of formal education. I was sent to the principal's office and all I remember is him taking me by one hand and letting fly as I hopped around in pain. I have no other memory of that principal, whether as a leader, a teacher or a human being.

Teachers then looked angry and aloof. Like the aunties in my home, they seemed to revel in inflicting pain on young children. One particularly nasty 'Miss' told a boy sitting behind me to shut up. He did not. She grabbed a heavy bunch of keys and threw it in his direction. I ducked in time and the keys hit the child with a thud. I cannot forget the blood on the boy's face or the guilt I felt about ducking.

I wish I could remember outings to the Kirstenbosch botanical garden, fish identification trips to the nearby ocean or something that stretched my learning about the rich fynbos that covered the area. None of that. Except for one visit to a museum in Cape Town where you could look at clumsy representations of your forebears, Bushmen and Hottentots, long before these racist images were transformed and renamed the San and the Khoi.

School was singularly unexciting and I tuned out early on. I was never at the top of any class nor anywhere near the bottom, just lingering somewhere in the middle, for I had found something else that truly excited me: the game of soccer.

In later grades I sometimes went to school early so that rival teams could get in a good hour of play with a small tennis ball in the sandy areas of the school. There was no grass or soccer field or athletics track, the kinds of things I envied every time I walked past Zwaanswyk Primary, the school for Afrikaans-speaking white children on the other side of Retreat railway station. Inequality was something you saw early in life.

We were particularly enthused the weekend before and after derbies between the two Cape Town teams, Hellenic (the Greek-named franchise) and Cape Town City. Since most of my friends chose City, I decided to support the opposition which, on reflection, became a character trait: never following the majority, finding freedom in doing my own thing.

Games of soccer were the highlight of my day as a primary school kid, and once classes started we selected the teams for the first break and the cherished longer second break. I had no interest in boring classes offered by what seemed to be perpetually angry teachers.

My passion sometimes caused pain at home. Since we did not have goalposts, those of us with shoes would volunteer a pair as posts on each side of the goalkeeper. Every now and again, when the bell rang, you rushed off to class and forgot your shoes on the field. By the time you returned, they were gone. My mother gave me a stiff hiding on more than one occasion and her teary eyes communicated a simple message: 'Do you know how hard it was for me to afford those Bata Toughees?' I felt horrible.

Fortunately, I discovered a less expensive school 'sport'. The English and Afrikaans classes in my grade had two huge guys. I invited them to wrestle each other after school in a corner near the gate at the far side of the teachers' admin building; that way we could not be caught. I was the school's Toweel, the surname of a famous boxing family who made it to the local news every week promoting one or other tournament. I would separate the two Standard 5 giants, and as I dropped my hand the fight would start. This went on for several months and I was proud of my organising skills until one day the two chaps turned on the Toweel-wannabe and that was the end of these wrestling tournaments.

Bored out of my mind, I would wander off with three or more mates to one of their homes for an extended lunch break and we would gradually make our way back long after classes had resumed. One of the teachers saw my group sauntering back to school and decided to make an example of us with a public hiding in the middle of the playground. The kids gathering on the balcony found this entertaining.

Otherwise, there was little to look forward to at school other than the athletics competition early in the year. I tried to take part in everything from the standing long jump to the sprints but was never really good enough to be one of the two children selected for a particular code, such as the 220-yard sprint. The Fords were the family that did well in track and my brother Peter was up there in the sprints, securing a place in the relay team as well. At least the inter-house school competition offered some respite from the humdrum of formal education.

Social welfare offered a comprehensive safety net for working-class kids. An organisation with an unflattering name, the Cape Flats Distress

Association (Cafda), dropped milk on Mondays and Fridays and soup on the days between. You were never hungry, even if the soup tasted steely and the brown bread was sometimes so dry it crackled. There were eye tests and dental checks, something that might never have happened to most children if these tasks had been left to their parents. In short, primary school was pretty ordinary and the teachers' colourless, but the basics were in place.

Even under these humdrum conditions you could not escape the grubby politics of the day. The 31st of May was the white people's Republic Day, the celebration of the apartheid government declaring independence from Britain in 1961. Every government primary school had to raise the flag and sing the anthem in a little ceremony.

I had very little political education at that point but enough of a conscience to know this was wrong. I hated the celebration and refused to sing the anthem. And from where I stood in the quad, it was clear that some of the teachers also felt this was nonsense but dared not do more than look their usual morose selves or they would be out of a job. It was a sad spectacle.

I observed one more piece of drama from time to time at Sullivan Primary. On the school's eastern flank, a high wire fence separated it from the council houses. Between the houses and the fence ran a long, narrow passage that you could use as a shortcut between Sullivan Road and Strauss Avenue.

Every now and then, two gangs would come running down this passage towards each other, and I once saw the sharp edges of spades and axes raining down on rival heads, blood spurting in all directions. There was no such thing as trauma counselling for kids in those days, but that clash remained lodged in my memory.

As I walked back and forth to school in my primary years, I became increasingly aware of the dangerous world I had to navigate and how easily one could fall into traps. A skirmish with a gangster one morning almost got me stabbed. You could be tripped up by any number of hoodlums lurking on the corners. I was lucky to be fortified on the inside by the steering values of Sarah and Abraham, but many of my classmates were not so fortunate and I saw them drop out of primary school and in greater numbers at high school.

By the time I reached Steenberg High I had still not found any excitement in learning, so Standard 6 started with the usual lack of interest in education and the mad attachment to soccer. Hellenic vs Cape Town City. I was alone again among the many City supporters, made worse by the fact that my evangelical parents forbade me to set foot anywhere near Hartleyvale Stadium to watch soccer at the weekend. I felt positively miserable on Mondays as I tried to join in on conversations about matches watched by my friends. I sometimes made up stories that I was there, but they would ask me questions about 'what was where' in the stadium and it soon became obvious that I had never been anywhere near this hallowed football ground.

One schoolmate was particularly fierce in his defence of City, especially when Hellenic won the derby. He was Alan Knowles, a bit of an entitled brat at the time, perhaps because his mother was a well-regarded teacher at Sullivan. I saw Alan on his bicycle one day and reminded him that Hellenic had won. He screwed up his face and spat in mine. The shock was so great that I just stood there, but I carried the anger for a long time. Alan would nonetheless go on to become one of my favourite preachers on the Cape Flats.

As I entered the gates for my first day of high school, things got off to a bumpy start. Two senior boys with thuggish faces must have seen the newbie and as part of their initiation instructed me to measure the perimeter of the school with a single matchstick. Saved by the starting bell, I eventually reached my assigned classroom.

The dullness of primary school continued into high school. First up was the woodwork class that every student had to take, even if in later grades you chose other streams like those with science and mathematics. In the first class we had to learn to do isometric drawings (graphic representations of three-dimensional shapes) that started simply enough with a single line across the page but became gradually more difficult until you were stranded.

The male teacher thought it would be fun to test our knowledge by lining up the boys (the girls did needlework) and having each one of them make the next line. If you were right in front, you made the first few lines and you were off the hook. If you were further back, by the time you got to the board it was a maze and the teacher whacked each boy as they made a mistake. Boys curled up in pain and others, out of sheer fear of a caning, simply cowered at the back of the class as the maniac of a teacher continued beating us rather than teaching us. I have hated woodwork ever since.

Teachers did not need a reason to beat you up. I remember one day coming down the long passage that ran from the outermost classrooms in a straight line along a well-polished corridor to the administration building where the principal and his secretarial staff were housed. As I started down the passage, I saw Mr 'Diff' Abrahams, so called because of his rather prominent forehead, coming in the opposite direction.

'Good morning, Sir,' I said pleasantly enough before he changed lanes and gave me an almighty smack as I sailed along the polished floor. In shock and on the edge of tears, I approached the teacher and asked, with some desperation, 'but Sir, why?' Another hard smack to the face and I went sailing along the floor again. To this day I have no idea what caused this assault by a grown man on a boy. I was, however, devastated enough to resent the man deeply.

It seemed as if cruelty was baked into the culture of the school and its operations. Mr Martin was the caretaker who lived just down the road from the school. He had fierce Alsatian dogs which he would bring to the school when there was a function that needed some form of crowd control. One such event was the annual interschool athletics competition. Mr Martin took great pleasure in pushing back the lines of non-athletes along the side of track by half-releasing the dogs on an extendable leash, scaring the children back behind the imaginary line separating athletes and spectators. This was provocative but at the time we did not think of such behaviour as something out of the ordinary. Cruelty was everywhere.

So was boredom. No teacher better represented the sluggishness of teaching than Mr EEEEEEE Ward. He used to string out the 'E' when he first introduced himself as the guidance teacher. Guidance was in effect a free period and, for as long as I can remember, one of the last periods on a Friday. This meant the teacher was tired and the children had one eye on the final bell. I cannot remember anything taught about guidance but I do recall planning a soccer match or doing the next day's homework while we waited for the bell.

When he spoke, Mr Ward seemed determined to put you to sleep. There was his favourite saying, 'It takes a live fish to swim against the stream,' and it seemed to take him five minutes to get to the end of that unlively sentence. In my memory, guidance is a blur, and that experience partly explains my suspicion of its current form, life orientation.

In this harsh and humourless environment, danger seemed to lurk in the curriculum. The end-of-year project for my woodwork class was to make an ashtray. I did not have the guts to tell the teacher it would cause problems in my family home if I came back with this worldly contraption that encouraged smoking. After all, *your body is the temple of the Holy Ghost that is in you.* You don't defile it with cigarette smoke.

In every woodwork class, I would work on the ashtray even as my fear of taking it home grew. I had to make a thick wooden base then carve out a semi-circular hole into which a piece of copper had to fit perfectly to hold the cigarette ash. In the middle of the ashtray we inserted a long, upright metal rod and before long the work was done. Forgetting the sinful ashtray for a moment, a neat range of skills was being taught here, from copper melting to wood carving, though mine did not resemble any manmade ashtray at all.

Eventually the year ended and we could take the ashtray to show our parents. I tried to think up excuses for not bringing home this contraption, but nothing sounded plausible. I could have dumped it, of course, but the teacher required a signature from one of the parents that they had seen the completed project.

I was sweating as I entered the house, and there in front of me stood the formidable Sarah. I felt like fetching the Port Jackson branch myself and getting this hiding over and done with, but then Sarah spoke: 'What a lovely little boat you made there.' I did not think it was *that* bad, but I felt such relief.

As in primary school, the dullness of schooling was broken by the daily soccer games and the annual athletics programme. Steenberg High had talented athletes who propelled us into the A-section of the provincial schools' competition at Green Point Track. One of the most fascinating duels in the middle distances was between boys known only by their surnames, Sakinari and Okkies. '*Hou, Sakinari hou*' became something of a war cry that egged on the brilliant runner when he seemed exhausted.

Then there were the yo-yo competitions that brought a huge Coca-Cola truck onto the school grounds. A boy or girl would win a box of Cokes for mastering yo-yo tricks like walk the dog, rock the baby and around the world.

You made your own fun, like playing cricket in the quad and being mesmerised by how Patrick Newkirk could spin a ball on tar. Or watching the dribbling skills of Clive Williams with a soccer ball as he twisted and turned around hapless defenders. Or being thrilled by how long-haired Michael 'Spike' Anderson showed off his wizardry with the table tennis bat. Thin as a rake, Spike's only other skill was his remarkable ability to 'tune' girls to go out with him.

Bored on the inside, we would sometimes stray outside the school perimeter. I occasionally wandered off with David Jason because we could watch movies at his place when few of us had Betamax or VHS video tapes or a television. Halfway between the school and his house was a fish and chip shop. Our standard practice was to send the man to the back of the shop to get the fish and chips, which gave us the opportunity stretch over the counter and steal three or four rolls. Years later, I went looking for the shop to pay for what we stole but it was no longer there.

Wrongdoing at school often brought its fair share of humour to carry you through the day. One such incident comes to mind. Examination rooms were usually decided in advance so the workers could put out the right number of desks for a particular subject, with enough space between them to prevent cheating. For some reason, a room was changed at the last minute. From where we sat in a classroom next to the large quad, we saw a junior boy scrambling as he carried his desk from one side of the yard to a classroom at the opposite end of the building. We fell apart laughing when told that the poor chap had the answers to expected test questions written on the wooden desktop; with the sudden change of rooms, he risked failure if he wrote on the wrong desk.

A more dramatic event would occasionally break the monotony. Not having encountered death among friends or family, I was traumatised by the death of a girl you could not miss seeing on any day of the week. That's because she had a haunting beauty about her. She moved along the corridors like a ghost, with short hair and an even shorter dress, and hardly ever seemed to speak. A bit of a mystery.

Then the announcement one morning that she had died. Officially, it was a brain haemorrhage, but student gossip suggested drugs. I attended the funeral wondering about the sudden loss of the mysterious schoolmate. The organ at St Andrew's Anglican church played *Peace, perfect peace, in this dark world of sin* and I had goosebumps.

For the most part, however, life inside the classroom remained dreary until an encounter with a teacher changed the course of my life.

As usual, I was enjoying a competitive soccer match on the tarred quad during the long break when a teacher called me out of the game. I tried to hide my irritation, given the limited time available to play, but of course you dare not disobey a teacher's instruction.

'Yes, Sir?'

Paul Galant taught me Latin and at the time I was in Standard 8 (Grade 10 today). He was one of the school's most dedicated teachers. Young and energetic, he started classes on time and always ran over time. The next period's teacher would peer into the room looking slightly annoyed that their colleague did not seem to know when to end his lesson. There was a passion that infused his pedagogy, even with something as mundane as conjugating the Latin verb '*amo*' in the indicative present. He taught rhythmically and melodically so that I remember the sequence to this day:

> amo
> amas
> amat
> amamus
> amatis
> amant

I had no desire to become a lawyer – which was one reason to take Latin – but I started to enjoy this subject, especially when the language was placed in the context of the great battles of imperial Rome. It would later have another advantage, I discovered, and that was helping me understand biological terms such as the names of phyla and species. Most of all, Latin was fascinating because of this young teacher.

Mr Galant was leaning against one of the pillars outside the classroom when he called me away from the soccer match. His message took me by surprise. 'I have been watching you,' he said. 'You pretend you know nothing but actually you're very smart. I have high hopes for you, my boy. You have potential.'

What? Nobody had ever spoken to me like this. I had not heard the word 'potential' before, except in the science class (as in potential vs kinetic energy) and there was no Google then. To say I was stunned would be an understatement. I momentarily delayed my return to the soccer game, wondering what had just happened. Could Mr Galant be right, that he was seeing something I had not seen within myself? Maybe Mrs Akoojee, my homeroom teacher, was right when she wrote in one of my reports: 'Jonathan's results have been rather disappointing. I fully expected a first-grade pass.'

It is hard to explain the reality of those times to young people when you are known as a distinguished professor. They think you were always smart. Up to that point, I really was not. Like any boy from the Cape Flats, my horizons were set by what I could see in the avenues and by my parents' level of education. Nobody went to university and just finishing high school was a worthy accomplishment. When I did think about a career, I thought of some white-collar clerical job if I was lucky, but anything actually to help my parents financially.

Now this message from Mr Galant.

As I fell asleep that night on the lower bunk in the small council house bedroom, I made a pledge with myself. I am going to try to prove Mr Galant right. I was going to study for tests and examinations. I would go to the local library, get a card and check out books. I would do my homework for a change. And I would pay attention in class.

Yes, pay attention. It took a 2023 reunion of my senior class at Steenberg High (49 years since matric) to hear how my mates remembered me in school. According to them, I did everything but pay attention until this turning point. They told me how I locked everyone inside the classroom and ran off with the key. They remembered how a teacher told me to get off the table and my response was to make the broomstick a guitar and imitate Percy Sledge, the black American R&B singer, who was playing at the Three Arts Theatre. In a pose, I apparently asked the class, 'Do you dig me?'

I don't remember this but I know that playing the fool was what I did out of sheer boredom. I recall a teacher saying, 'stop walking round', as I preferred to hear the last word. 'Not true, Miss,' I responded. 'I am walking in a straight line ($y = mx + c$).' That kind of silliness.

The first subject I was going to do well in was Latin and I started to study hard. Suddenly, my marks went through the roof and I could sense the other teachers were taking notice. Mr Joorst, who did not even teach me any subject (he was geography, I did history), now noticed me and would not pass me in the corridors without a word of encouragement. Mrs Akoojee, my biology teacher, told me bluntly that she expected an A from me in the subject which would become my favourite. The old Greek with the perpetual pipe who taught me English, Mr Cokinis, was suddenly talking to me about studying literature beyond school rather than my first love, science.

It was good to feel noticed for something other than tomfoolery. Next, I was called to the principal's office and told I was one of two students chosen to go on a leadership camp at Esselen Park, a high school with boarding facilities in Worcester on the other side of the mountain pass. It was a distinctly Afrikaans affair and I felt lost at first then perturbed as I listened to the childish stories of some of the boys' sexual exploits. Even more discomforting was the realisation that the camp was organised by 'Coloured Affairs' and a Dr Quint featured prominently; I hated these sellouts who bought into the arrangements for racial and ethnic education. Some of them like Quint went on to join the tricameral arrangements of the apartheid government for whites, Indians and coloureds while excluding Africans.

Even so, I was chosen to represent my school and that made me proud. When we were invited to present something at the talent evening on the closing night, I chose to play a classical piece on the piano and it was quite a hit. '*Uitstekend*,' said Dr Quint as I left the stage.

Strange how being recognised for leadership pushes you into acting as a leader. I noticed that our school did not have an organised soccer team to play in the interschool league. After approaching one of the teachers, I called a meeting of all boys interested in playing for the school. The room was packed and we chose a senior team and some reserves based on reputation alone. I made myself the temporary captain until we could sort out something more permanent. Off we went to play against other schools, including the 'naughty boys' in the Porter Reformatory who apparently did not need soccer boots because their feet were naturally hard. I did not think of this as leadership, but according to my friends I started doing a lot of that around the school.

I was so appreciative of what Mr Galant had done for my change of direction that I sought out other opportunities to come under his influence. He was in charge of middle-distance running for the interschool championships and announced that there would be trials in a few weeks' time for those interested. I signed up, knowing I did not stand a chance with the likes of Alex Thomas, the 800-metre specialist, in my year group. After all, I had never represented my school in any athletics programme. My brother Isaac would later do the 400 m, Denzil excelled at high jump and Peter did well in the 100 m and 200 m. I was the weakest link when it came to athletics but let's give it a go, I said to myself.

What happened next was the most intense physical preparation I had experienced. It turned out that Mr Galant trained his 800 m charges with the same intensity that he taught Latin. Up and down the dunes of the Cape Flats, including those near the family home. Fast bursts of running on an open field followed by 'cooling-off' runs and back again to sprints. This went on for weeks almost every day after school. The trial date was set and there I was among 12 or so other boys to decide which two would go to the Green Point Track for the interschools.

The starter's pistol went off and we ran on a track with fading lanes marked by whitewash and a whole lot of thorns to torture you if you did not have spiked shoes. After one lap I was surprised to find myself on the heels of Alex Thomas and not yet tired. On the final bend, with the rest of the competitors far behind us, I even thought of passing him. I chased him hard but Alex still won and the two of us represented Steenberg High in the championships. 'I was wondering who was chasing me down like that,' he said as I tried to regain normal breathing.

On the day of the interschool championship, I lined up on the far side of the track under bright green trees. My heart was pounding and I noticed those boys from the Porter Reformatory with hard soles that could do more damage than spikes. In that race was Cookson, the record-holder in the 800 m from Harold Cressy High School. This was going to be tough. As we came around the track before the main pavilion where the different schools were sitting, I realised there was no way I was going to make the top five, or ten for that matter.

Fortunately, just before the pavilion there was a little side gate off the track and I ran through it and walked among the crowds as if it was the most natural thing to do. I was not going to be that boy who comes across the line long after the other competitors are in the shower, only to receive sympathetic applause from mildly amused spectators. I was not interested in the spirit trophy.

I was nevertheless overjoyed by my relative success and learnt a precious lesson: that success in one area of school life, such as academics, can spawn success in a completely different area, such as sport. The key, of course, was a committed teacher, and that success I credit to Mr Galant.

It was fortuitous that around the time I experienced my Latin teacher's intervention, a boy about my age came to the Steenberg assembly with his parents. His name was Archie Lennie Dick, and I went to introduce myself after a meeting. Lennie was somewhat shy, the only boy among three sisters. We would become lifelong friends and the first thing that connected us was our shared love for soccer. Lots of our socials were organised around the beautiful game and one other thing – studies.

Lennie went to a more fancied school, South Peninsula High (SP, as it's called), and it had instilled in him a studious spirit. One day, he invited me to 'study through the night' with him on a Friday. What? It's the weekend, man. Let's play soccer and when the sun sets, chess and table tennis indoors (a cheap net across the kitchen table worked). But the SP man studied from mid-evening on a Friday until the sun rose.

I was curious, so I went over on the first Friday and slept through, except for the eating breaks he had organised; I woke dutifully to consume the koeksisters and other goodies his mother had prepared. Eventually, spurred on by the motivating words of my Latin teacher, I joined Lennie in Friday night studies. Now I was on a roll in the final years of high school.

There was an added advantage to studying with Lennie. Though we were born in the same year, he had been promoted two years forward in primary school so he was in Standard 10 when I was in Standard 8. The young Lennie must obviously have been supersmart for this kind of progression, but it worked to my advantage because he could explain things to me that he had already passed. More than that, Lennie instilled in me the habit of systematic study.

He was also a pioneer from the streets of Steenberg and Retreat, the first person I knew to go to university. 'What do they do there?' I once asked him. 'Study,' he replied. 'But you just finished studying,' went the banter. We had, after all, burnt all our schoolbooks together after a train ride down to Long Beach in Simon's Town. More studies? I would follow him to university to do the same. He studied library science while I registered for the biological sciences.

Looking back, at just the right time, halfway through high school, two important role models came into my life to smooth my academic path. My Latin teacher and my soccer buddy. My late mother Sarah would say this was God; my less religious friends would use the word serendipity to describe those happy accidents that sometimes mark the good life.

I became aware of these transformations in my life in the middle of high school. I was now officially a jerk. Two girls from the 2023 reunion remembered how Alan Newkirk and I chided them for playing soccer outside when they could have spent their time more productively doing schoolwork. This was also a time when I was becoming a budding evangelist, so most students thought I was weird even though I got along well with most of them. But this serious bloke was not the kind of chap they wanted as a prefect, and girls avoided me like an Old Testament plague. Who, after all, wanted to hang out with a guy who would regularly remind them that *the wages of sin is death*?

The prefects were chosen democratically, votes split more or less equally between students and teachers. They made a brilliant choice in Jean Solomon and a disastrous choice in Bobby somebody. Jean was decent, well-spoken, charming and a leader. Bobby, a boy from upcountry, was an everyman who was always in trouble with the school authorities for one or other misdemeanour.

And so, you had the strange phenomenon that at the school assembly on a Monday morning those who committed misdeeds, such as smoking in the toilets, were paraded on the stoep above the open-air tarmac where we gathered for assembly on the theory that exposure in front of the whole school would be a deterrent for bad behaviour. Bobby was a regular but everybody liked him.

While I was disappointed not to be a prefect, I had discovered in the final years what kinds of subjects made me excited about learning. It was clearly the sciences but there was a problem: you were lucky ever to learn science except through the denseness of a textbook. I enjoyed it when Mr Poyo, who taught us science, tried one or two 'experiments' on us, like showing the action of sodium and potassium metals darting across water in distinctive colours. Someone (I'm not telling) got his hands on too large a piece of those metals and dropped it into a bowl of water with spectacular consequences.

But it was the science of living things that really got my attention. Mrs Akoojee was a motherly teacher who ensured that you understood a concept or principle in biology before she moved on. Quiet, unassuming but determined, she took us through our paces with enormous patience as we sidetracked her with silly questions about the reproduction of the gastropod, *Helix aspersa* (how do snails actually do it?).

Early on, she noticed my interest in 'bio' and actively encouraged me to go from a solid B to an A. But we did not perform a single experiment in those two senior years, nor did she do something even easier, and that was to stand in front of the class and use demonstration as a method for teaching. It was a gap in my education that cost me dearly in my first-year science classes at university and one that I fiercely compensated for when I became a bio teacher years later.

In the trio of school subjects (mathematics, physical science, biology) that made up the science stream, maths was the most poorly taught. I still remember an old white man called Mr Gilloway standing in front of the board, his back half-turned away from us, reciting meaningless theorems like this one by the great Pythagoras: 'the square on the hypotenuse is equal to the sum of the squares on the other two sides.' Over and over again, and still I had no clue what he was talking about. This was mathematics as procedure, not mathematics as understanding.

For much of the year I thought 'the square' referred to the square shape as opposed to, for example, the rectangle. Thanks to Lennie, I grasped almost too late that it was the square of a number. Gilloway was reputed to have written maths textbooks but the poor soul simply could not connect his expertise in mathematics to where we were as students. He knew a lot of maths (content) but he simply could not convey it well (pedagogy), and that explains the fate of millions of children in the South African school system except for an added difference – many of our teachers do not even know enough mathematics content.

You were lucky to find teachers in our schools who were subject-matter experts and excellent pedagogues – one of whom we were exposed to by accident. A language teacher was absent and, to our great surprise, in stepped principal Lochner. This was going to be interesting, I thought, since I didn't think too many heads of schools then or now actively taught classes.

A short, bronze-tanned man, he proceeded to write one word on the chalkboard. Monotonous. He then did a deft explanation of the etymology of the word, its Greek root, then made it simple for us by splitting mono (single) and tone. From there he demonstrated the meaning of monotonous by imitating the preaching of a dominee, which was all too familiar and, to give life to the word, apt. Then he left the room. I have never forgotten that brief moment of powerful teaching or the word 'monotonous'. Gilloway was not a pedagogue.

However, apart from the missionaries at church, Gilloway was one of a handful of white people I came to know at close quarters. White teachers in coloured schools gave us further exposure to those on the other side of South Africa's racial divide. Some were liberals for whom teaching across the colour line was their way of showing off their credentials as open-minded whites. Odd ones were radicals from the University of Cape Town who showed solidarity with us, the oppressed. And then there were those, I suspect, who were either bored or could not get a job and thought teaching coloured kids might be a useful way to pass the time.

One woman among the small group of white teachers at our high school intrigued me. She was in her late 20s or early 30s and taught us Afrikaans. Like many Afrikaans teachers, she was very focused in her preparation and intense in her delivery. I cannot for the life of me remember the name of the setwork piece we had to cover, but its content is unforgettable.

It is a story about a white family (of course) in a small *dorpie* who were faced with removal, not due to their race but because of the advent of modernity. The dorpie was about to be turned into a modern town, with big industry moving in, fancy shops being built and lots more opportunities for the locals. The white family would have to yield to the developers but they refused point blank. Much of the setwork is about the small and large ways in which this brave family resisted being uprooted from their home, which stood smack bang in the middle of the developers' plans.

As this teacher taught the setwork, and in the way she looked up at us, I could swear she was asking the class to make the connection between the plight of the old white couple being forcefully uprooted from their home and the forced removals under apartheid. She emphasised resistance and I sensed she was a kindred spirit. Being white and Afrikaans, there was no way she could make her political leanings explicit, for that would cost her more than her job.

What flattened our feelings towards these white teachers, however, was the discovery that they were being given 'danger pay' or 'inconvenience pay'. Danger pay, because they took the risk of coming into violent black areas to teach and therefore needed to be compensated for what other teachers did every day. Inconvenience pay because they were doing us a favour; they had options and now had to put up with inconveniences like sharing a toilet or a staffroom with coloured teachers. I used to wonder how many of them refused to take that extra pay since they were already being paid more than coloured teachers anyway for being, well, white.

To be sure, there were a few socially conscious teachers at Steenberg High as well, but they did not make their feelings too public like the teachers of the known political schools such as Trafalgar, Livingstone and Harold Cressy. Some of their teachers went to prison or were banned, and at least one ended up on Robben Island alongside Nelson Mandela. Still, one or more of the Steenberg teachers arranged for transport to Hewat, a teacher training college in Athlone, to listen to radical poetry from stalwarts such as James Matthews and Richard Rive. James' poetry had an earthiness to it that spoke directly to your soul, like this poem published in the 1970s with Gladys Thomas in a banned collection called *Cry Rage*:

> Suffer little children
> and forbid them not to come to me
> the words of Christ, the Master,
> have lost their meaning
> when his natal day is celebrated
> with separated seating
> and little black and brown angels
> not wanted in the cast
> all they can do is sit and watch
> Christ and his message of love
> turned into a mockery
> little black and brown children are to suffer
> and not wanted, a damn!

This was my real education and for the first time I could make direct connections between literature and politics in a way that ordinary school teaching did not. I was mesmerised by the eloquence of these poet activists and how with few words they could make your experiences of repression become real. The atmosphere in the hall at Hewat was charged and you felt like marching on the regime after listening to this feast of struggle poetry. This was my real education, outside school. Years later I remembered words attributed to George Bernard Shaw along the lines 'the only time my education was interrupted was when I was in school'.

What I experienced at Hewat on more than one visit to the college was a tradition of political education that distinguished the Cape from politics in the north. I am not sure if it was the legacy of the Non-European Unity Movement, a radical left organisation led by some of the Cape's most influential intellectuals, that saw education not as something to be boycotted but an arena in which to continue the fight against apartheid. When I became a young teacher, I would find great encouragement in what was called 'alternative education'.

My understanding of the concept was that while you did what was necessary to have your students pass the government examinations, you did your utmost to present in parallel an alternative education to what was required in the state curriculum. The Hewat classes did exactly that for me as a high school student; they expanded content beyond the official curriculum, negating it and enriching it in equal measure so that you knew what was necessary to pass and what was essential to live a life of conscience. Yes, there were school boycotts from time to time, but the notion of 'liberation now, education later', heard in the north, did not find much of a foothold in the Cape.

Fired up, I now saw things that would otherwise have escaped my social consciousness, and in small ways I acted on them. One event could have ended badly. My mother and I went to see her parents in Montagu and had to use a railway bus for the long journey. Immediately, I noticed that there was a comfortable section for whites in the front of the bus with two or three passengers but the other 10 or more seats open. There was also a rudimentary air-cooler in that section, so comfortable all round on that hot summer's day.

There was just one problem. As we picked up coloured people along the way, they became packed like canned sardines in the segregated back section of the bus. It was hot there, the passengers were sweaty and half of them were drunk. Sarah and I tried hard to keep our composure. What drove me mad was that I could see the open spaces in the front of the bus; could they not take some of the passengers to the front and relieve the overcrowding, if not the stench, at the back? I was fuming.

When we eventually reached Montagu, I went to the driver's section and told the middle-aged white Afrikaans man what I thought of him and the racist arrangements on the bus. To my surprise, he said absolutely nothing, dropping his head as if in acknowledgement. To my even greater surprise, Sarah said nothing as she witnessed my tirade against white authority. She did not reprimand me, nor did she bring up the heated speech at all. In fact, she seemed proud of her 16-year-old taking a stand against injustice without herself uttering a word.

That was a tumultuous visit to the place of my birth. My grandmother asked me to go town (the *dorp*) to buy groceries at Brink's, a shopping chain in these parts. Off I went in my Steenberg High tracksuit top, expecting to return within half an hour or so. On my way back up the inclined road, I was walking past the rows of white homesteads where coloured people used to stay, and thinking about the impact of that upheaval on my proud grandparents. Then a brick landed with a thud on the pavement just behind me.

In shock, I looked up to see a boy about my age sniggering, and I knew then who the assaulter was. Without thinking, I rushed him, and just as I was about to wring his neck (at least that is what I imagined) his father came out, a large Afrikaans man who informed me he was an off-duty policeman. The man was apoplectic, more so because I could even think of attacking a white youth. For the next two hours I felt my life hanging in the balance.

He threw me into the back of his car and drove off, destination unknown. I started to fear something really bad was going to happen. I wondered if I would see my family again because not too long ago a black man had disappeared in that area, raising all kinds of questions about the police. Those were the heydays of apartheid, the early 1970s.

Then a strange ritual unfolded. The angry driver asked me a question in Afrikaans, like where was I from, and when I answered he would slam on the brakes and lean back as if to slap me. After a few of these to-and-fros I realised what was happening: I was giving incomplete answers. I should have said '*Ja baas*' like the locals did in every interaction with whites. He could go screw himself as far as I was concerned, there would be no *baas*.

We arrived at Montagu police station. The off-duty policeman stomped up and down, asking permission to sort me out from the huge officer in charge, elevated in a high chair. I began to think I would get a severe beating or worse. At that moment, my mother's youngest sister, also Naomi, came flying into the police station, pleading to take me 'home' and sort me out. For some reason, the sitting policeman let me go. Now I was angry all over again as we made our way back to Cape Town.

Politics was not the only way in which I learnt about the world outside school. I worked in every school holiday to bring in some much-needed cash. There was no chance of lazing around under Sarah's roof. Holiday jobs included helping Mr Jacobs, a jovial brother in the church, with his fruit box business. He collected broken plank boxes from farmers and the local market, fixed them, then sold them back to these clients for crating apples or potatoes. He did a roaring business transporting and selling thousands of these repaired boxes. My job was to sit in his backyard with pliers to remove old nails and a hammer to bash in new ones. The compensation was meagre but it was better than nothing.

A snake oil salesman took Neal Dreyer (my dentist student friend and fellow Christian) and me off the streets one day and convinced us that selling a miraculous soap would make women lose weight. Soak-and-Slim was the product and the science was as simple as that. A woman would take a bath at night, apply the soap and lose weight. We bought into the magic story and sold hundreds of these packages to unsuspecting clients. You did not need a degree to know it was nonsense but we kept going from door to door down the avenues. For a long time, we avoided certain streets for fear of retribution.

The only person who did not pay me was a man who had Rodney (a dear friend in the church) and me try to clean up the oil that filtered into the concrete where trucks stood. This was an impossible task but we persevered with all kinds of strong liquids in the misguided belief that the oil could be soaked up. We were not paid a cent.

The nicest holiday job was acting as a postman's assistant to Sydney Alexander, a co-leader of the church youth. He worked from Muizenberg station at one end of the beach and started by sorting letters by street. Then, along that beautiful ocean-side road to Fish Hoek, he dropped them off in mailboxes. I did much of the running up the steeper slopes to houses in that area. That job is responsible for my theory that white dogs can identify a black person and charge when they do not do the same for white strangers. This was long before the University of Cape Town psychologist Wahbie Long wrote about white people and their dogs in his celebrated book, *Nation on the Couch*, or my Stellenbosch University colleague Sandra Swart wrote about police dogs and other animals in her stunning work, *The Lion's Historian*.

It is no longer a theory. Years later, I was doing that scenic morning walk along Fish Hoek beach when I saw many white people with their dogs. I grew tense, as always, as I was about to pass an older woman with her pet. Suddenly, the dog charged me and the woman's response floored me: 'Well, he does not normally bite black people.'

School holidays were not all work, though. We had a tight group of male friends from church. Our fathers were senior brethren in the assemblies and we bonded early in friendship. One thing we liked doing was cycling around the Cape Peninsula and ending up in the vicinity of the Simon van der Stel buildings in Constantia for lunch. The De Vries twins, Lennie Dick, Raglyn (who would tragically jump from an upper floor at Groote Schuur Hospital, killing himself) and myself.

Each of us brought one item for the meal in haversacks strapped to our backs. My commission was to bring dessert. The trip started in Steenberg/Retreat then continued to Muizenberg, from where we cycled along the coastline past Cape Point then over Chapman's Peak via Hout Bay to Constantia. After the rolls and meats, everybody was hyped for dessert.

Rushing out of the house before the trip, I had grabbed several tins of those no-label syruped peaches in bold grey cans. Except, when we opened the cans in Constantia, they contained tomato puree. The discovery dampened the whole day and I was never allowed to forget the no-show dessert episode.

It was also with this group that I had an alternative education of the conservative kind. Every Friday night we gathered at the De Vries home for concentrated Bible study under the leadership of the senior elder, Ernest, or Ernie as his contemporaries called him. He was an intense man with a reputation as a fiery dual-medium (English and Afrikaans) preacher, though he was also known to be abrasive in his manner. Ernie would take us through ways of analysing holy writ.

I quite enjoyed these in-depth studies of the Bible as much as I looked forward to hanging out with my friends on a Friday evening. The Brethren were dispensationalists, which means they believed there were distinct periods in which God governed the earth by different rules. The age of law, for example, was under Moses and the prophets in the Old Testament, when God's followers had to abide by a strict regime of legal prescriptions. Today is the age of grace, when the regnant principle that governs believers is faith in Christ. Knowing these different dispensations was a wonderful way in which to do systematic thinking and scriptural analyses, which gave me skills way beyond matters of the soul.

Needless to say, I found a tight classification of the ages a bit too rigid (as I would in the social sciences for any kind of categorisation) and asked questions for which Ernie did not seem to have answers. I could see him becoming irritated with me, as I in turn did with any form of dogmatism. Ernie meant well but he was not a trained Bible scholar; what he taught us he learnt mainly from the missionaries coming in and out of the assemblies. I doubt he finished high school even though his basic biblical literacy was superb. But the dispensations are complicated stuff.

My questions got too much for elder Ernie, so he instructed his boys not to pick me up for the Friday night Bible study. Peter, the shorter of the twins, drove the large family car while straining his neck to see the road ahead. He would collect Lennie and the others but not me. We then made a deal. Peter would indeed pick me up but then drop me off close to their home so it appeared I had walked to the Bible study all by myself.

Being disinvited from events for asking questions and having a viewpoint would become a life-long personal and professional hazard.

Lennie and I had both achieved PhD degrees and over time I learnt that Mr Galant also taught him at Steenberg Primary before he encountered me at Steenberg High. Both of us remembered an energetic and inspiring teacher who made a lasting impact on our lives. As two boys from Steenberg and Retreat, where few people obtain doctorates to this day, we decided to do something special for him.

By this time the famous teacher had retired from normal teaching and done a post-retirement stint as a principal at a small school in Hout Bay. Lennie came down from Pretoria, where he was teaching at one of the universities, and we collected our star teacher and his second wife for a fancy dinner on the town. We took turns at the dinner table to thank him for changing the trajectory of our lives and those of countless others.

Paul Galant died shortly afterwards.

4
Undergraduate struggles

'The function of education, therefore, is to teach one to think intensively and to think critically.'
Martin Luther King Jr

Most of my class missed the inorganic chemistry lecture in N7 (the large science lecture hall) that day in 1976 because of the protests on the University of the Western Cape campus 'in solidarity with the comrades in Soweto'. The few who were in attendance must have been weirdos with no social conscience, I thought at the time. Shortly afterwards we received the date for the critical quarterly examination and word leaked that what we had missed in that one lecture might play an outsized role in the assessment: how to calculate the half-life of uranium.

Some of us sensed that this was potentially bad news. We asked the sellouts but they were not sharing their notes. There was no textbook readily available for reading up on uranium, nor were there any internet search engines. I was in a serious panic but comforted myself with the knowledge that there was, after all, a whole quarter of teaching, so even if I missed out on uranium's half-life I might make up marks with the many other examinable topics for which I *did* attend lectures.

On the day of the examination, there was one main question: calculate the half-life of uranium. We failed like flies. That day I understood how in the hands of an apartheid functionary the exams could be used as a political instrument to punish those who participated in protests. Dr Botha* is still the most miserable lecturer I have encountered anywhere on the planet. His demeanour was sulky and he barely looked up at the sharply ascending rows of long benches where more than 100 science students furiously took notes.

His English was terrible and he taught mainly in Afrikaans. The result was that those of us who were not first-language Afrikaans students really struggled, not only with chemistry and translation (*suurstof* was not remotely close to oxygen, even if you could make the link between *koolhidrate* and carbohydrates) but with making sense of what this poor creature was saying in the first place. It was rumoured that his kind were the less intelligent Afrikaner academics who had not made the cut at the elite Afrikaans institutions, such as Stellenbosch University, and were therefore handed down to the nearby not-white campus where many (certainly not all) coloured staff and students spoke Afrikaans.

Other lecturers shared Botha's mean-spiritedness. After a test, some of them would take the time to arrange the marked scripts in descending order of marks obtained. The lecturer would then read out the marks from top to bottom and students would rise from their seats to collect their papers. The goal was humiliation. If you got 80–100 per cent, you were only too happy to rush forward, smiling broadly at your terrified classmates. But by the time the gleeful lecturer (this was one of the few times Botha smiled) got to 'Maarman 10 per cent' or 'Fataar 2 per cent' these poor students had already fled through N7's back door.

The organic chemistry lecturer was a Frenchman, Georges Delpierre, who seemed determined to be more obnoxious than white South Africans. Perhaps he needed to confirm his credibility as a member of the white tribe. Delpierre shared Botha's disregard for students but with a more open, professional face that pretended nothing else was happening in the country in which he taught chemistry. There were also allegations that Delpierre worked with the police and carried a gun to his lectures, for which actions the university tried to discipline him.

It did not surprise us that one of his lectures had to be abandoned because he sensed the smell of petrol – a possible petrol bomb in the cupboards under the large science bench behind which lecturers stood. We had to rush out of the back and front of N7 on that potentially dangerous day. That was not the last I saw of the Frenchman.

I was dog-tired from a late lab session the previous afternoon, which meant I missed the bus back to the southern suburbs and arrived home after dark.

The next morning, I had to make my way back to Bellville in the northern suburbs using a taxi, train and bus (which broke down), meaning that from Athlone I had to do the last leg of the journey to campus using my hitchhiking thumb. The long final stretch of road to and from campus was called Modderdam Road, meaning dam of mud, as if in the very naming of the street the city fathers were intent on communicating misery to the thousands of students who used it every day.

Once there, I ran for all I was worth from the university entrance through the middle of the water sprinklers that some idiot always placed right over the path students followed into the science building.

I entered N7 wet, exhausted and just wanting to sit down and take in the lecture. Delpierre saw me. 'You are five minutes late,' he said. 'Turn around and leave my chemistry class now.'

I was dumbfounded, I was angry and I was immensely sad. At that moment I decided to give up studies and become known as one of the many dropouts from UWC. This is too hard, I told myself. Far too hard. Far too damn hard.

Delpierre had no idea what happened every other morning at No 51, nor did he care. He did not know that when I woke my mother after a night of nursing to ask whether she had some money I could use to get to UWC, she would scratch in her flat floral purse, knowing it contained nothing but odd papers. Nor did he know how the tears welled up in her eyes, meaning no words were needed to say, 'I can't help you this morning.' Nor did he know how long I waited on such mornings for a random lift, hoping that at least one of the many passing cars might eventually take me in the direction of Bellville South. All he saw was an empty figure at the back of N7 who was five minutes late.

I left for the UWC cafeteria, picked up that day's copy of the lowly *Cape Herald* (decent people read the *Cape Times* and the *Cape Argus*) and went straight to the classified pages at the back. There was a job at nearby Anchor Yeast and they offered me an assistant's post alongside a haughty young Englishwoman fresh from the mother country. I was a first-year dropout without much chemistry, let alone lab practice, so they asked me to leave. For weeks I sat at home dejected and not knowing what to do.

Sarah prevailed on Uncle Martin, my dad's cousin and fellow Brethren leader, and asked him to take me back to UWC. A kind-hearted man, he did not have much difficulty persuading me to jump into his VW Beetle and head to Bellville. I was a student again but the year ahead was going to be hard.

I failed the first year for several reasons. I had missed too many classes after dropping out. I did not understand science in Afrikaans. I struggled with the pace of university teaching, thinking I could study only before exams, like at school. And I found the stress of travel from so far away and the unpredictability of available funds too much to bear.

When I failed, there was a heavy-heartedness in my church. By this time, I had moved to a smaller and more modest assembly on the border of Grassy Park and Retreat which gathered in the garage of Uncle Japie and Auntie Babs James. That's right, the cars stayed outside while the inside of the garage was made up beautifully to give it the feel of a church; neat rows of chairs and a pulpit stand in front with a vase containing a white arum lily or two. These people believed in me, and the fact that I had failed was not only my disappointment – it was theirs too. I had seldom felt so bad; I had let down people who really believed in me. If I did well in my academics, I realised, they too would feel good.

I took refuge in that little assembly and decided to study during the day from the garage of the Jameses with my dentistry student friend, Neal Dreyer, who also joined this small church. With or without him, I showed up early and stayed late, studying hard to ensure I did not fail again. On church nights, I would stay all day then freshen up, put on my shirt, tie and jacket, and be ready for the Bible study or prayer meeting. But failing my support group again was not going to happen.

The James family was my anchor in those dark and difficult days. Auntie Babs would show her love and support in a special way. Three times a day, every day, she would feed us: coffee and snacks for the mid-morning break, a wonderful lunch and an afternoon tea with cakes. On campus days, I missed those treats but especially the little chats with this wise and gracious woman. After delivering the trays of goodies, Auntie Babs would stay for a few minutes and we would talk about a scripture from the previous night's meeting or some advice I needed on a personal matter. She did not gossip.

Amid the blessing, a crisis was brewing. Having failed and lost my bursary, I would have to pay my own registration fee for the next academic year. I must have shared my anxiety with Uncle Japie or his wife, and one night after the prayer meeting their only son, Ernest, called me to his little room attached to the outside of the main home. He was older than us and quite accomplished as a senior engineering student. Ernest worked for Murray & Roberts during the university holidays and earned a modest stipend to support him during his studies.

Being summoned by Ernie was odd. We had more of a relationship with his three rather feisty sisters, all active in the little church. He seldom interacted with us and was rather spare with words. But we looked up to him not only as the girls' older brother but as a student who paved the way for many of us. I entered his small room and Ernest held out a R20 note, a lot of money in those days. Whether he said anything, I can't remember, but it was the exact amount I needed to be able to register for continuing my studies at UWC. I never allowed myself to forget that enormous gesture that made all the difference.

Slowly, my shaky confidence came back and I started to be competitive in the smaller classes, showing some mastery in the majors, botany and zoology. Getting to this point was not easy. There was a built-in culture of low expectations at UWC that explicitly told students they would fail. It went something like this.

The lecturer arrives in class and welcomes the students to Biochemistry 134. Then he says: 'By the end of the first semester, half of you will have dropped out.' Sometimes it was more specific and I heard two more versions of this academic putdown: 'By the end of the semester, those of you remaining will be able to fit into the campus telephone booth.' And even more directly: 'We have only 25 spaces in the second-year laboratory so we are going to wean you out so only 25 pass [in a class of more than 100].'

We laughed nervously when these statements were made but they were remarkably predictive in their accuracy.

This awareness of coming to university with a more than average chance of failure was deflating. It wasn't like there were no other forces also making you doubt your choice of UWC. On pragmatic grounds alone, I wanted to go to the University of Cape Town (UCT) because it was so much closer to my home in Retreat and would have saved me time and money. But when I showed up to enquire about applying, two white women had that white kind of English smirk (those who know will know what it looks like) on their faces when I showed them my matric certificate; apparently, being the first in my school to obtain a first-class matric pass was not good enough.

Years later, when UCT offered me an honorary doctorate in education, I fleetingly thought of turning *them* down for a change. I didn't, of course, but I mentioned that moment in my acceptance speech to make a larger point about access, opportunity and decency.

There was, however, another reason for not wanting to go to UWC. I was under the influence of friends who had their baptism in the Non-European Unity Movement, and its puritanical beliefs as a leftist organisation in the Cape made no bones about the fact that UWC was a 'bush university', built in the Bellville bush. The same was true of the other black universities established at the same time and condemned to the rural nothingness of Bantustans such as Transkei or Zululand. All of them were creatures of the cynically named Extension of University Education Act of 1959.

In the minds of my Unity Movement friends, by going to UWC I was advancing the racist and ethnic project of the apartheid state. These folk looked down on you if you even considered going to 'Bush', the shorthand name for UWC at the time.

Of course, hypocrisy was written all over the pretentions of the anti-UWC crowd. They went to UCT, a colonial university by virtue of its origins and which had a prominent statue honouring the British imperialist who had carved up southern Africa, Cecil John Rhodes. This monument to empire stood not far from Jameson Hill (the Jammie steps, to students), named after one of Rhodes' henchmen in fleecing African mineral wealth. No shame at all, at least not until 2015 when student rage brought down the Rhodes statue.

At the time, though, the criticism stuck.

It was, however, not only the discouragement of the two smirking Englishwomen that discouraged me from pursuing a UCT application. Even if I had been accepted, I am not sure I was prepared to apply to an apartheid minister to study there on grounds that some of the courses I wanted to take were not available at the university for my kind. Factually, that would not be accurate since UWC and UCT both offered the BSc degree. Politically, that was reprehensible since you were now begging for a place at a white university.

I had one more dilemma to work through. Then and now, I detested being called coloured, a designation I would be accepting implicitly if I went to UWC since it was set aside for people classified by this strange designation: mixed race. I knew from my limited knowledge of history and biology that most South Africans were mixed race (by official definition). In fact, the very notion of mixed ancestry applied to one group of people was so ridiculous that every year in the apartheid parliament the minister of the interior would announce a list of names of people who had been reclassified in all directions of South Africa's complicated colour schemes. Moreover, to designate one group of people as mixed race was to assume the existence of pure races on either side of them, and at that point you slide into the realm of national socialism (Germany under Hitler), with gas chambers in sight for the impure.

I am not, never was, coloured.

But I needed a degree to get my family out of their financial struggles and to give myself a chance of a better life. In the end, I had little choice and found myself registering for the first-year BSc degree with majors in botany and zoology.

At every step of the admissions process, I was reminded in small ways that perhaps I did not belong on a university campus. We had to fill out a form indicating our subject choices for the three years of the degree. A white professor of zoology, Jan Skinner, did not even look up to greet me but took a red pen to correct my spelling of 'physiology' without saying a word. In the registration line I stood behind Lewis Jonker and his future wife, whom I did not know at the time but with whom I became good friends in later years. The taller Lewis, who went to a more fancied school called Spes Bona, grabbed my matric certificate and wondered out loud among his friends how I obtained a first-class pass with the subject marks I had. It took me a while to forget that dig (and writing it here means I did not, even after his passing). It felt as if your self-confidence was constantly being pummelled by everyone around you.

When you are in such a zone of low confidence as I was as an undergraduate at UWC, you start to believe that maybe you're not good enough, that the backlogs of science knowledge and practice from high school have eventually caught up with you. You expect to struggle and even fail, and when lecturers predict your demise your subjective self takes this to be true. After all, I had no role models in the family or among friends who were accomplished in anything, let alone in scientific endeavour.

Even at that time there was more than a hint that these subjective states of a lowly undergraduate might not be the whole story. Slowly we became aware of earlier UWC undergraduates who struggled to excel in the sciences but went to the US and other countries for postgraduate studies and achieved PhDs, some even becoming professors.

One example was that of Dwight Triegaardt, one of the more courageous UWC alums I would meet. Dwight failed chemistry solely because he was a political activist on the campus; insiders like the 'demmie' (the demonstrator in science labs) who saw his papers noticed that he had passed. But when the results came out, they showed he had failed. Eventually Dwight passed 'chem' and went on to do his master's and PhD in the US, obtaining a doctorate there in, yes, chemistry.

One of his friends, future UWC vice-chancellor Jakes Gerwel, showed the dissertation to his former tormentors in the chemistry department to see whether they were interested in reading it. They declined, perhaps out of embarrassment or not understanding this advanced work in chemistry, or both. Dwight went on to become a leader in science, science education and engineering in South Africa.

With this knowledge of the Dwights of UWC, I made a simple calculation that would inform my thinking and action in education for decades to come. In such cases, I realised, the problem was not simply the underprepared student or the demanding curriculum. It was the context in which they were taught and required to learn.

'What words do you want on your gravestone?' my daughter once asked me in a light moment between us. 'You know,' I told her. 'I say it in every speech to school and university students alike.' It's quite simple: you are smarter than you think.

On campus I nevertheless continued to struggle with confidence that was challenged in every way, including how you dressed. It did not help that I was tied down in what was at its core a conservative campus culture. I believe I was at the tail end of a practice where students had to wear jackets and ties. This was not unfamiliar from my church dress code, so I fell in line even in the heat of summer. I did not think about this much until, in conversation with other students, I realised how ridiculous this practice was across the Afrikaans-speaking universities, black and white. Attuned to the model of European universities and the hippie culture of the 1960s, the old English campuses in South Africa had students wearing jeans and sandals.

It was not really about the jacket and tie in conservative Afrikaans universities. It was about complying with a quasi-religious institution in which there was very little distinction between the university and the church. Even as late as the early 2000s at universities like Pretoria, I sat there as a dean, watching every senior management meeting, senate and council open in prayer, if not also a Bible reading. The tightness of the social, cultural and ideological fit between church and campus was also deeply ingrained in the everyday life of an earlier UWC.

But this compulsion around dress had another intention with respect to black students: to keep you in check, to mould you according to regnant values, to keep you on your knees. Gradually, student resistance – with one eye on what was happening at UCT – broke this social practice and students were free to dress for lectures as they pleased. However, not all campus spaces were as constrained or conservative.

I realised early on that the 'caf' (cafeteria) was an academic death trap. It was where students bunking classes went to play *klawerjas* (a popular card game) or pool. I only went there for the stand-on-the-table lunchtime political lectures of Allan Boesak and others. A caf regular was one of the Brethren children whose family was quite close to my parents. Roddy 'Porky' Hendricks, who later married a Muslim, made a reputation for himself in the caf. I was not to follow in his footsteps, a fellow believer warned.

I noticed another Brethren student who seemed to lose her way at UWC. The strikingly beautiful Joy ran off with a library science lecturer. All the Brethren kids on campus gave me a wide berth, perhaps knowing that my holier-than-thou attitude might get them reported to their elders. Others just found me irritating, like my future sister-in-law, whom I greeted heartily one afternoon with 'Praise the Lord, Faith!' to which she responded, 'For what?' It was perhaps the first time I realised that I was probably quite annoying to members of my church.

Then something happened that fundamentally changed my politics. UWC at the time was the home of local stirrings of an international movement called Black Consciousness (BC) with its origins in the US. Thanks to struggle stalwarts such as Steve Biko and Strini Moodley, here was a politics that did not distinguish black people according to their apartheid classifications as Indian, African and coloured. You were black, period. Black, moreover, was not a colour but a consciousness. It was a status that recognised oppression as the common bond that united us.

This meant the oppressed were brought together by solidarity rather than variations in skin tone. BC was also a force, not a timid acceptance of the terms of your existence dictated by whites; it struck back, as Biko did so gratifyingly when he beat up those interrogating white policemen in the movie *Cry Freedom*. Watching the film for the first time in San Francisco as a student, I saw the audience jumping out of their seats in glee when Biko smashed up those cops. BC fought back.

Ever the evangelical Christian, I was less attracted to the confrontational force of BC than its compelling message that I was black. It was a political consciousness which some of my friends demonstrated with clenched fists and huge Afros. I was tempted to grow one myself but the Brethren were strict about the regulation of men's hair: *Doth not even nature teach you that if a man have long hair, it is a shame unto him?* I remember lengthy discussions with the elders and among ourselves as youths about existential questions such as, 'How long is long (hair)?'

Buoyed by these powerful BC ideas, I found their theological expression in Black Theology (US) and a related movement, Liberation Theology (Latin America). Here again, Allan Boesak was the local exponent of these worldwide trends and I was a regular at the lunchtime meetings in the caf where the short man with a high-pitched voice stood on a table and educated us about God, human suffering and political salvation. Years later, Boesak led the charge to expel the Dutch Reformed Church from the World Alliance of Reformed Churches for its apartheid theology. I don't think some of his white compatriots ever forgave him.

These were the contending influences shaping my political becoming at UWC – evangelicalism, Black Consciousness, Black Theology and a growing irritation with white authority.

One day, I was leaving an urgent prayer meeting on campus where we had asked God to open the eyes of the riot police on campus. To our astonishment, God had answered our prayers because right in front of a military vehicle called a Casspir ('Casspir is not a friendly ghost', was a familiar protest placard), a group of armed white men had taken off their khaki caps and were gathered in prayer. Miracles, at last.

After the 'amen' they put their caps back on and rushed at us prayer warriors, and others in the area, with batons and rifles. I ended up running through the bush with scores of other students and discovering a railway line on the other side of campus. Here again was an abiding challenge to my faith: white Afrikaners living comfortably while oppressing black people and at the same time being devout Christians. The policemen genuinely thought they were praying to God before levelling their weapons at us. How was this even possible?

It was only many years later when I wrote *Knowledge in the Blood* that I came to understand the powerful role of different socialising agencies (home, church, school, cultural clubs) in indoctrinating Afrikaner youth in the intertwining logics of white supremacy and Christian nationalism. For those praying and shooting white policemen, there was no contradiction.

As far as my own evangelical faith was concerned, I still believed fervently and shared the gospel with anyone who cared to listen. A tall student in the botany lab did not appreciate my attempt at outreach. As I started to share the good news with him, he launched into a loud public and personal attack on me. Who did I think I was? He came here to study, not to be harassed! And on, and on, as I tried to fade into the brown lab bench out of sheer embarrassment.

The next week, in the same class, there he was again but this time with his entire face bashed in and extensive wrappings of white medical gauze hiding his wounds. Apparently he had been beaten up at a weekend nightclub. I tried very hard to resist drawing a link between his public reprimand and the assault that followed.

By the time I reached my second year academic (third year, if you count the repeat of the first), I had settled much more comfortably into UWC. There were fewer classes and fewer classmates. We started to form friendships in the class and relationships with lecturers were a bit more relaxed. '*Eerstejaars is nie mense nie,*' the professor of zoology once shared with us seniors and we laughed politely. We had successfully run the gauntlet of first-year studies at the hands of the Bothas and Delpierres.

It was around this time also that I started to become aware of the awkward spaces occupied by 'the firsts' at a slowly changing UWC. These were the coloured lecturers in small numbers who were becoming more visible. We admired people like the lab assistant Martin Hendricks, whose demeanour in the zoology labs was friendly and helpful, in contrast to the white senior lecturers and professors. Martin would take a final-year group to Paternoster for a science weekend devoted to one of his favourite research subjects, barnacles.

Then there was Frans Weitz, a much more intense botanical sciences lecturer who was also friendly but frowned a lot. His speciality was conservation biology, and he impressed us with his knowledge of flora and fauna with the species name *Capensis*, of the Cape. Both of them were Afrikaans, like other junior lecturers or lab assistants, and slowly made their way through the system to become doctors in their disciplines.

We admired these bright young minds and perhaps envisaged for ourselves such eminent status one day as 'demmies' (demonstrators, or lab assistants) with white coats in 'bot' or 'zoo'. But there was little question that at UWC in the middle to late 1970s, they were junior partners to the more senior white Afrikaans academics. We could see how lightly they trod around these men (there was one woman who came later, a Hofmeyr) and how moments of interaction required more than the necessary laughter at what was said by their superiors. It was sad to witness how these men walked the tightrope between the freedom to be themselves and a cultivated adulation of those whom, in most cases, were also their master's or doctoral supervisors.

Every now and again there was a senior black academic in our midst and we would be starstruck by these rare specimens. One was Professor Ismail Jacob (Josef) Mohamed in mathematics who, with a colleague, made a discovery in group theory that is central to abstract mathematics; the Heineken-Mohamed Groups in mathematics refers to this great thinker. It was also clear to some of us that Mohamed had a political streak and would not bend to or accommodate white authority in his professional life. Shortly after he made a stirring political speech he was arrested and banned, after which the cowardly UWC terminated his contract.

He stood out also because the black science academics (as opposed to those in the arts and theology) were by and large conservative and Afrikaans and not likely to give offence to whiteness; they were also the ones who were comfortable with being labelled coloured. I used to envy the arts students who boasted among their lecturers the likes of Jakes Gerwel in Afrikaans and Rhoda Kadalie in anthropology. Jakes wrote a brilliant thesis in Brussels on stereotypes of coloured people in Afrikaans novels before becoming dean of arts and then rector of UWC. The feisty Rhoda became a pioneer in women's and gender studies at UWC. In other words, the *radicals* were not in the science faculty, unless you were referring to molecules that contain at least one unpaired electron.

Probably the best black lecturer in science was Cecil Leonard, who became Dr Leonard and, after I left, professor of anatomy. Leonard was probably the best teacher in higher education I have encountered. He was knowledgeable and systematic with the enormous gift of sense-making for undergraduate students. It was his teaching that convinced me that among the best university teachers are those who first honed their craft in high schools.

For what good schoolteachers do well is to give meaning to that profound insight about learning left for us by the psychologist David Ausubel that, 'The most important single factor influencing learning is what the learner already knows.' Leonard made that connection so powerfully that his teaching did three things in quick succession: recognise your knowledge, engage your knowledge and transform your knowledge into new learning. A master teacher, in other words. Teaching the anatomy of the platanna, Leonard would also relieve our everyday anxieties with humorous moments like this one.

Apparently, the police arrested a family of three frogs in Grassy Park for excessive nocturnal noise. 'What do you have to say for yourself,' the magistrate asked the father, who responded, 'Your honour, we were only making bubbles.' 'And you ma'am?' the magistrate asked the mother. 'Your honour', she replied, 'I also was only making bubbles.' 'And you little one?' he asked the baby frog. 'Your honour,' said the smaller frog, 'I am Bubbles.' We laughed also out of relief, given all the stresses around us.

Leonard was not alone among the impressive young black academics. There was Merlyn Mehl, who taught me optics with a wry sense of humour. There was no question that the man was brilliant as a scientist and a teacher, and he became a world authority on science learning and cognition among disadvantaged students, allying himself with famous university networks on the east coast of America.

Colin Johnson was also a rising star in botany, and he reported back to our undergraduate class on a sabbatical during which he had the use of one of the most powerful (and at the time, novel) electron microscopes in the world. I was in awe.

Then there was Jan Persens, who studied 'ill-posed problems' in partial differential equations at Cornell University. At UWC, Jan was one of my more thoughtful lecturers and taught us calculus. We would become good friends at Cornell, an Ivy League university in upstate New York, where he was finishing his doctorate while I was pursuing my master's in science education. I suggested to him at some point that his obtuse research topic was itself ill-posed.

However, no matter how good or funny they were, my university teachers could not solve a major gap in my education. I did not have a solid grounding in the practical component of science. It is a horrible feeling as a first-year to enter a lab never having seen a microscope. In the botany class, for a moment I did not know which side to look through, threatening to treat the microscope as a telescope. I had never done a simple dissection of anything and suddenly there were strange instruments in my hand which I did not know how to use in opening up *Xenopus laevis*, or simply the platanna. Even simple things like titrations were foreign to me and the difference between a pipette and a burette was opaque. I felt completely disempowered in such moments, when you are super-aware of other students looking at you fiddling around.

I think of my life as a series of moments in which I made firm decisions that would be taken up later in life. One decision I took after I tampered with a microscope was that if I ever found myself teaching the biological sciences, no matter how poor the school or the students, they would learn to do science.

Not that science teaching was my first choice of career. I was stuck in a situation familiar to thousands of my generation. You went to university to study microbiology or sociology then discovered you had a major problem. The only funding available for black students was for those professions which the apartheid government had decided were worth supporting; that is, graduates who could populate the racially and ethnically based civil service. There were bursaries for librarians, policemen/women and, of course, teachers.

My plan was to do the BSc and teach high school biology while paying off the bursary, then return to do an honours in biochemistry, an early fascination. However, something became clear on my first day in the classroom: I was born to be a teacher. I suspect many of my contemporaries had the same experience and stayed in their professions even if they originally had other plans.

Because I had already wasted a failed year and had no intention of becoming a teacher, I did not study the additional year in the education faculty to obtain a teacher's certificate. In other words, I graduated as an uncertified teacher, later completing the qualification through part-time studies once it became clear that teaching was what excited me.

My world at UWC as an undergraduate student was therefore confined to the faculty of science. And because South Africa does not have a liberal arts tradition which enabled you to study across faculties, my intellectual world was limited – something I was determined to change as a university leader.

I also became aware of the limits of the institutional curriculum; that is, the range of offerings available or not available for study at UWC. When you looked around campus as an incoming undergraduate student, you could not help noticing an anaemic curriculum. There was the standard fare of the arts, science and commerce disciplines but no medicine, engineering or architecture, the high-status disciplines that top students often wanted to pursue. UWC, like the other 'bush' universities, was not meant to prepare graduates for independence or the private sector; these were training grounds for the civil service which required functionaries to make the apartheid system work. That much was clear.

It was only on reflection, having studied elsewhere in the world, that I became aware how narrow my undergraduate education at UWC really was. Instead of riveting lunchtime seminars on one or other topics in the natural sciences or the humanities, we were left with little by way of a broader education other than one mass meeting after another. Politics, in other words.

Make no mistake, there was some entertainment value to these mass gatherings as we waited for the political students to get proceedings under way. As students trickled into the full hall they would be greeted. A lone soul, looking shy, might hear someone shouting, '*Ou aap!*' This meant you were an old hand at UWC, implying that you had failed one or more years and thus earned the moniker, 'old (stretched out for emphasis) ape!'

It got worse. When you were suspected of having been at UWC forever without much progress in your academic status, the shrill voice from the crowd would announce the incoming veteran as '*oer aap!*' That '*oer*' (as in primeval) was really stretched in the mouth of the assailant as '*ooooooooeeeeeeeeer aap*', for effect. The crowd would roar in laughter as the embarrassed student, head down, scurried to find their seat.

One day, the '*oer aap!*' announcer met his match. It was a theology student, and these older men were known for their eloquence and aloofness in equal measure. When they spoke in public forums, they might as well have been preaching from the dominee's pulpit on a Sunday morning with those quivering voices. '*Oer aap!*' came the announcement and the bearded theology guy stopped dead in his tracks, looked in the direction of the noise, and said, '*Verskoon my, meneer, derde jaar akademies, derde jaar histories.*' The room fell silent and all you heard was muffled laughter, this time directed at the *aap* who had tried to take down a *tokkelok* (an affectionate name for a theology student).

I experienced much more serious extra-mural education in UWC mass meetings. A man called Ahmed Deedat would provoke Christians with a clever and systematic takedown of their core beliefs. University campuses like UWC were happy hunting grounds for the Indian-born imam. One memorable clash was with Frank McConnell, a Brethren missionary with a profound understanding of the biblical scriptures. I attended a few of these debates and Deedat ran rings around his Christian opponents, much to the delight of Muslim students and the dismay of Christians in attendance.

I was intrigued by his fluency but after a few of Deedat's performances I discovered why he always won these debates. The man had refined a few rhetorical skills which he wielded with great effectiveness. He made literal what was figurative (the earth created in five days); mathematical what was symbolic (of the trinity, how can three be one?); and humorous what was serious (the divinity).

Deedat's style of religious polemics was extreme and divisive, and eventually lost traction among Muslims in the Cape, given the broader inter-religious solidarities being developed under anti-apartheid movements like the United Democratic Front. But, for a brief moment, Deedat brought a provocative energy into undergraduate life and at the very least challenged Christians, who were the more active proselytisers, to *give a reason for the hope that was in them*.

It was during these mass meetings in the undergraduate years that I discovered something about myself that was an enduring disposition. The entertainment value apart, I did not like following the majority in these large meetings. There was a mass psychosis in crowds that made me uncomfortable. What I found deeply satisfying, intellectually and politically, was the gift of thinking for myself and not being buoyed by crowds.

Mass gatherings, especially in South Africa, are performances where people with otherwise sedate personalities would be swept up in the emotion of the moment to say and do things they would never contemplate without the incitement of the throng.

These events often reminded me of a choice passage of scripture about a mass meeting in which *some cried one thing and some another for the assembly was confused and the more part [most of them] knew not wherefore they were come together*.

This kind of mass behaviour was for me the opposite of thoughtfulness. My almost instinctive reaction was to take the opposite viewpoint to that of the majority, an instinct that would serve me well in my future scholarship. That disposition I acquired from observations of mass meetings, not from the UWC undergraduate curriculum.

The narrow curriculum nevertheless raised an interesting question for me as I looked around at what was on offer. Why would the state fund a dentistry department at UWC? This too was an elite, sought-after discipline that was expensive (like medicine) to operate and sustain. Was it because of the overwhelming oral health needs of the Cape Flats population? Or was it some sop to coloureds in last-minute negotiations about the institutional curriculum of this newly established bush university? Regardless, apartheid logics meant that the white and coloured dentistry faculties were on different floors of the same building with different entrances for their racially coded clients.

When democracy came and a swashbuckling minister Kader Asmal merged universities, his department decided to combine the dental facilities of Stellenbosch and UWC, giving this prized faculty to the black university.

At some point in my first year of studies I discovered that I lacked a subject. To complete the degree, you needed to do at least one additional subject outside your majors. The first year was simple enough (physics 1B, chemistry 1B, mathematics 1B, botany 1A and zoology 1A). The Bs meant those subjects were less demanding, aligned with your majors, and would not be done beyond the first year. But you needed a 'filler subject', and after consultation with fellow students I chose geology.

At this point I discovered a major hurdle to my academic progress. In the first session, a practical, we were called on to imagine the rocks before us in multiple dimensions and draw them from those many-sided angles. Try as I might, this was not something I could easily do. So, after two weeks I changed plans and decided to do mathematics 1A, the one for majors in the subject. Now I had to knuckle down because I had wasted enough time and missed classes in this course.

It was a soul-deadening experience. Like Mr Gilloway in high school, Mr Gonin, also an old white man, could not teach to save his life. He drawled on in front of the class without making eye contact with the students or even enquiring whether we understood what he was mumbling. He, too, was a well-known maths textbook writer (Gonin, Archer & Slabber) but pedagogy was not his forte. Since I was now in my second year, I dared not fail any other subject. I then got lucky.

In the sparsely populated university library, I stumbled upon a set of mathematics books called the Schaum series. What was amazing about this collection is that it offered a simple and systematic set of problems for every topic in the curriculum. You did not need to understand mathematics (which, of course, was the fundamental problem); you simply had to identify the category or topic being discussed then work your way through the self-guided problems with neatly worked-out answers for each of them. I was now learning mathematics as procedure (another problem), and with a reasonably strong memory I sailed through mathematics 1B and 1A as if I knew what I was doing. It was a joke, really.

Speaking of teaching as jokes, I was now in my third year and for some reason I had missed the class by De Vries on evolution. I enjoyed this topic very much, even if it rattled my fundamentalist understanding of the origins of man (sic). God created man and out of his ribs, the woman. It was nice and simple, but evolution threw me an initial curveball until I rationalised that the means for human creation could very well have been via evolution. But I digress.

I had missed this class and because we were now in the final year of the degree, it was acceptable to go to the lecturer and ask for 'the notes'. Mr De Vries, with a rumpled manner and an amusing demeanour, obliged. I found a photocopier and returned the yellow notes which from the fading print suggested that he had taught the same content for years; but that was not the main shock. The first paragraph had a definition for evolution. Then, before the next substantive point in the handwritten notes, there was an interjection: *'maak 'n grap'*. The man was reminding himself to make a joke.

Not all UWC lecturers were this pathetic and one who stood out among the whites was a curious personality called Kristo Pienaar. He had a Sunday evening television slot, *Veldfokus*, which was part of an environmental programme, *50|50*, designed to show the balance between human beings and nature. In this slot, Kristo would show off his extensive knowledge of garden plants with an incredible wit and presentation style that won him an admiring audience. This was one of the few lecturers I knew who adored his discipline and loved to teach it well.

Surprisingly, he was the only white lecturer who took the class on excursions, such as one to the Kirstenbosch botanical garden, where he made sure we knew the genus and species of the major specimens in this remarkable place. On another trip, he took us botany III students on a drive through the town of Darling to show us the rich flora of the area. At one stage, and to the surprise of us students, he fell to the ground in front of a carnivorous plant, *Drosera capensis*, and with great passion explained how it devoured flies. Easily the most enthusiastic of university teachers.

Kristo seemed to enjoy international esteem. At one stage when he was in full flight, teaching us in the late afternoon, someone summoned him for an urgent overseas call. He went to his office for several minutes and returned with a remarkable story. An American scientist was calling because he was interested in Pienaar's research on certain plants in the middle of roads and highways that flourished as a result of the carbon dioxide emissions from vehicles. This sounded awesome to a budding scientist.

Kristo, whose wife Christina was a writer of popular Afrikaans books, went on to become a councillor and mayor of the Bellville area and even enjoyed honours from the South African military. Then and now, such a 'normal' existence raised deeper questions about how many white South Africans lived their lives so fully and freely as if this crime against humanity (apartheid) did not exist and as if their students were perfectly normal specimens in a botany classroom which could exist in any part of the world. There were many whites like Kristo who enjoyed a normal life on campus during the day, only to retreat into their white enclaves at night, enjoying their racial privilege while receiving pats on the back for their efforts to uplift *die kleurlinge*.

More than these white lecturers, I harboured strong feelings against coloureds at UWC who sold out. These were conservatives who desired power and privilege for themselves within white-sanctioned structures. I thought it was a joke when the more radical rector of UWC, Jakes Gerwel, declared years later that UWC was to be 'the intellectual home for the left'. As a future ideal, even an ambition, that would be nice. But his categorical distinctions between the liberal universities like UCT and the conservative universities like Stellenbosch, pitted against the home of the radical left, meant it was always going to be an intellectual flight of fancy.

Gerwel, in my view, had underestimated the deep roots of coloured nationalism at UWC, the kind of conservatism embedded in the culture, values and politics of this institution. Right next door to the university were the buildings of the Coloured Persons Representative Council, the white government's attempt to give some form of self-governance to coloured people as representatives. It was a hated body among progressive students at UWC and its location next to the university was no accident; this was probably the point of absorption for coloured intellectuals graduating from UWC, if not also a lame attempt at demonstrating that the government cared for their voices after all.

Whether it was coloured rugby players in what was called the Federasie (as opposed to the South African Rugby Union, the more political players' union) or the coloured sellouts in the representative council, I detested these people who could not see that they were being played by the white man. Not long afterwards this dummy representation took another form, the tricameral parliament, where once again the apartheid government experimented with partial rights for whites, Indians and coloureds at the expense of the black African majority. So intense was the resistance from progressive forces on and off campus that the tricameral experiment gave rise to the largest anti-apartheid force in South Africa, the United Democratic Front, which gathered its membership from all sectors of society.

However, long before that moment, many of the coloured intelligentsia played footsie under the table with the apartheid authorities. Right next to UWC was a technical campus, Peninsula Technikon, headed by some of the coloured intelligentsia. One moment they were leading the coloured teachers union, the Cape Teachers Professional Association (CTPA), the next they shifted their politics towards the ANC as soon as there was word of the unbanning of the liberation movements and the release of Nelson Mandela and other political prisoners. The CTPA was in fact the first formation to adopt the Freedom Charter. It was a sight to behold.

During my undergraduate years, these men were very susceptible to coloured nationalist politics and representation in order to enjoy a seat at the white man's table, and I resented their duplicity. UWC had produced many such conflicted quasi-political figures over the years I was a student, not least the first non-white and compromise rector Richard van der Ross, whom the more conscious students regarded as part of the problem. He was appointed after student protests against the last white rector.

Dickie van der Ross, as he was known, spoke and wrote comfortably about coloured people as if they alone were struggling for rights of inclusion rather than demands of liberation that included the African majority. The progressive students resented him and I remember clearly how Van der Ross courageously showed up one morning to address an angry group. Without warning, a brick came flying in his direction, and with unbelievable calm he simply moved his head away as it flew right past his face. I was in shock and remember having some admiration for the man for not backing off in a hostile situation.

Years later we shared a platform at Stellenbosch University in one of those interminable debates on the future of Afrikaans. In my invited presentation I reminded Van der Ross, the chair of my session, of the event just described. He seemed to recall the incident and asked me, somewhat playfully, 'But I wonder who threw the brick?' I was angry with him because, in my student mind at the time, Van der Ross was a coloured stooge but I was never violent towards any human being. Since then, Van der Ross' acceptance into UWC's broader democratic project has become complete. During a tribute to his role at the university at the time, headlined by six of us as current and former vice-chancellors, we all praised his leadership during those perplexing times.

In the foment of the time, though, there was little to forgive and nothing to yield.

For example, in my undergraduate years there was something approaching admiration of a supposed coloured authority in the form of Erika Theron, who at the time enjoyed the status of chancellor of UWC. This was a ceremonial position but it gave a white Afrikaans woman enormous stature, based, I suspect, on her role as chairperson of a commission of inquiry into political rights for coloured people within the constraints of apartheid ideology. Most seemed to forget that at Stellenbosch University she was a protégée of Professor Hendrik Verwoerd, the man often credited as the father of apartheid.

In short, as more progressive students in time pushed for radical change on a non-racial basis that included all South Africans, there was this surrounding turmoil among people who took coloured identity and politics seriously even if it meant foregoing the rights of Africans and accepting narrower terms of ethnic participation under white domination. What this group did not recognise was that the political floodgates were opening and the demand for one man one vote, as it was posed at the time, was already a non-negotiable.

Conscious of these broader struggles for ethnic inclusion among conservative coloureds, I had earthier and more immediate concerns on the ground. I was struggling with the back and forth travelling from Retreat to Bellville.

I used to envy students who lived in on-campus residences or rented in nearby Bellville South. They could walk to lectures and take naps in 'res' between classes. They also formed a tight-knit community and had time for sports and weekend parties at on- and off-campus hangouts. Every day I would hear them regaling each other with funny stories from residence life. How nice, but my parents definitely could not afford on-campus accommodation.

This meant I missed out on all the fun the hostel students seemed to be enjoying. On Monday mornings we commuter students could only listen to stories about dances, pranks and drinks. Not that I would have been able to participate in these sinful activities but at least those living on or near campus had built among themselves a camaraderie and an identity. Every now and again there would be a sad story. The university news would report that a student had drowned in the campus swimming pool near the residences. The subtext was difficult to miss; only a drunk student would climb over the fence after hours and swim without any lifeguards nearby.

I was left to spend most of my time feeling tired and trying to figure out how to commute without money. Hitchhiking was safer then but when you got to campus depended on whether a car stopped to pick you up and how far it was going in the direction you wanted. On more than one occasion I abandoned a hitchhiking effort and went home to study because no cars were stopping.

When there was an examination the next day, I would stay over with family friends, the Sheldons, in Belhar to avoid the risk of not getting to campus on time. Maureen and Abe Sheldon were close friends of my parents. I discovered later that my mother, Sarah, served as a confidante and mentor to the younger Maureen over the years. The Sheldons delighted in offering me accommodation during examination periods, almost as if they understood their role in the broader network of support that made it possible for me to study and succeed at UWC.

Eventually, I found a dentistry student, Husain Brey, travelling down Retreat Road to UWC for classes, and for a long time in my senior years I could wait on the corner for his yellow VW Beetle to show up. It was such a relief, even if the bespectacled Brey, as we called him, hardly ever spoke.

There were other notable characters in the mix of random lift opportunities from UWC back home. One was Howard Beyers, an older theology student whose car ran on fumes and God's grace, as the saying goes. I remember him driving in pouring rain with the left hand on the steering wheel and the right hand reaching outside the car and acting as a wiper to clear the windscreen. You could but pray in the back seat as the car-shaped lump of metal on wheels hurtled down Modderdam Road.

Then there was a real gentleman from the dentistry faculty, Dr Jairam Reddy. He was kind and generous towards students hitching a ride and always had genuine questions of interest for all of us lucky to travel southwards with him.

Years later I would appoint him as chair of the council of a dysfunctional Durban university where the minister had asked me to 'take over' and restore governance and management. At the time, I allowed myself a thought about how unlikely this appointment action would have seemed to me then, an awestruck undergraduate getting a lift from an esteemed professor.

Back in my UWC classes it was becoming clear, for the first time, that I would obtain the BSc degree. You could feel more respect coming from the professors and a sense that the first-years were looking up to you; some would even ask for advice.

Also, as the large class thinned into the senior years my classmates started to bond as 'bot' and 'zoo' majors. Many had endearing nicknames which further cemented the relationships among us. I was JD (to this day), my initials used to distinguish me from the other Jansen in the class, my cousin Edwin. If there was any distinction among us, it was one of language. The Afrikaans speakers were in the majority and that was the language of classroom banter and engagement with each other and the lecturers.

Naturally, the English-speaking students tended to form their own groupings. One was always aware, though, that the English speakers were regarded as snobs from the southern suburbs who looked down on Afrikaans speakers who were mainly country bumpkins. As an English speaker, on the other hand, I thought they had a distinct advantage in terms of their access to the Afrikaans lectures and lecturers. The Afrikaans students certainly held their own in academic performance, so there was no need for any sense of inferiority.

Gradually UWC lost the Afrikaans profile of its student body when the university became deracialised and speakers of the African languages started to study there. In later years, I discovered that the loss of an Afrikaans majority identity at UWC because of its coloured student population was a major defeat for conservatives at the white Afrikaans universities since UWC provided a convenient fig leaf for Afrikaner nationalist drives to maintain the language. Sometimes their arguments were embarrassingly dishonest: we fight for Afrikaans on our (white) campuses for the poor rural coloured child who would otherwise be at a disadvantage with English in the lecture rooms.

It was time to prepare for graduation after four years (1975–1978). The big day itself is a blur but I remember my parents feeling very proud without saying so. It was those days, of course. What I did tell myself, however, was that I would never want to study further at UWC, this ethnic institution that had caused me so much distress.

I had had enough.

5

Back in the classroom

'Your profession is not what brings home your weekly pay cheque, your profession is what you're put here on earth to do, with such passion and such intensity that it becomes spiritual in calling.'
Vincent van Gogh

I was standing inside the biology classroom of Vredenburg Secondary School when I heard the sudden whoosh of students running past the open door. Seconds later came another whoosh, this time of policemen in blue uniforms with whips swishing ahead of them. It was 1980 and the student uprisings that had started that year in Cape Town, almost 150 km away, had come to this rural school on the west coast. From that moment, everything changed, including my understanding of the politics of education in schools. However, to understand the moving sands of school politics, I first had to grapple with everyday life in a semi-rural Afrikaans school where I was the urban, English-speaking stranger from the Cape.

When I graduated with a BSc degree from UWC, I had a sense of mission. Like my father, I wanted to serve outside the relative luxury of Cape Town and for me that meant teaching in rural schools. The department of education required you to list three choices and it made the final decision on your behalf. I listed schools in Beaufort West, De Aar and Vredenburg, the one chosen for me.

There was a problem, though. Until recently, there had been no high school for coloured children in Vredenburg, only one for whites in the *dorp*. As a result, most primary school graduates either dropped out to work or went to Malmesbury or further afield for their high school education. For those who sought work, Saldanha and its fisheries was a popular choice. By the time the new high school was completed, some of the students returning to class were more or less my age as a fresh graduate from university. I was in for a series of shocks.

Then and now, teachers in South Africa's dysfunctional schools seldom started teaching in assigned classes on day one of the new term; this practice continued even though teachers came in two days before the learners in mid-January, the start of the academic year.

The delay in teaching was a huge surprise to me. You were given a temporary class to supervise, one you may or may not teach a few weeks (or months) later, while senior teachers worked out a timetable. By the time the timetable was completed and the seniors had worked it out in their favour (no teaching for them in the last period on a Friday), it was time to prepare the children for athletics.

Athletics started with a school-based competition from which the top students in track and field were chosen for the Boland interschool competition. Those who came tops in this regional competition would compete for provincial colours, hoping to represent Western Province in the national championship.

I was dismayed that months of potential teaching time could be wasted in such a reckless manner. That experience would inform much of my thinking about why education in South Africa was so difficult to reform. At the heart of school dysfunction is the wastage of the single most important resource in the national budget – teaching time. When, as a junior teacher, I pointed out the waste of time and the effects on student learning, the older teachers laughed at me. '*Ag, jy verstaan nie*' (shame, you don't understand) was the response.

I took things into my own hands. Whether this was going to be my eventual class or not, I was going to start teaching them the basics of biochemistry, the first chapter in the biology book. At the end of the lesson on day one, I assigned homework to be handed in the next morning. The Standard 9 students (there was no Standard 10 class yet) looked at me as if I was completely crazy – no other teacher did this and I might not be their eventual teacher anyway. Early the next morning as the class drifted in, I told them to put their homework on the desk in front of them.

Things went well until I got to a chap called Haas (rabbit, in English).

He lay with his head on the desk and did not bother to display his non-existent homework. '*Huiswerk!*' I demanded. Haas appeared to be snoozing. The other students were smiling with glee. What better *afleiding* (distraction) than a fight between a young teacher and an overage student who looked like he spent weekends beating up random people.

What happened next I am still embarrassed about. I lifted Haas clean from his desk and delivered an almighty swipe to the body that ended the standoff. Unfortunately, from that day forward, several teachers with 'difficult' students would send them to my classroom to be sorted out. On the upside, if there is one, I never again had problems getting homework from my students.

I taught biology for the next two years as if my life depended on it. Or rather, as if their lives depended on it. I lived in the hostel on the school grounds which allowed students from distant rural and coastal areas to attend Vredenburg Secondary (the white school, like everywhere else, was distinguished from its coloured neighbour by being called High School). Unlike UWC, I got to and from my class with a couple of hundred steps.

Full of energy, I asked my students to come in on weekends and holidays so I could 'reinforce' what they had learnt during the week. Those in the hostels had no choice and those living in the surrounding neighbourhood, Louwville, sometimes came.

If I had any doubts about a career after the science degree, I knew instantly that teaching was for me. I loved the thrill of making complex things plain, like the Krebs cycle in aerobic respiration or the double helix structure of DNA. To see a child move from frown to nod is a priceless reward that only a teacher can fully appreciate. I taught my heart out, and then followed disaster.

The results came in from the first school-wide quarterly test and I was devastated. The students had done poorly despite my intensive teaching. What on earth had happened? I did lots of soul searching, talked to older teachers, asked the smarter kids and even consulted the enemy at the time – the subject inspector from Coloured Affairs, the government's department of education. What was I doing wrong?

Inspector Schroeder was a highly organised and efficient public servant who took his job seriously. He was also a master teacher in biology. I was teaching the concept of pH, an indicator of a solution's degree of acidity or alkalinity. He stopped me halfway through the lesson and asked if he could take over. Within minutes, I understood where I was going wrong.

Schroeder taught them as if they were high school learners; I taught them as if they were first-year university students. I marvelled at how he made things accessible by using ordinary language and bringing in everyday examples of substances from their kitchens and gardens. The youngsters came alive when he taught.

It then dawned on me why I was not making those connections. I had come straight to high school teaching without a teacher's qualification, that additional year you do after a first degree when you learn how to teach through a combination of theory and immersion in teaching practice. I had only the BSc degree, and it showed.

A little irritation on the side was the parents of Lewis Jonker (the fellow student who joked about my matric results), especially the mother, who took every opportunity to remind me that I was an unqualified teacher while her son stayed at UWC for an extra year to do his teaching diploma. I did not bother to tell her my parents could not afford that luxury. Lewis's father was the school principal and his mother had an administrative role on the property, which included a boys' and girls' hostel.

What made the poor results of my biology class feel even worse was what I saw in my first pay cheque. I could not believe it. Less than R300, which even at the time was a disaster. How could I work so hard, including weekends, and earn so little? One reason was my unqualified status.

I needed to do something about this and immediately enrolled for a teacher's diploma with a distance education institution, the University of South Africa (Unisa). The content of much of the curriculum was absolute nonsense. The regnant approach to education was something called fundamental pedagogics. It was the underpinning philosophy of apartheid education and a bastardisation of Dutch phenomenology.

According to its key tenets, the purpose of education was to instil in children the values of compliance, obedience and submission to the divine; that is, the white Calvinist God. Children were not-yet-adults rather than unique human beings on their own terms. As such, they had to be moulded through education into adulthood. Education was neutral and therefore not to be used as a political weapon, for that is not the true purpose of education. Instead, its purpose is that a fully formed adult leads an incomplete and insecure child to adulthood.

You did not need to be a specialist in education to realise this was dangerous. By framing the child in this infantile way, you not only cancelled out their uniqueness as creative human beings but you laid the groundwork for indoctrination. To further claim that education is neutral when the entire apartheid system was indoctrinating children with state ideology was rank hypocrisy. And to give adults this elevated status of fully formed human beings was to beg the question about the racist mind that devised and sustained this system of white supremacy in the first place.

The problem remained that I needed to get this qualification, so I studied what I did not believe to be true and scored distinctions in most subjects. What made matters challenging was that the authors of fundamental pedagogics, all white Afrikaner men, wrote in arcane language deploying circular reasoning about impenetrable concepts. There was only one way to pass: memorise the nonsense. And I did.

I discovered one helpful component of the teaching qualification. Student teachers would meet in small groups and be taught the basics of teaching. You would then present a lesson from your subject, in my case biology, and the travelling lecturer would give instant feedback. This I found very useful, in part because the focus was on the mechanics of teaching, which was the minimum I needed for the diploma.

In Vredenburg, my teaching improved and my salary increased. By now the study bug had bitten me and, buoyed by distinctions, I decided to do an honours degree (it was called the BEd at the time, now the BEd Honours). Once again I gained distinctions in most subjects. My confidence in the classroom increased and there was a further jump in the salary scale. Like many students before and after me, Unisa offered a lifeline for those who could only study part time because of the need to work and earn simultaneously.

I was now in full flight and my students were getting As and Bs. But I had to deliver on another promise I had made to myself long ago: my students would do practicals. In an ideal world, you would do a theoretical lesson on, say, the functioning of the human kidney, then have the students do a dissection of a pig's kidney. However, this was difficult for three reasons. One, the classes were quite full. Two, the equipment and solutions were not readily available; I needed time to buy or borrow some of the essentials. Three, I needed more time for experiments (setting up and cleaning up) than the standard 40-minute period would allow.

I planned a week in which all my students would conduct and write up at least 12 scientific experiments and negotiated with the school leadership to give me a week of double periods for this purpose. I then set up the rudimentary science lab with 12 stations around the room, each of which hosted an experiment, with 12 worksheets on hand. Students would move from one station to the next doing a titration at one stop, a microscopic investigation at another and a small dissection at the next. All of this took an extraordinary amount of planning and not a small amount of money from my meagre salary.

Fortunately, being a new school, Vredenburg had a clean laboratory with a reasonable supply of basic science equipment such as volumetric flasks, retort stands with clamps, and of course chemicals. I was in my element, so to speak.

Until tragedy struck.

Another whoosh of students past my classroom followed by police with whips in hot pursuit. This time things were escalating fast as students took on the might of the apartheid regime. Some were arrested and recirculated into the student population. The students were angry and the staff gathered to discuss how we could help them not only with making up for missed classes but offering all kinds of material and social support. What started in urban Cape Town was now a national movement of student protests.

During one of those whooshes past my office I was not present. It is possible that I left the lab's storage room open, a space heavily stocked with equipment; either that or one of the students got hold of the key without my knowledge. I do not know how but students got in there, destroyed the little room and ran off with expensive equipment. This was the first time I had to make sense of something I still do not understand: how students could destroy on one day what they needed for their learning the next.

On the one hand, I understood the anger of the activist students, especially since their lives were at stake. They were lashing out. On the other hand, I wondered why they would do this when education was the one weapon they had to deny apartheid's intent, which was to educate them for barbarism, as the Cape Town Trotskyist, IB Tabata, so poignantly put it.

After a short investigation, the department of education found me liable for the damage to the lab and the loss of materials. I wrote back saying this was ridiculous; I did not do this, and for all I knew the key might have been stolen. The department's response was to start deductions from my modest salary, and that was it. I was angry for a long time, even as I started to understand their political minds: if the teachers can't control the students, let them pay the price.

I would never again trust officials of the education department to take the interests of teachers seriously. I needed to join a union but the papers handed to me were for membership of the Cape Teachers Professional Association, the coloured union of which my first principal, Mr Jonker, was a prominent member. I tore up the application forms and threw them in the bin. Colleagues warned that I might lose my job, because in the rural areas everybody was obliged to join this ethnic association of teachers.

My confrontations with officialdom were far from over. During a break one day, I wandered over to an empty classroom with a newish piano. I started to play the only thing I knew, gospel songs, when the principal walked by. 'Meneer Jansen,' he said in Afrikaans, 'you're just the man I need. We lack a music teacher for the senior classes.' I protested vigorously; I was not a trained music teacher.

His response was to enter my name into the timetable to teach music. So, I taught music from my limited repertoire of praise and worship songs and an even more limited ability to teach the subject competently. Shortly afterwards there was a panel inspection. This means a team of inspectors arrives at a school for a comprehensive evaluation of all subjects.

I had to perform, and my class had to perform, for the white man sitting at the back of the make-believe music class. His report card on me had one line: 'his choice of music is *eensydig* (one-sided)'. 'Of course it bloody well is. That's what I tried to say all along,' was my unspoken thought. Regardless, that damning criticism went into my official evaluation record as a new teacher. Once again, I felt powerless under the might of bureaucracy.

I could understand how inspectors came under deadly fire in places like Soweto, the centre of student protests during the uprisings of the mid-1970s. Their government cars were torched and they had to scamper for their lives. These men were the enforcers of apartheid policy at school level. They made one deadly mistake in African schools which led to the historic Soweto uprising of 1976: in their nationalist hubris, the Afrikaner government decided to expand the teaching of Afrikaans to more subjects in the curriculum. It was one of the dumbest moves in the history of education policymaking in South Africa and provoked fierce protests that some argue contributed to the eventual fall of the apartheid state.

In my small world as a beginner educator, the inspectors were the face of the government, and apart from a brief and pleasant intervention by my biology mentor Schroeder, I resented their presence on the school grounds.

Nothing, however, would stop me from my 18-hour day commitment to teaching my students to the best of my ability. And so, when the senior teachers were looking for volunteers to help in the different athletics codes, my hand shot up first and I offered to do the middle-distance training for the Boland school championships. After all, I had had the best coach for the 800 m at Steenberg High, my Latin teacher.

I took all the boys and girls who won middle-distance races (800 m, 1 500 m, 3 000 m, 5 000 m) in the interhouse event at Vredenburg Secondary and put them through their paces. I knew only two things: the importance of stamina and the value of strategy in a multi-lap race.

For stamina, I took the group of 12–15 students through an exhausting regimen of long-distance running and on-the-field sprints every day after school. One of the most memorable stamina training episodes was to run with them from Vredenburg to the Paternoster coast about 12 km away early on Saturday mornings. I seldom made the full distance myself and would follow the runners by car.

For strategy, I would teach them the basics of how to run a middle-distance race. Never run in front. Always hang back in second or ideally third place until the final bend. Recognise a rabbit so that you don't exhaust yourself following a pacesetter who will drop out at some point; a rabbit from an opposing school's team might be there to confuse you for the advantage of his or her running mate. Never pass wide on a bend; it takes too much energy. And in the final stretch release everything.

At the Boland meet, Vredenburg Secondary won all the middle-distance races and everyone took notice. I was asked to coach the Boland team going into the provincial competition. Again, several of our athletes won their races and a clear standout was the under-14 boy John Carolus, who was so fast he sometimes won his 800 m by more than 100 m.

The next year, one of the senior teachers decided it was his time to shine so he made himself the school's middle-distance coach without consulting me. I was bruised but I was a junior teacher without power. Long story short, we won nothing in the Boland middle-distance races that year.

Back in the classroom, I was still the master of my children's destiny, so we continued teaching in school, after school and on Saturday mornings. I could start to discern the ones who promised to do great things way beyond the semi-rural confines of a lowly coloured school. Ivan Meyer (Vredenburg) was a solid biology student who went on to senior leadership in politics in the province. Christina Amsterdam (Hopefield) trained for her doctorate in the US and become a professor of education finance. There were many others, such as the bright sparks Derek and Jolene Abrahams, whose parents owned a shop up the road from the school. The talent of these students, like young people anywhere, simply required the launchpad of a good education.

They found that at Vredenburg Secondary. I was astounded by the talent of the teachers on offer. Mr Esterhuyse might have been old-school but his booming voice could be heard through the door as he revelled in teaching history. He had the wonderful ability to make his subject plain and pleasant. The students adored him and he called his fellow male teachers *meester*, an Afrikaans words that has so many beautiful meanings, including master of your discipline. He was erudite, knowledgeable, cultured and an impeccable professional.

Then there was a teacher who taught Standard 6. She did not have higher qualifications, perhaps only a basic primary school teacher's diploma from a college. But I watched her take her students through the basics of science. She would have them memorise parts of a plant or the natural elements. Even then, I recognised that there is a place in schools for getting children to recite and memorise the basics as a foundation for constructivist learning later on. This teacher used every second available in the classroom and her children did well. When the teachers' colleges were closed years later, hers was the kind of talent we lost.

I was fortunate to enjoy access to these outstanding teachers and to learn from them. But Vredenburg offered me much more. I was the joint head of the boys' hostel for out-of-town children, and this was a new experience for me. You were with these youngsters during the day in school hours and had to care for them in the hostel afterwards. It was generally pleasant, but every now and then there would be hysterical episodes on the girls' side which involved seeing ghosts or something like that. The food was horrible, but I was saving money by having to pay only a modest accommodation fee.

On weekends off I travelled back home, especially at the end of the month. I found myself trapped in an age-old custom on the Cape Flats where you gave your pay cheque to your parents. They would then give some of the money back before taking their fair share. It was a silly tradition but I respected it.

It was now time to prepare Vredenburg Secondary's first matric class for the final examinations. I had taught them for two years, since the matric paper was set on the basis of subject teaching in standards 9 and 10. From senior teachers I had learnt a valuable strategy. You would teach in such a way that you completed the syllabus in the middle of the second year. In that way you could use the latter half of the final year to do revision of everything learnt previously, enhancing students' chances of success at year end. After all, which student will remember what was taught almost two years earlier? It worked like a bomb and all my students passed, including some with excellent marks in biology.

I had one more shave with officialdom. I was invited and then applied to be a sub-examiner in matric biology. I thought this would be a great way for a young teacher to see what counts in the marking process, working off expert memoranda. It was an invaluable experience and I adjusted my teaching accordingly. This was also a useful way of making some extra money for the holidays.

However, shortly before the end of this first marking experience the chief examiner, a white Afrikaans man, asked if we sub-examiners, all coloured teachers, had any questions before he dismissed us. I raised my hand and asked whether it was ethical for the two young boys in front, his son and a friend, to be working for him and making money through their roles as 'checkers' – they tallied our mark allocations in case mistakes had been made.

The white man's face turned an angry red. He had no answer for my ethics question and mumbled an inadequate response. Today we would call that corruption. I should not have been surprised that I was banned from ever again marking matric scripts for the provincial education department.

It was time to move back home after learning the foundations of teaching practice at Vredenburg Secondary, later renamed Weston High School. A post was advertised at Trafalgar High School in District Six, Cape Town, and I could not have entered a more different environment than that of my former west coast school.

If Vredenburg Secondary was a new school with possibilities for shaping its future direction, Trafalgar High was steeped in history, culture and politics. I had hardly arrived when I was told about the intellectual and political heroes of the school, from the great struggle lawyer Benny Kies to the famous poet Cosmo Pieterse, both banned for their politics.

Unlike Vredenburg, here I felt I was walking on sacred ground as the names of great teachers tripped off the lips of the old-timers: Apollis 'Polly'

Slingers, Hassan Bavasah, Ernie Lennert and, still there at the time, Ernie 'Snoekie' Steenveld. Even the retiring teacher I was replacing, Cynthia Fisher, was presented to me as one of the great biology teachers of her time. I felt in awe of these greats, perhaps a little intimidated.

The majesty of the teacher greats was offset by the derelict state of the buildings. In the first class I was asked to supervise, the student walked through the door without opening it; there was a massive hole in the wood, carved out over the holidays. For a moment, I played around in my head with the thought of how to discipline a student who does not open a door but walks through it.

No part of the old building was worse than the biology lab in which I was to teach. Even to use the word 'lab' is to stretch the imagination. There was a fume cupboard stuffed with garbage. The five or so white basins per row of benches were filthy. The gas outlets were ornaments; there was no gas. The shelves running the length of the lab had one or two specimens in preservative fluids but they seemed to have died of shock as large eyes stared outwards through the glass. Old newspapers and magazines were stacked next to the specimen jars. The weary-looking periodic table lacked several elements that seemed to have been torn off at some point. Uranium was still there, though.

I immediately got to work after hours and in free periods to make this lab an attractive space for learning the queen of disciplines, the biological sciences. As I was cleaning up late one afternoon, two women teachers walked past. 'New brooms,' one of them shouted, as if to indicate I'd be an old broom soon and become like these lousy ones who would not leave their own homes in such a state of despair. While I will never forget that cynical comment, it was all the motivation I needed: I will show you.

My motivation for rebuilding the lab was simple. Even though I did not have the research to back me up at the time, I was already convinced that classroom culture and climate had a bearing on children's attitudes towards learning the subject.

I had a strong political motivation as well: why must black students get anything less than white students simply because of who they are and where they went to school? In other words, I had long ago discovered through my own journey that, given the same opportunities, all children can achieve at the highest levels in their school subjects.

That commitment would be tested soon enough. I bought some rabbits, put them to sleep and decided my 'Trafs' students would learn how to do a mammalian dissection and see the large, well-distributed organs inside the body. Having announced the plan, I did not think much about the request from a Muslim student that he be able to speak to the media about his faith-based opposition to the dissections. 'Of course you can,' I told the young man, unsure what the Muslim objection to science practicals could possibly be. Sensitive to his concerns, I asked senior Muslim teachers at the school whether I was violating anything sacred in Islam and they told me the student was making things up.

Still, I wanted my students to know that in a democratic classroom, if not a democratic country, you could have your own views and express them to the media even if your standpoint was at odds with that of your biology teacher.

The next day I had a visit from the Society for the Prevention of Cruelty to Animals (SPCA). Two officials came to challenge what I was doing. I was ready for them and asked the white men whether they had gone to any of the elite white schools along the main road of the southern suburbs to complain about dissections those privileged kids performed. The poor fellows were rather shocked at my impromptu lecture on racial equity in science education. They backed off soon enough and I never heard from the SPCA again. The *Cape Argus* reported the dispute and my friends had a field day teasing me about all of this.

My struggles were not only from the outside. Inside the school, a few strong voices argued that I was doing too much. As my driving partner to and from school put it, 'you are making the apartheid system work.' In other words, do the minimum, get the kids over the line, but don't make the system shine. I was confused initially since these were highly principled activists and good teachers. After some reflection, I took them on with a simple message: if these students can do well despite the intents of apartheid education, I am going to do everything to make sure they succeed in the one area where I can make a difference – biology.

Fortunately, there were other teachers, older and experienced, who shared this view. They were exceptional professionals and I tried to model my teaching on their example. Right next to my bio lab was the physics lab of Saleh Adams, the two classrooms separated by a storeroom for chemicals and equipment. In my free periods, I would often listen to Saleh's teaching through the door on his side.

He was mesmerising as a teacher and unintentionally funny. He taught chemistry and physics to the senior classes in ways I had yet to learn. There were practicals for every section of the syllabus and frequent classroom tests to check on learning and reinforce what was taught. 'My boy,' he said to a student who had lost concentration, 'I will dissolve you in sulphuric acid.' During the lunch break I suggested to him that hydrochloric acid had a much more powerful corrosive effect. We had a good laugh about all of this. The students admired him for his expert teaching and for devotion to his faith; Saleh was a *hufadth*, one of the few who had memorised the Qur'an.

He had the habit of speaking with a degree of pomposity that sometimes resulted in hilarious outcomes. On occasion, he visited us while I was a doctoral student at Stanford University in Palo Alto, a Californian city in the heart of Silicon Valley. On a return visit home, Saleh and his wife had us over for an exquisite lunch of curries in Bo-Kaap, the Malay quarter situated above Cape Town city centre. Welcoming us with the usual bombast, Saleh made some announcements before dinner: 'I must tell you I had an absolutely wonderful time in Alto Palto.' I scrambled for the toilet with an undefined emergency and put my head in the towel to muffle my laughter. He was too senior and dignified a person to laugh in his presence, let alone correct his pronunciation.

If Saleh was the cultured and captivating physical science teacher, Ernie Steenveld was the socially conscious English teacher. From Ernie I learnt the language of politics. For some reason he included me in a small group of activist teachers who met in the school library to talk about the state of politics in our country and what we as educators could do about it. I felt privileged to be part of these stimulating discussions on history, politics, economics and change.

Ernie was an active member of the Teachers' League of South Africa (TLSA) associated with the Unity Movement, which produced *The Education Journal* for radical teachers. Quiet, principled and determined, Ernie's life reflected the struggle against apartheid from the perspective of his movement.

It was said that when Philip Kgosana, a former UCT student, led a march against the pass laws over De Waal Drive and past Trafalgar High towards the city centre, it was Ernie who opened the school gates to allow students to join the African people's fight. He paid a heavy price for his activism, never being allowed to become principal even though he had all the qualities of an exceptional school leader.

One day I came up the steep flight of stairs leading from the parking lot entrance to the school's administration floor. I looked for Ernie in the deputy principal's office but found him at the far end of the passage in the broom room that doubled as the caretaker's space. I was puzzled and asked him what was going on. His office had once again been turned upside down by the security police for no other reason than harassment; nothing stolen. I rushed to his office and found drawers on the floor and papers scattered all over. I felt the anger course through my veins. Why do this to such a devoted teacher whose only crime was to question power?

It took me a while to understand the politics and history of the school. With great patience, Ernie taught me what I could not see. One day I complained to him that during breaks students would gather in the classrooms; things disappeared and a mess would be left behind. 'It is time for us to lock the doors during the breaks,' I told my vice-principal. Then lock the doors, said Ernie, with a pain in his face that I tried to decipher.

It hit me soon afterwards how shortsighted I was. In those days of my teaching at Trafs (1981–1983), the apartheid government was doing the last round of forced removals in District Six, right where the school was located. I taught biology to the 10C class and from that vantage point had a direct view of the bulldozers taking down the last flats as families were moved to faraway places like Mitchells Plain. The children were being uprooted and thrown out of their homes, so the last thing any sensible person would want to do is to put them out of their classrooms during break. It hit me with a thud and I felt like a lout. I apologised to Ernie for my lack of empathetic consciousness.

The forced removals of people from District Six uprooted every aspect of their lives. Ordinary routines became complex as children were separated from their schools by 20–30 km. One day, a student called Fatima told me she would not be able to attend my biology class because of heavy bleeding during her menstrual cycle. She would remain in the sick bay for the rest of the school day, then walk to the train station (a good 20–30 minutes down a long, sloping road then over a main road and a bridge) to wait for a train to Mitchells Plain.

If she had lived five minutes away in her original home, Fatima would have been able to change and return to school within no time. I had somebody take over my class and I drove the young student all the way home to Mitchells Plain and then returned to school. These finer meanings of upheaval were not always obvious when the focus of protests was on legislation and policy and the attention of media on the physical aspects of removal. The pain was in the ordinary, and in the case of Fatima the dignity of a young woman trying to live and learn amid the ruins of her family's life.

As the last of the homes were bulldozed and the rubble was cleared, the real intentions of government and capital became clear. New buildings went up and whites moved in. It was a bitter pill to swallow because I had a ringside seat to this display of state criminality. On one of those sad days the newspaper carried a headline of a bomb threat in the area; I was not at all surprised.

Which raises the question: Why was this coloured school not also flattened? That was never clear to me because two other institutions in the area also survived the removals: a church and a mosque, which stand to this day. But between and around them white residences were built. Later, the Cape Technikon (now the Cape Peninsula University of Technology) was built a short walk down the road from Trafs.

The traumatic memory of removals meant Trafs had a laid-back position on informal dwellings going up around the school. I drove in through the main gate one day when I saw two 'bergies' (homeless people, so named because they used to live in the bush on the slopes of Table Mountain), a man and a woman, having a fistfight in front of the school. I went to separate them and the couple turned on me. 'This is what they do every morning,' said a more insightful teacher. 'You are interfering with marital routines.' I was never quite sure of that explanation.

Today there are mushrooming informal housing structures on the doorstep of the school. At any other institution, the parents would have rallied to remove the dwellers on grounds of the safety of their children. But this is Trafs, and this was District Six.

Soon afterwards our students started to become involved in the most dangerous times of student protests in the mid-1980s. Biology students would disappear into prison and come back days or weeks later with blank stares in their eyes as they sat at the back of the classroom. There was no question that they had been tortured but nobody spoke about it. It was tense in the school and once again our small group met under Ernie's tutelage, including woodwork teacher Alex Marshall and the history teacher John Marincowitz, an Englishman. I was learning how to think and do as an activist in the presence of these educators and I discovered an interesting approach to the politics of education.

These men and women did not believe in boycotting education in the way unions boycotted work. Education was, for them, a political instrument in the struggle against injustice. You worked to get more of it, not less of it. However, content mattered, so the task of the teacher was to figure out how to teach what was necessary to pass the government exam and how to teach to pass the examination of life. This is why alternative education flourished in the Cape and in schools like Trafs. It was an understanding about education and politics that would shape my own.

This is what made my second school such a fascinating place. It had a quiet but determined politics, a way of standing up to authority when necessary – such as the inspectorate. As at Vredenburg, I could not escape these henchmen of 'Coloured Affairs', the shorthand and dismissive reference on the Cape Flats when referring to education and other government departments. Unlike my previous school, there was a healthy disregard at Trafs for these functionaries of the apartheid state.

One man, however, inspired a measure of fear among my senior colleagues. He was inspector Africa. I was puzzled by the nervousness about his upcoming visit. The principal warned us that this was a very difficult character and that we were to be on our best behaviour and not provoke him under any circumstances.

The day of his visit finally came and it was announced: 'The continent is on his way.' Except, Africa did not ascend the sharply rising set of stairs to the admin section of the school for some time. This was strange. Word later reached us that Mr Africa got out of his car and saw a Standard 6 girl standing outside her classroom. The Standard 6s studied in half-submerged classrooms at the front of the school which were referred to as the dungeons. The child had been put out of her class for being disruptive.

At that point, the story goes, the haughty inspector approached the youngster and said in a loud voice: 'And WHY are you not in your classroom?' The poor girl, clearly not briefed on the arrival of this self-important man, stood up to him, put her hands on each side of her head with thumbs in ears, stuck out her tongue, and said 'where-where-where-where-where', which in Cape Flats lingo meant get lost (there are stronger terms for this).

Oh. My. Word.

The continent flew into a rage, choking as he gasped for air, and asked the poor kid the equivalent of 'Do you know who I am?' He dashed up the stairs to the principal's office and spluttered out what had just happened. With a straight face, the principal apologised and lied that the sternest action would be taken. After Africa left, the teachers were told the story and we roared with laughter.

What I did not tell my colleagues was that the continent had come to my lab and opened the door, inviting himself in. I was in the middle of teaching and, pretending I did not know this was Africa, told him firmly that he could not come in since I was busy and that he should wait outside. To my relief, Africa left and I never saw him again. I suspect there was some understanding on his part that you do not disturb a teacher in the middle of teaching and, if that was the case, I would have respected the man.

One way in which I responded to the gloom of those times was to devote myself to the whole lives of the students for whom I was responsible. It was a practice I had started at Vredenburg Secondary. I would visit every student in my register (homeroom) class in their homes.

The problem was that my family home was in Retreat, on the other side of Cape Town, while most of my students lived in and around the city in places like Walmer Estate, Woodstock, Salt River and Bo-Kaap; others, of course, in Mitchells Plain much further away to the south. On these night visits, I would sleep over at Brethren friends, the Hankeys from Walmer Estate assembly, so I did not have to make the long trip home then back to school early the next morning.

The home visits were revealing. I found out who the spoilt brats were with state-of-the-art music stereos in their Bo-Kaap bedrooms. I discovered why students like Shaik hardly did their homework but also spent far too much time with his beautiful classmate, Abdea. I could talk to his parents and was surprised by their generous agreement about a spoilt son.

Then there was Marlene, who begged me not to come to her home in Walmer Estate. When I got there, I could understand why. There was not much in the house and I had little sense of the parents being present in the lives of their two daughters. Years later, Marlene called me from the UK to tell me she had earned a master's degree. She thought I should know. I was overwhelmed with emotion.

You teach differently when you know where and how your students live. Such insight brought respect at the interpersonal level but also affected teaching strategy. However, home visits almost cost me my life.

On a Saturday morning I was visiting the home of one of my students in a small fishing town, Velddrif, about 24 km from Vredenburg. The fisherman father was alone and it was painfully clear that there was nothing in that home besides the sparsest of furniture. Suddenly, the burly fisherman brought to the table a bottle of strong wine and two glasses; this was around 10 am. Since the evangelical brother had never tasted wine in his life, except for communion (and then it was often grape juice because of unresolved disputes in the Brethren), this was going to be a major challenge. I remembered that episode from my youth when with my father I was at the home of farmworkers where pap with flies was on the menu. I recalled Abraham's unspoken message with his eyes: if that is all a poor family can offer, eat it – or in this case, drink it.

During feedback on his matric daughter's academic progress, I sipped slowly from the glass, feeling the unfamiliar burning sensation down my gullet. 'Who the hell drinks this kind of poison?' I asked myself. The fisherman watched me and must have been amused at the slowness of the swallow. I tried to distract his focus on my drinking with discussion about his daughter's marks in a biology exam.

Eventually, I was done. At that very moment the fisherman grabbed the bottle and was about to fill up when I made an excuse about having to be back in Vredenburg as soon as possible. '*Is jy seker?*' Oh yes, I was *seker*, I told the man wielding the bottle.

What happened next was reckless in the extreme. I started to steer my yellow Ford Cortina back to Vredenburg and the car went swerving across the road as trucks rushed by. I was drunk, sleepy and only half-aware of how close to death I was. The little consciousness I had told me to get off the road and so I did, and promptly fell fast asleep. A few hours later I woke up and continued the drive to my hostel on the school grounds feeling simultaneously miserable and guilty. I woke up sometime on the following afternoon.

Back at Trafs, I was in the full swing of biology teaching. Not required by the syllabus, I nevertheless wanted my students to complete a group science project as part of their overall biology education. We would then have an exhibition at the end of the year and invite parents and communities. There were careful guidelines for how to do these projects, each of which had to have some connection to the syllabus. I was surprised by how inventive these young people were. At the exhibition, I invited some of my tutors from UWC, the 'demmies', to judge my students' work. The students enjoyed the recognition and I felt so proud of them.

Years later, one of my Trafs classes asked if they could take me and two other teachers for a 'thank you' dinner at Bo-Kaap Kombuis (kitchen). It was exciting to see these wonderful young people who were now married adults – with some of them grandparents even before I was. The evening went well, then some of the former students got up to say nice things about us as their teachers. I was curious to hear what they remembered about biology lessons. To my surprise, none of them mentioned how I taught the double helix structure of DNA (my favourite subject) or the workings of the human heart; what they recalled was the energy and the enthusiasm of teaching, and the connections made with them as learners.

In the Trafalgar lab, my students were going to be taught biology in ways I never was. I again planned a week of experiments using double periods in the timetable but needed more chemicals and equipment. I borrowed some of what I needed from UCT nearby and the rest from the more well-stocked competitor school at the other end of District Six, Harold Cressy. Cressy was in fact the first principal of Trafalgar in 1912 and, according to the record, 'the first coloured person with a degree' in South Africa.

Harold Cressey High had a much stronger academic reputation than Trafs and produced formidable leaders such as Trevor Manuel, a former Minister of Finance, and the SA Revenue Service commissioner, Edward Kieswetter. The highly regarded principal at the time was Victor Ritchie, who ran the school with an iron fist. He also had a reputation as a top mathematics teacher and would teach the challenging subject for years into his retirement.

I drove the short distance to Cressy to fetch equipment for my week of experiments at Trafs. A tall, kindly man, Lionel Adriaan, was the school's senior biology teacher and as I walked with him along the upper balcony he bent over as if he had injured himself. 'Why are you walking like that?' I asked. 'Oh,' he said, 'Mr Ritchie must not see me outside of my classroom.' I sat down to laugh even as I appreciated for a change a school culture in which being present in your class and your teaching was something to uphold.

Eventually, my biology lab looked like a place in which people did science. The walls had the latest charts representing most sections of the syllabus, including biochemistry, plant life and animal and human biology. Near the door was an adult-sized human skeleton. 'What is this, sir?' asked a nervous-looking Standard 8 student when he entered my bio class for the year. 'That's a boy who did not do his homework,' I replied.

What I really enjoyed was that students would hang out in the bio lab during lunch breaks while I sat at the demonstration table marking tests and assignments or having consultation sessions with individual students who were falling behind in their work. At that point I was probably the happiest teacher on planet earth. My plans had come together beautifully and I felt I could do much more beyond the school.

I decided to start an association of biology teachers, beginning in the Cape. It would be a professional network in which we could share ideas on the best ways to teach nucleic acids or where we could purchase some of the pricier microorganisms (I was using my own money to buy some of these critters from a lab in Grahamstown). So, I went to principal Goosain Emeran with the idea, and he said he would canvass his fellow principals in the circuit to see what they thought of my plan. He reported back that they were not enthusiastic and, without explaining, told me to drop the idea. I was deeply disappointed but realised I had no authority over such matters as a young teacher.

At that point I decided to leave the school and apply for a promotion post at a boys' school, Spes Bona. Contacts there told me I was the preferred candidate, so even before I heard from the department of education I started to prepare for the transition. There was definitely a problem, though, because no letter came, whether to confirm the appointment or otherwise. I found that really strange.

Many months later I discovered the likely reason: a senior person (I know who it was) at my current school had gone to the department, where there were several old Trafalgarians, and told one of them to remove my application from the file so I could be retained as a biology teacher at Trafs. I was furious but in a way felt complimented; I was valued at my school.

I still wanted to branch out, and in the process earn extra money. I was pointed in the direction of Savio College in Lansdowne, which offered evening classes to adults who had dropped out of school and wanted to complete their matric years (Standards 9 and 10). It was an incredible experience because there were new things to learn. While the subject-matter was the same, I now had a highly motivated group of adult learners who *wanted* to be at school. For them there was an immediate material benefit if they could get a matric certificate, but there was also the novelty of learning as an adult.

From my side of the classroom, I had to learn how to teach adults. The awkward word andragogy – the science of teaching adults – was bandied about, but it sounded like a species of fundamental pedagogics so I never used the term. But there were other benefits to this new assignment: I had adult company after a day of teaching children, and I could expend the energy I always felt left in me when the school bell rang.

Being over-energetic reminds me, by the way, of a memorable experience when years later I addressed parents and teachers on the open lawns of one of my favourite schools, Cedar House in Kenilworth. After an energetic talk, the principal asked the parents whether they had any questions for Professor Jansen. Right in front of me, a boy raised his hand, got up to speak, and floored me with this question: 'Sir, do you have ADHD?' I could not stop laughing. If I had this neurodevelopment disorder, it must have gone undiagnosed. A more likely explanation is that I simply enjoyed – and still enjoy – the thrill of teaching.

There is something interesting about the ease with which children in privileged schools would approach adults without a hint of reservation, let alone fear. I was invited to another of my favourite schools, Westerford High in Rondebosch, to give a talk to a speakers' club organised by the students themselves. I went to the room where I was to speak and waited for classes to end. One of the student organisers came in and asked, 'Are you Professor Jansen?' 'Yessir,' I replied.

Then this, as he stood with one hand in his pocket and the other pointing towards me: 'I would like to thank you for how you dealt with that racial situation in the Free State (that is, the University of the Free State, see later chapters).' There is a thin line between arrogance and confidence, and the young Budlender fell on the right side. Today he is a distinguished lawyer on the right side of justice.

None of my students at either Vredenburg or Trafalgar had those facilities of exchange, nor would they dare in the culture of black schools to approach a teacher with such informality. What enables these dispositions on the part of the two boys in this story are confidences of race, class and gender, with upsides and downsides in equal measure. The obvious upsides are the facility for questioning, position-taking and an independence of mind. The more obvious downsides are arrogance, entitlement and the disregard of others. The most important and challenging parts of high school teaching, I found, involved helping children understand the upsides and downsides of human interaction. Otherwise, they are all the same.

At one point I was working with students in one of the more dysfunctional high schools, Oscar Mpetha in Nyanga, Cape Town. Around the same time I was a guest teacher at one of the most affluent educational institutions in the world, Castilleja School for girls in Palo Alto (Steve Jobs' daughter went there, to give you an idea). As I moved between the two schools I was struck by something that was obvious to me intellectually yet not so obvious emotionally: there was no difference between the children. They had the same capacity, the same intelligence, the same devotion to learning. The only difference was opportunity to learn. At Oscar Mpetha, teachers were sluggish, often not showing up in their classes (I once taught a class waiting for a teacher who never arrived but was lounging in the staff room with rubbish all over the place). At Casti there was a notice on the board about an upcoming excursion to some learning site in Europe. But the children are the same.

That simple but powerful belief drove my biology teaching at Trafs, and I pushed for As in matric biology while making sure every student passed this final examination. Things were going well but I was still restless.

I was always looking for opportunities to teach outside my comfort zone. I shared this with a fellow teacher who mentioned that they were looking for science and maths teachers at St Francis in Langa, one of Cape Town's oldest townships. This was exciting because it would allow me to break out of the apartheid constrictions of coloured education and teach students classified as African. I immediately signed up with the nuns and was asked to teach revision classes in biology to the matriculants on Saturday mornings.

Two things struck me about that experience. One was the absolute dedication of the students. They packed the hall, and I was up against the board with very little room to move. It was crammed, it was hot, and I was going hell for leather teaching the life cycle of the fern as sweat rolled down my face. Another was the relative deprivation of African education compared to coloured education; it was normal for classes to be overcrowded, the students told me, and there were even fewer qualified teachers.

An exception was Nat Bongo, who taught at one of the Langa schools; I watched him teach the other biology group at St Francis and realised he was so much better than me. It was also fascinating to witness him moving fluently between English and isiXhosa as he explained biological concepts; the students were hooked.

I remember sitting down with Nat and wondering out loud when this madness would end with four departments of education operating according to apartheid's racial categories: white, African, coloured and Indian. It was so clearly a farce to divide children on grounds of alleged differences in their racial and cultural essences, if not also their social and academic aspirations.

But my comfortable Trafs life, with expanding contexts for teaching at Savio and St Francis, was about to change completely.

I became aware of an opportunity to study in the US under a scholarship advanced by then Bishop Desmond Tutu and an American clergyman-activist, David Smock. They set up the Educational Opportunities Council (EOC) in Johannesburg in the 1980s with the simple goal of recruiting black South Africans for master's and PhD studies in the US in preparation for their becoming leaders in the new South Africa. That was a bit of a stretch of the imagination of my generation because we were in the thick of apartheid and did not think 'the Boers' were going to give up that easily. It turned out to be a visionary and prophetic stance, but at the time the end of apartheid did not seem even remotely close.

John Volmink was a family friend from a Brethren church who had also won a scholarship through the EOC to do his PhD in mathematics at Cornell University. John was the one who encouraged me to apply. My childhood friend Archie Dick was also a recipient, and he did a master's in library science at the University of Washington in Seattle. With these pioneers ahead of me, I thought this would be an exciting venture if I were selected by the EOC.

There were, however, two problems. One, the invitation to apply came at the height of the student protests and upheavals in national politics. I remember being concerned about the shootings in Langa, Uitenhage, that left 35 people dead and 27 wounded in April 1985. How could I possibly desert my students at a time like this? For weeks I tossed and turned about going if selected. Two, I was not sure I was good enough to study at an American university. Yes, I had a good sense of myself as a teacher and things were humming along nicely in my classroom. But this was next-level serious academic work; could I succeed in such a demanding context?

The good news finally came. I had been selected and Cornell was my destination. There, I would work with a guru in science education, Joseph Novak. 'Should I go?' I asked some of my senior teacher friends. Even before I asked I was developing my own rationalisations for going. You can only teach the life cycle of the fern in so many ways, then you get bored.

I was not convincing myself until I asked Mr Potgieter, a kind-hearted white Afrikaans *meneer* at Trafs, whether I should go. In Afrikaans, he told me that South Africa and its problems would still be here when I returned from the two-year master's. 'Go and be a good ambassador for South Africa,' he added. I did not want to unsettle my dear friend by asking him which South Africa I should be an ambassador for.

There was one final rationalisation that made sense to me at the time: if I came back with a postgraduate degree in science education, I would be able to reach hundreds if not thousands of student teachers over time and make much more of an impact on South Africa's school system than in the few classes at Trafs. That would become true.

In the two years running up to my departure from South Africa, I had met Grace through our family and church connections. She was just perfect in every way, the foil to my outgoing, forthright, take-no-prisoners approach to education and life. Grace is more refined, cautious and forgiving than I was, and balanced out my rough edges. I was in love before she was, but eventually she came around and we both left for Cornell. Her companionship was critical to my later academic success.

Two of my teacher friends at Trafalgar with fancier cars than my little white Toyota offered to drive the wedding party and the family. I smiled at what was beautifully unannounced: that Muslim teachers were driving Brethren families on the occasion of a most Christian wedding.

6
New horizons

'It's one thing to communicate to people because you believe they have something of value to say. It's another to communicate with people because you believe they have value.'
John Maxwell

As I stood in front of the office door of Professor Joseph D Novak, I was nervous. I would finally meet the man whose work I had read, if not always understood, on conceptual change in science learning and on the use of conceptual maps as a heuristic in science teaching. What would I say? How would he respond to me? All kinds of insecurities rushed to the fore and I felt completely inadequate. But here I was.

I knocked on the office door and a short, white man with a friendly face and reddish cheeks appeared. 'Ah,' he said, 'you must be the man from Africa.' Then, without any further small talk, he turned round and went to the shelf in his rather small office, returning with a thick manuscript. 'This,' he said, 'should have been with my publisher already but I was waiting for you so that I could first have your comments on the work before I send it off.' I felt I was going to wet myself in public. Me? What? This?

Shaking slightly, I took the work of the great man and returned to Hasbrouck graduate student apartments on the far side of campus, terrified of the unexpected homework assignment. I read and reread the manuscript several times. Much of it did not make sense and I saw certain words for the first time, the most memorable being 'epistemology' and its adjective, 'epistemological'. I must have written and rewritten a page or two of notes (there was no computer at the time), thinking the man was going to send me right back to Africa for blatant ignorance.

To my surprise, Professor Novak accepted my typewritten notes and insisted that I call him Joe. A few days later in his class of master's and doctoral students, he told me how much he appreciated my feedback. Much later I realised what Joe was really doing, something completely different from my South African experience:

He believed I had something to say.

That simple act of faith in a postgraduate student (Americans call them graduate students) deeply changed my understanding of what I could do at this stage in my higher education pursuits. I was thrilled, over the moon, that Joe acknowledged my feedback. I was now a serious Ivy League student and I bounced to classes every morning.

It was still a difficult transition. The classes, a mix of master's and doctoral students, were relatively small, a dozen students at most. This meant you were easily exposed if you did not do the readings. A typical pattern of teaching graduate students in American higher education goes as follows: the professor assigns three or four readings per seminar session. Then they show up, make some introductory remarks, and ask individual students to lead the comments on one of the readings. The rest of the class then pitch in, and the role of the prof is to steer the discussion, ask pertinent questions, but generally allow the students to shape the content and direction of the seminar.

In the first class of any seminar there is an announcement by the professor that puts the fear of God into students from Africa, Asia or any country where lectures dominate instruction. Going through the assessment plan, the professor says 30 per cent (it varies) of your mark will depend on classroom participation. In other words, if you come from a social and academic culture where sitting back and taking notes is the primary mode of engagement, you're finished right there.

I remember how nervous I was in a small class of graduate students. What made matters worse was that the American students talked all the time; they were fluent and seemed to know so much more than I did. I felt embarrassed that I had nothing to contribute. It did not help that some of the professors did not make allowances for international students, so you had to scramble to catch up with acronyms from the New York state school system or even everyday terms such as 'bunting'. I asked what bunting was and immediately felt looked at, that I was delaying the point being made since I obviously did not understand baseball.

In the first few weeks I sank into despair. There was only one way out: I decided to speak up by raising questions, taking a position or comparing an observation about American education with something from South Africa. Slowly, my courage grew and I became a more active participant. I noticed that the more I read beyond the prescribed texts, the more it seemed my inputs were appreciated. The other students started to ask me out for coffee and professors put a reading or two in my pigeonhole in the graduate student lounge. Now I was on a roll and felt my voice carried in the seminars.

The campus beyond the classroom remained intimidating. Though situated in upstate New York, several hours from what most people think of as New York – the built-up borough of Manhattan – this rural campus nevertheless reflected the culture of the state. It was brash, in-your-face, fast-moving and cold. The opposite of Cape Town, in other words. I used to fear going for a meal in Memorial Hall. By the time you reached the front of the queue, you'd better know what you wanted.

There was a whole new language to learn. How would I know what 'over easy' means for eggs or that strange question that sounds like an order, '4here2go?' For here or to go? I had no idea and the burger flipper shouted his irritation to the self-conscious newcomer: '4HERE2GO?' I was holding up the long queue. Before long, I was shouting like the rest and on a visit home my mother said, 'Why are you speaking so loudly?' I had to adjust quickly or sound obnoxious in my hometown.

What was supposed to help incoming South African students was an orientation session hosted by Denison University in midwestern Ohio, a few miles from the state capital of Columbus. Before the 60 or so postgraduate students dispersed to their respective campuses, we were all together to learn about American culture and universities.

At that time in the mid-1980s few of us had regular contact, if any contact at all, with African, coloured or Indian students outside of our classification. So this first sustained interaction was new and liberating. I sang the African liberation song, *Nkosi sikelel' iAfrika*, and felt goosebumps on my skin. When at night students sang and explained the hauntingly beautiful song *Senzeni Na?* (What have we done?), we understood why apartheid separated us. There was a powerful coming together of emotions, politics and common cause: the struggle against apartheid which we had all experienced in common and different ways.

It helped enormously that the American leaders of the orientation were themselves diverse. White and black (in later language, African-American) professors, gay and straight staffers, young and old. Two of the young American staff were both lesbian Lisas. This was new to many of us and a timely demonstration of humanity after the suffocating social, cultural and political environment we had just escaped.

It helped that senior South African students had come before us and could help translate into South African idiom some of the customs and expectations of American culture and classrooms. Among our student leaders were Mzamo Mangaliso from Cornell University and Edna van Harte from Teachers College, Columbia University. Even more exciting were the South African students and political leaders from the exiled community who spoke to us at Denison.

For the first time we met those who had fled the country, particularly after the Soweto uprising of 1976. I remember the brilliance and commitment of the exiled community. Individuals such as David Ndaba (his protected name) from the ANC and Henry Isaacs from the PAC were insightful, eloquent and inspirational, and our spirits were lifted by these amazing warriors.

The seminar sessions were organised in ways that modelled what we would later experience at our US universities. Small groups, recommended readings, lots of questions and open participation. I lapped up the unfamiliar pedagogy that took students seriously and gave us a voice. Every now and again there was a session to reflect on what was going on 'back home', and a mix of guilt (having left to study) and determination rested on all of us to continue the struggle from wherever we were placed.

It was time to experience American culture 'live', and off we went on

Sundays for lunch with families around the little college town of Denison. These were the first of many visits that gave me insight into the enormous generosity of Americans. At that time, many Americans had not yet heard about apartheid or Nelson Mandela, so ours was an education job. Even in the late 1980s, US citizens were more likely to know Africa because of *Tarzan* movies rather than through documentaries, life histories or the media. Those would come shortly afterwards but we had to swallow our pride in some of those home visits when ignorant questions were asked about lions in the streets or modes of transport (thank you, Tarzan).

There was something strange about this new culture. I remember walking with my lunch mates (Job Mokgoro and Reuben Mosidi) to our Sunday hosts and seeing children's bicycles and other toys lying outside in the street. We looked at each other, wondering how long that bike would lie there on the streets of Johannesburg. I was astounded that you could put a quarter (25 cents) into a metal cage that opened for you to take one copy from a stack of newspapers. The first time this happened, I opened the cage after the deposit and looked around: would anyone notice if I took a few more and sold them down the street? There seemed to be a level of trust built into society. All of this was strange to us.

The Ohio State Fair was huge and the weekend visit there was a welcome break from orientation. There was lots of food, and we noticed that Americans ate humungous portions of just about everything. To my pleasant surprise, one of many music shows was hosted by the Gaither Vocal Band, a popular gospel group in South Africa, who added to the bill the wildly successful singing duo of Larnelle Harris and Sandi Patty. I was thrilled.

One Sunday, I visited a black Baptist church. I had listened on radio to the stirring messages of Martin Luther King Jr, replayed after his death from Ebenezer Baptist in Atlanta, and I knew there was a distinctiveness about preaching in the black church. There seemed to be little separation between salvation and politics, so different from the anaemic gospel of the Brethren. Most of all, I enjoyed the call-and-response style of preaching that sometimes brought me to the edge of open laughter. One memorable visit to a Black church had me in stitches:

> Preacher: What did Jesus do when he got to the fig tree that bore no fruit?
> Congregation: He cut it off, pastor.
> Preacher: And where were you last Saturday, brother John?
> Brother John (standing up): Out drinking, pastor.
> Preacher: And what must Jesus do with you, brother John?
> John: Cut me off, pastor!

I struggled to contain myself. Such honesty eluded me in the stiff and starchy gospel meetings of my home church or the formal liturgy of the Anglican or Catholic churches. Wherever I studied in the US, visiting a black Baptist church became an outing I really enjoyed to lift the spirits.

Back at the state fair, I was reminded of the racialised pasts shared by the US and South Africa. Students from a local college were giving free haircuts, I suppose as part of their community service. I needed one and approached the young white student to ask for a haircut. Sure, she said, but I noticed just a little bit of hesitation – something I would also experience later in New York and California.

The student looked at the top of my head and started to cut rather gingerly with her scissors. 'I notice you have an accent,' she said. 'Yes, I'm from South Africa.' 'What do they use to cut hair in Africa,' she asked. Slightly irritated, I said 'lawnmowers'. 'Okay,' she repeated without a hint of surprise, and then screamed: 'Lawnmowers!'

Now that orientation was over, it was time to disperse to our respective universities. Before leaving, the senior students encouraged us to become active in the Student Representative Council (SRC), the body representing South African students in the US. We were liberally funded by the US government via two managing entities, the International Institute of Education (IIE) and Aurora Associates, a 'minority' firm (which in the US means black, Latino etc) which had by law to be included in federal funding of this kind. I happened to be in the Aurora contingent but there was little difference in treatment whether you were in this group or under the IIE.

There was some resentment about the Educational Opportunities Council students and their funding among those who were in the US independently or as part of the exiled groups. Those students relied on smaller scholarships from the United Nations Educational and Training Programme for Southern Africa and the Canon Collins Trust in the UK. Politically, however, we were all connected in our common goal to free South Africa.

In this coordinating task, the SRC for South African students in the US was a key vehicle. At one of the meetings of the SRC in Boston, the secretary was urgently called home to work with the South African Council of Churches. Immediately, he terminated his studies in journalism at Boston University and returned to South Africa. That man was Saki Macozoma and I was asked to step up from deputy secretary to fill his position. What made a lasting impression on me was the way Saki relinquished everything and flew home because of the urgencies of the struggle.

Now in Ithaca, New York, I was beginning to settle in to my two-year master's degree. While I began with an interest in Joe Novak's work in cognitive psychology and education, I read a report from South Africa saying the country needed skilled curriculum developers for the design of the post-apartheid education system. I instantly shifted to studies in curriculum theory, design and evaluation with George Posner, a colleague of Joe's in the small education department which happened to be in the school of agricultural sciences. A land grant institution, Cornell combined components of a public and a private university. Education was part of the rural development thrust associated with agriculture on the public side of Cornell. As a result, your degree was an MS (Master of Science) even if it was in education.

I wanted both Joe and George on my master's committee but there was a problem. For some reason, the two men did not speak to each other. Our supervision sessions were hilarious. There was Joe advising me followed by George making suggestions on a draft chapter. They were not openly hostile to each other but there was no eye contact. I remembered a prescribed Afrikaans book from high school where an old couple spoke to each other only through their children. I had the best of both worlds with Joe and George in my corner and was amused by the strange relationship between them.

My intellectual interests in curriculum theory came alive under George. He brought to his teaching a depth of knowledge on design issues in curriculum studies, inspired as he was by Mauritz Johnson, who invented conceptual schemata for the systematic study of curriculum based on intended learning outcomes. I would push George in our seminars for complementary perspectives to the technical design approach by introducing critical theory and the politics of curriculum, topics which he generously allowed me to lead in class.

In response, he brought one of my heroes in curriculum theory from the University of Wisconsin-Madison to Cornell for a series of lectures. I was overjoyed. The fact that a professor would allow me to help shape the curriculum for his seminars was simply mind-blowing. I remember the detail of Mike Apple's talk to this day and the feisty but friendly engagement between us.

When you study at a place like Cornell, it transforms you intellectually not just because of the excellent professors but as a result of the academic environment. I was captivated early on by the founding statement of the university, written by Ezra Cornell just after the US Civil War: 'I would found an institution where any person can find instruction in any study.' Just imagine how radical that idea must have been in an era where the classics dominated at universities like Harvard and Yale and white men dominated enrolments.

Any person, any study.

What this meant was that I could take any classes at Cornell without the usual prerequisites or minimum courses per department common throughout the world. I could not believe my luck: I did gender studies with Chandra Mohanty, African studies with Locksley Edmonson, and even audited classes in microbiology and other sciences. Auditing a class in American universities means you can attend without the obligation to write the examinations. I was in curriculum heaven.

I knew to stay close to my curriculum home base in part because the education department was so small. I also knew I had to find a South

African connection to my work. In the physics department was a professor, Hugh Helm, who had come to Cornell from Rhodes University in Grahamstown, and he became the third member of my master's committee. Hugh was also involved in the research programmes of the department of education because of mutual interests in the exciting area of misconceptions in science education. Hugh and his wife Jill became lifelong friends who supported Grace and me during the two years in Ithaca, especially during the critical period when our first child, Mikhail, was born.

Cornell was also the place where my political education began in earnest. Locksley, my African studies professor, was a Caribbean scholar who spent much of his life supporting the anti-apartheid struggle. To honour the academic boycott of universities, he had refused to travel to South Africa. I was embarrassed to find in his classes that he knew much more about my country than I did – and he had not set foot there.

It was also through Locksley that I met another professor in his Africana Studies and Research Center on Triphammer Road. He was a cofounder of the ANC Youth League, a gentle man called Congress Mbata. What an incredible person, a scholar who was cultured, sophisticated and an inspiration to us young South Africans. Congress took us under his wing.

Politics was only one part of the wonder of Cornell. There was also the sense that you were in the centre of significant intellectual accomplishment. When I drove through campus to our student family apartment, I passed on the left the lake house of Carl Sagan, the great astronomer whose *Cosmos* series was popular on South African television. On the right of the road, higher up, was the office of Urie Bronfenbrenner, the psychologist who gave us ecological systems theory. Near the department of education were the offices of a retiring Nobel laureate, Barbara McClintock, who won the prize for her groundbreaking work on genetic transposition in maize plants.

One afternoon I was sitting on the grass waiting for the campus bus to take me to Hasbrouck apartments. It was alumni weekend, when universities show off their development projects and secure confidence and funding from wealthy alums. I introduced myself to an older man sitting on the grass. He shook my hand and said he was Heimlich. 'Wait,' I said, 'as in the Heimlich manoeuvre?' 'That's right, I'm Dr Heimlich.'

I could not believe how lucky I was to be in such an exciting academic space. I wanted to earn my place in this hallowed company as a student from Africa.

The politics of South Africa cast a long shadow on American campuses. The big thing in my time there (1985–1987) was the divestment campaigns. Cornell and other US institutions were rocked by student campaigns demanding the withdrawal of university investments in companies doing business in South Africa. Frank Rhodes, the president of Cornell, resisted and students wondered whether his surname connected him to the imperialist Cecil John.

One protester more than any other made a huge impact on my life.

Uncle Bob Smock was an old but feisty professor in post-harvest pomology; a professor of apples, he would laugh. Every day, even during the harsh winter months when snow lay thick around Day Hall (the administration building), he would march in a circle holding a placard demanding that Cornell divest from South Africa. As a white man, his singular devotion to ending apartheid in such a small way made a lasting impact on me. Uncle Bob was white, he was devoted, and he was so different from what I knew at the time about privileged South Africans.

Uncle Bob would drop a bag of red apples at our apartment every Saturday and at his funeral he required those paying tribute to read out some of his funniest greeting messages. It was his son who started the Educational Opportunities Council scholarship programme with Bishop Tutu.

It was much more difficult convincing white South Africans visiting Cornell and New York to emulate Uncle Bob's steely determination in the fight against apartheid. As secretary of the SRC, I was asked to go from Ithaca to the Yale Club in Manhattan and debate Stuart Saunders, then vice-chancellor of the University of Cape Town, on apartheid, divestment and the government's last-ditch reforms. I developed a massive headache as I entered Manhattan from my idyllic, rural campus. I was also a little nervous, but by this time I was somewhat experienced in weekly debates on South African politics, in large part due to Locksley Edmonson's insistence that I participate in such events.

Saunders' main mission was to raise scholarship funds to allow black students to study at UCT. I could not believe his audacity, and in my response at the Yale Club I told him to go back to Rondebosch, Newlands and Bishopscourt and tell the rich white alums of UCT to compensate for the theft of South African wealth and property by themselves paying for those scholarships. What a cheek, I argued, coming to America and begging for money when the answer was right there on UCT's doorstep.

Needless to say, Saunders was upset, and I don't think he ever forgave me for that stinging criticism of his mission to America; when he came to Cornell afterwards, I said more or less the same thing. The American education leaders in the room made it clear through their questions during the talk and in private conversations afterwards that they supported me. That was encouraging since I was only a student and not sure how my message would land.

In the last year of studies, an incredible joy came our way. Our first child was born in Tompkins County in Ithaca, New York. Grace and I were overjoyed. We named him Mikhail after the Soviet leader Gorbachev, who made such an impression on us intellectually during his political sparring with Ronald Reagan at one of their summits.

How my retired mother pieced together the money for a trip to New York I do not know, but she came all the way, determined to help Grace with the delivery and reception of her first grandson. Friends from all over Africa and other parts of the world gathered in our small apartment to welcome Sarah, whom I fetched at Kennedy Airport and drove the five hours to Ithaca.

As the door opened, David, a dear friend from the Congo, greeted my mother with outstretched arms wearing the most beautiful, flowing African dress from his country. 'Welcome, my sister from Africa,' he announced loudly. My mother, never fazed, said 'thank you' and in familiar style added, 'Listen here, I'm not from Africa, I'm from Cape Town.' David laughed more than I did.

It was a joy having our mother to help with the baby. Sarah was mostly cautious, offering support to Grace, having brought five children into the world, but holding back for the new mother to bring her own common sense to feeding and caring for our little boy. Being Sarah, she opened the cupboards to see whether there was enough food and the right kind of food. Then disaster struck.

Whenever we had friends over from anywhere in the world (except our Muslim friends), they would bring a bottle of wine. Since we did not drink, the bottle usually went into a kitchen cupboard. Over time, we had accumulated lots of them.

Well, Sarah opened the cupboard and her face dropped. In Brethren scriptures, *wine is a mocker, strong drink is raging, and he who is deceived thereby is not wise.* We were clearly deceived, not wise, and possibly worse. Mother went into the main bedroom which she occupied (we slept with the baby in the lounge) and closed the door. After some time, I slowly opened the door and there she was on her knees, praying for her wayward son and his wife.

The life of a student was impecunious and Grace worked on campus to bring in vital income that enabled me to study with less stress. At one point she did childcare at Cornell for families from the area, one of which was a happy-go-lucky couple who must have been hippies in their day; they had a chubby little girl, and *ouma* (they learnt the word) would help. *Ouma* would see the huge holes in her clothes and bring needle and wool to mend them. Her parents smiled politely.

Cornell is one of the most beautiful universities in the world, with lakes and waterfalls studding the campus. 'Ithaca is gorges,' read some of the familiar marketing posters for a campus that included a swing bridge and ample picnicking spaces. Those deep gorges with bridges above also made Cornell a campus with one of the highest suicide rates in the US. Later, the university authorities installed huge nets in places where students jumped to their deaths.

The long, cold winters were the worst, especially when the beautiful snowfall gave way to hard, icy, dirty remains. You could break a leg if you did not wear the right boots and learn quickly how to walk on hard ice. One day, I was waiting for the bus from Hasbrouck to lower campus when the temperature suddenly dropped below freezing. I had not yet experienced severe cold of that kind and thought this was an epiphenomenon of sorts, perhaps even the second coming. I rushed back from the bus stop to the apartment across the road and did not emerge for days.

Studies continued in winter, and I remember writing an examination set by the education statistics prof, Jason Millman, on Christmas Eve. I felt like a martyr, dressed in several layers of clothing that included what I swore I would never wear as a real man: John Wayne underwear.

But then summer came and the compensation for winter in this part of the world was more than adequate. With graduation around the corner, I went to see my adviser, George Posner, to say thank you and tell him I would be returning to South Africa shortly afterwards. The man looked to be in shock. 'Wait,' he said, 'I have just been to dogs and told her you are the best curriculum theory student I have ever had. She agreed to give me a scholarship for you to do your doctorate with us.'

I almost fell off the chair, but first I needed to clarify something. Dogs? Oh, the dean of the graduate school, he laughed. I had to do my sums quickly. The master's had been a huge hurdle for me as a simple biology teacher, and I had never imagined myself being capable of a PhD. That was beyond my imagination and yet George Posner at Cornell, like Paul Galant at Steenberg, clearly saw something in me that I had not recognised in myself. A doctorate?

I discussed this new development with Grace. Okay, if George thinks I can then maybe I should try my luck and apply to other graduate schools, rather than stay at Cornell. After all, in this small department I knew the work of the few gurus, such as Kenneth Strike (philosophy), David Deshler (adult education), and Joe and George. I had read all their books and attended their classes. Four more years would be boring; if I were to stay, I needed to stretch myself intellectually, so I applied to Wisconsin, Stanford and Harvard. All three responded with offers.

My first choice was the University of Wisconsin in Madison because that was where Michael Apple taught and held his famous Friday seminars in curriculum theory. I considered Harvard because Noel McGinn was doing interesting work there in comparative education, and Stanford because Martin Carnoy had written a riveting book that resonated with my anti-apartheid thinking, *Education as Cultural Imperialism*.

There was a snag, though. Wisconsin and Harvard required me to pay for my doctoral studies. I was disappointed but then the phone in our apartment rang; it was Carnoy, and in laid-back California style he offered me a full scholarship that would include bringing my family. The only requirement was that I serve as a part-time science supervisor of master's students in the Stanford Teacher Education Program. I consulted Grace and a friend advised us on our choices: we could freeze in the east or shake in the west. Shortly after we arrived in California there was a massive earthquake, but we were delighted to be there.

But first we needed to go home for the summer break to show off our little boy. There was a problem, though. South Africa was burning at the height of the protests and passport officials said it was not safe for Mikhail to go there. We were baffled. 'But he is *our* son,' we said. 'True,' said the straight-faced official, 'but he is an American citizen.' After some back and forth we were allowed to take the young American with us to our homeland.

Shortly after landing in Cape Town, I had an urgent mission. I drove the rental car to UWC and went straight to the office of Dr Botha, my former inorganic chemistry lecturer. I marched in without an appointment and found him with the same miserable face, head down in some papers. I informed him that I had just achieved my master of science degree despite the terrible chemistry education I received in his classes. My impromptu lecture must have gone on for several minutes but the man sat there without saying anything. Then I got up and left after telling him what a horrible lecturer he was and how many students had had their lives and learning crushed by his cold and brutal teaching.

The break in the South African winter was a much-needed respite from studies. We stayed with friends who had broken away to form their own little church because of the conservatism of the Brethren, especially over who could break bread on a Sunday morning.

At about this time, a relative called and said there was a temporary position to teach biology for a few months at a high school in Manenberg;

this, in my calculation, was a wonderful way of getting back into teaching but also of earning a few rand, what with a new baby added to the family budget.

The school was called Phoenix but there was every indication that it was yet to rise from the ashes of apartheid education. The principal was a kind-hearted man without the toughness needed to lead teachers and children in one of the more violent and unstable areas of the Cape Flats. Two students tumbled into his office through the roof, where they were up to no good. Many of the teachers were slack and the other biology teacher spectacularly incompetent. He asked if I would sit in his class and give him feedback, which I did. During breaks, the young man seemed to be in cahoots with the gangsters hovering around the school fence.

I taught my classes with great excitement and energy and invited students to come in and consult with me during the breaks on any part of the curriculum they did not understand. Even as I taught, I was conscious of the political protests in schools around the Cape, and some Phoenix students were aligned with those struggles. Then came the end-of-term exams and I walked towards the principal's office to return the student scripts.

As I approached the admin building, two or three boys intercepted me, grabbed the scripts and set fire to them. There was nothing I could do, nor did I want to, in part because I was there for only a few weeks and also because I respected the larger struggle for education going on in society. But I did wonder, and still do, how to tell the difference between genuine protests and mindless, opportunistic disruptions or even gangsterism.

It was time to return to America, and as the plane landed in San Francisco I already knew this was a very different culture from the brash, fast-moving east coast. Waiting for us was Bakary Diame in his capacity as president of the Stanford African Students Association (Sasa). The smiling and friendly Senegalese was a senior graduate student at Stanford and was incredibly helpful in the settling-in period.

We moved into Escondido Village, the graduate student quarters on campus, and everybody was friendly. Surrounded by students from Malaysia, Belgium, Brazil and elsewhere, we felt right at home in this mini-United

Nations interspersed with a fair number of American families. The hilly campus of Cornell was replaced by the flatlands of 'the Farm', as Stanford was fondly called from the earliest days of its founding. Everyone seemed to have a bicycle, including the lecturers, and I had to learn quickly how to walk in a straight line without sudden changes in direction as cyclists whizzed by on either side.

After settling in, I attended my first doctoral seminar. The professor was Charles Drekmeier and the class was on the book *The Structure of Scientific Revolutions* by Thomas Kuhn, the philosopher of science who popularised the term 'paradigm shift'. Since I came from Cornell and felt I had mastered the dynamics of the American university seminar, I was thoroughly prepared. I read the book twice before the first class. In addition, I developed a set of questions and observations that I would throw into the pot as debates and discussions got going.

Oh, my word. I was reduced in that seminar to a spectator at a tennis match. As the debate swirled, my head moved from right to left and back again as other students discussed the text at a very high level. Stunned, I tried to figure out what was going on. Then it hit me: these students had not only read the seminal text, they had also read all the major commentaries on it, as well as some of the author's responses to his critics. This was next-level preparation and I slumped into bed that night thinking this was a serious mistake. Yes, Cornell was Ivy League, but this was something else. I could never compete at this level. To save myself the embarrassment, I would make up some excuse and return to South Africa.

By dawn, however, I had made a decision. I was going back to that class and would read even more than my fellow seminarians. This meant I would have to get by with less sleep, since I also had other classes and my Stanford Teacher Education Program obligations. I spent many hours in the Cecil H Green and J Henry Meyer libraries. I read up on all the major journals in the field related to upcoming seminars. I subscribed to those closest to my emerging research interests in curriculum studies and comparative education. I started to attend the major conferences of the Comparative and International Education Society (CIES) and the American Educational Research Association. I became confident in my classes and ready for any discussion on that week's readings. The professors noticed, and so did my fellow students. It felt good.

I learnt a lasting lesson in those months of readjustment. American professors take graduate students seriously only if they show up and stand out. Suddenly, I had dinner invitations to professors' homes and offers to lead sessions in class. One professor asked me to copresent a term paper with his own at the CIES conference hosted by Harvard that year. Perhaps the biggest compliment of all was when Martin Carnoy asked me to design and lead a major seminar for senior World Bank officials on the place of curriculum in international education development. I was seriously chuffed, and they paid me.

The programme in which I was enrolled was in a department in the School of Education called the Stanford International Development Education Center, or Sidec. It was the school's most diverse department, with students from around the world. Unlike Cornell, you had to take a common core of subjects in economics, anthropology, politics and sociology of education. During the two years of immersion in these social science courses, you would also prepare a proposal for the PhD defence and, if approved, you were let loose to do fieldwork anywhere in the world.

Initially, I did not like the core courses in the social sciences since they were taught by specialists from the disciplines, not by people who understood schools from the inside. These professors had joint appointments in a school outside education and could not engage me on, for example, the meaning of the economics of education for classroom teaching, assessment practice or curriculum design. I must have been a real irritant, but my professors were patient with me as I told them what schools and classrooms were really like.

Then I did something that really paid off. I decided to extend my curriculum experience by taking courses in science education and curriculum theory outside Sidec. Myron 'Mike' Atkin, the dean of education, said I could attend his classes in science education. After one semester, I asked him if I could teach my own class to other graduate students and whether he would be my sponsor for the course. It happened. Since it was not my major, I could not attend the overflowing classes in curriculum with Elliot

Eisner (or teaching with Lee Shulman) so I asked Decker Walker, the other curriculum professor, if he would guide me in a self-study of curriculum reform across Africa; he obliged.

I was not done. I wanted to be an activist teacher introducing American students to the history and politics of apartheid. There was an outlet for such courses called Swopsi, the Stanford Workshops on Political and Social Issues. My class was approved and oversubscribed. I was excited to teach these eager undergraduate and graduate students. Some of them later visited and worked as volunteers in South Africa.

This fullness I experienced of living, learning and leading on a world-class campus that regularly ranked among the top two or three universities on the planet was easily the happiest time of my life.

Bakary insisted that I lead the African students on campus, so I became president of the Stanford African Students Association (Sasa). The apartheid struggle was an important anchor for my term but I was conscious that I also needed to pay attention to other conflicts around the continent, such as those in Sudan and Namibia. I worked with activists in the Bay Area and we loaded a plane to take medicine, medical equipment and other vital resources to southern Sudan. It was a special thrill to see the plane taking off and realise that my team had pulled off this amazing venture.

Sasa hosted an annual meeting called Africa Week. The theme for one of those weeks was education and activism in the Namibian struggle for independence from apartheid South Africa. It was a complicated struggle that also involved Angola, the Soviet Union, Cuba and the US. This was one of the dramatic theatres of the Cold War and we had teach-ins on the complexity of the region and the case for liberation from white rule.

I made a major mistake as Sasa president in that important week. In the spirit of openness and debate, I invited two men to be our headline speakers. One was Helmut Angula, the South West Africa People's Organisation representative at the United Nations in New York. The other was Chester Crocker, the assistant Secretary of State for African Affairs appointed by Ronald Reagan. Crocker had been recommended for this position by a Georgetown University colleague, Jeane Kirkpatrick, who would become Reagan's ambassador to the UN. Why Crocker? Because he had come up with the concept of constructive engagement which became American policy for dealing with southern Africa. In other words, rather than condemn apartheid and its leaders outright, engage them constructively towards ending what the UN had called a crime against humanity.

As African students, we were outraged by this policy, but I thought the debate between the two men would expose the ridiculousness of constructive engagement. In the weeks leading up to this event, I started to have some doubts and a lot of anger. The South African Defence Force had committed another atrocity that killed innocent civilians on the Namibia border. I thought of calling off the event but decided to go ahead.

The problem was that Crocker ran circles around Angula. He knew the territory, he had eloquent arguments, and he had contact with all the protagonists in the southern African struggle. Angula was dry, emotionless and clearly out of his depth. It was up to us, the students and the Stanford faculty in attendance, to challenge Crocker. I had taken a risk and it failed.

I had to deal with two other sad realities as Sasa president. First, the Nigerians wanted their own association. As at Cornell, I was struck by the arrogance of the brothers (they were men) from West Africa. They thought they were better than the rest of the continent, an arrogance South African students themselves were not immune to. Many meetings later, the Nigerians decided to go their own way.

The other challenge came from black Americans (later called African-Americans). They felt the Africans on campus received special treatment and ample scholarships while they had to struggle for the same attention within their own country. It made sense to me, but they too preferred to continue in their own organisations; very few were seen at our anti-apartheid campus rallies.

It was mainly white American undergraduate students who independently took the struggle for divestment to Stanford's administration. They joined us in protests whenever the board of trustees met on campus – a body which at the time included alums William Hewlett and David Packard. Stanford, a private university, would not budge on its investments in American companies working in South Africa. It preferred the Sullivan

Principles, a code of conduct advanced by a black American businessman, Leon Sullivan, whereby American companies would be allowed to stay in South Africa but promote equal pay and non-segregation, among other concessions, for their black and white staff.

A group of undergraduates then descended on the admin building and occupied the president's office. The Stanford response was swift and consequential for the protesters. They were removed from campus. I was angry and felt utterly helpless even as we protested about their exclusion. I came to appreciate how these young Americans would sacrifice their careers for a country they had never visited and a people they deeply cared about.

Back in classes, I was thriving academically. I passed my core courses well and won approval for my proposal from an examination panel of professors. I was ready to go and do my fieldwork in Zimbabwe before returning to write and defend my doctoral thesis. There was just one problem: it was almost impossible to get a study permit from the Zimbabwean authorities, and for good reason. Every now and again there would be an incident where a bomb went off because of infiltration by South African agents.

I decided to go first on a tourist visa and try to convince the comrades there to give me a researcher's visa. While everybody in State House was nice to me, I could not swing the visa. I started to collect as much curriculum documentation as possible and conducted interviews with key leaders, including Fay Chung, the minister of education and former head of Zimbabwe's curriculum development unit for schools.

I returned to California and waited a few more months for the visa. When it did not arrive, I went back to Harare on the back of a consultancy opportunity to help the Zimbabwean government with curriculum implementation.

Why Zimbabwe? The country was reaching the 10th year of its liberation from colonial rule and was touted among black South Africans as a possible model for educational change after apartheid. I was fascinated by the prospect of curriculum change in a country with a strong school system.

Zimbabwe had announced radical curriculum reforms based on Marxist-Leninist principles. Even from a distance I sensed this was not possible for a whole host of reasons, not least of which was the retention of that most colonial of assessment systems, the Cambridge O- and A-level examinations.

I interviewed every official who wanted to talk and sensed reticence. The name Jansen probably did not help. Chung was exceptionally nice to me and there was mutual respect. Eventually she handed me a bag of documents and when I went back to my residence in Harare I had a good laugh. One of the documents, a set of examination papers since independence, had passed up and down the hierarchy of the ministry of education with each official putting down a written opinion.

Some said, 'give it to him, he's a comrade.' Others said, 'we cannot be too careful … do not give it to him.' And so on. I could have bought those exam papers at a local bookshop, but such was the paranoia among civil servants and politicians that a simple decision could not be made easily.

I wrote up my dissertation, presented it to the examination panel and passed in record time. There was about a year left in my scholarship and I decided to use the time to write an edited book, *Knowledge and Power in South Africa: Critical perspectives across the disciplines*. I approached South Africans from around the world with a simple question: how does knowledge/power show up in your discipline? There were interesting chapters on everything from dentistry and urban planning to sociology and anthropology. Skotaville Publishers in Braamfontein, Johannesburg, put out my first book on a subject unrelated to my dissertation.

I published in journals in almost every year of study at Stanford, mainly on the politics of curriculum in apartheid South Africa. There was something special about seeing your work in print. However, looking back, neither the book nor the dozen or so journal articles were very good. In fact, I wished nobody would read my dissertation. But that was how I learnt to research and think and write, and I hope my publications have improved since those early attempts to put ideas into the public domain.

Rejections were not easy, so I went to see one of the most prolific authors on campus, my sociology of education professor, Chiqui Ramirez. He looked at my disappointed self holding another rejection letter and did something I will never forget. He showed me a huge pile of paper in the corner of his office. 'These are my rejection letters,' said the famous sociologist, and I felt much better. This is simply part of the academic game, I concluded that day.

In the meantime, things were looking up on the home front. Grace was working hard to keep us financially at ease by caring for and educating young children while their parents worked, and she took charge of the graduate student neighbourhood as coordinator of events. When the 1989 earthquake hit, she knew where resources such as water and canned food were buried underground and where residents should go for their safety. Her income enabled us to travel over weekends to places like Los Angeles and Nevada in our rickety but reliable family car.

Around this time, our daughter Sara-Jane was born in nearby Redwood City. Now we had a pigeon pair of children and our joy was complete. Four-year-old Mikhail adored his little sister and we felt blessed as a small family. Sara's birth was fully covered by our insurance but Mikhail's was not. We therefore arrived in California with a massive health bill that we were paying off because of an unexpected Caesarean delivery. It was tough on our student budget.

An American neighbour whose wife was a doctoral student used to pop in regularly to see me. He was genuinely interested in South Africa and wanted to know everything about it. One evening, he did something I did not expect. He asked if he could give me $10 000, then a lot of money, to help support us during my studies. At that point, he knew nothing about our financial situation, let alone the health bill we were paying off. I said 'absolutely not', fearing, in part, what dependence or attachment such a gift might entail. The offer was made again, and again we said no. During another visit, he left a cheque on a table and vanished into the night. We decided to use it to pay off the remaining debt. The question hung in the air: how did he know?

Those four years also opened our eyes even further with respect to our narrow Brethren upbringing. On some Friday nights we enjoyed Shabbat with Jewish fellow students. We went as a family and enjoyed those sacred moments; I could not but sense resonances with the Old Testament. My evangelical eyes were opening but there was a major challenge ahead.

I became close friends with Bruce King, a fellow student who shared my interests in critical theory and education, and we decided to organise lunchtime debates with leading scholars in the field. The graduate school of education covered guests' travel costs and, for those who insisted, a small honorarium. Great scholars such as Patti Lather, Henry Giroux and Peter McLaren addressed our seminars.

Bruce was in Curriculum Studies and Teacher Education and I was in Sidec but we shared a passion for critical teaching. These debates also rallied together students with similar interests in education and social justice.

One day, Bruce did not appear for a planning meeting and I had no idea how to contact him. A mutual friend told me he was in hospital in San Francisco and wanted to see me. In hospital? I rushed through in my car and could not believe what I saw. My good-looking, athletic friend was thin as a rake. I hugged him and the questions flowed: 'Bruce, what is wrong? What happened, man? Why did you not call me?'

'Jonathan, it's been difficult to tell you, but I'm gay, I have Aids and I am dying.' I sat down and cried openly. 'No, it can't be true. Please tell me it's not true,' I begged. Shortly afterwards, Bruce was dead.

I had to deal with one kind of bigotry that I had not yet confronted. How to be with gay people. My socialisation into Brethren dogma on the issue was strong, and because I had not had a Bruce in my family or circle of friends (or so I thought), I had yet to confront what I really believed about gay identity and the scriptures.

In the week of mourning before Bruce's memorial service in the education school, I had one of those conversations with myself. If Bruce and I could be so close as friends, why would this have to change simply because I was told he was gay? Even more disturbing questions haunted me that week. If, in a gay-friendly region like the Bay Area, Bruce could not share this treasured identity with me, what does that say about me? Did he sense my prejudice and fear the loss of friendship?

From that day onwards, my upbringing apart, it was clear that homophobia had the same roots as racism. In my conscience, the matter was resolved.

It was almost time to return to South Africa. During those final months I reflected on what I had learnt about university life in America. Since Cornell, I had started to think about the possibility of an academic career, so I did what I always do: try to learn from the context in which I was studying or working in order to emulate what I observed. What did I see?

I noticed how hard academics worked in the US. Martin Carnoy, my adviser, regularly put out great scholarly books and worked late in his office, as did his secretary. He genuinely enjoyed academic work, developing theory and doing empirical research on topics like education and income distribution in Latin America.

I had not seen Martin for a few years after graduating and knocked on his open office door with a loud greeting. As usual, his chair faced away from the door as he pored over data coming off dot matrix printers. Eventually he turned towards me with the ream of printed paper in hand. Rather than greet and hug, Martin was jumping up and down saying, 'Jonathan, you must see this data on labour earnings and employment from Mexico.' I wanted to be that kind of academic for whom there was sheer joy in the pursuit of research and discovery.

I noticed the high importance American universities placed on hiring and retaining the best scholars. Without fail, I attended presentations by potential hires at Cornell and Stanford. I learnt from the tough questions resident professors asked candidates for a faculty position. I saw how deans pursued leading scholars. What stood out was the attempt to lure the Nigerian scholar John Ogbu from Berkeley to Stanford.

Ogbu became famous for his theories about why minorities performed differently in their learning attainments. He described black Americans as involuntary minorities in that they came as slaves and developed particular cultural dispositions towards education. Those dispositions explained their underperformance relative to voluntary minorities such as new immigrants from Asian countries, who came with the goal of doing well academically. I found this kind of bold thinking inspiring, to say the least.

In the end, and despite Stanford's offering him the world (a wealthy private university can do that), Ogbu decided the opportunity costs of coming across the bridge from Berkeley were too high. He died far too soon aged 64.

It was at Stanford that I made a simple observation: a university stands or falls by the quality of its professors. This meant recruiting the right scholars and promoting only those who met the highest standards of academic rigour and accomplishment. The US academic system has something called tenure. Your initial appointment is for a trial period. After five or so years, you come up for review and what follows is one of the most thorough and intense evaluations of your scholarly work.

At the top universities, like Stanford or Princeton, very few assistant professors are retained as tenured academics. Young scholars who work hard to meet the standard often fail the test and have to look for other jobs, frequently at less prestigious universities. The tenure track system is not without its critics, but given the low standard of higher education in South Africa, where mediocre academics often became professors simply for being white and male or, after apartheid, being black, I was sold on the model.

I also observed how much time, energy and resources American universities put into undergraduate education and undergraduate students. Making the contrast with my UWC experiences was perhaps inevitable and saddened me, to be frank. It was not only the countless number of competitive athletic, cultural or out-of-classroom educational opportunities that were available to undergrads. It was things I thought unlikely, like the university president visiting the student dorms dressed in a nightcap with tassel to read students bedtime stories from a great book.

There were constant efforts to reform undergraduate education, and at Stanford that led to sometimes intense curriculum struggles in the public domain over what was called Western Civilisation, where students learnt the great classics of, well, western civilisation. White men dominated those curricula and other regions of the world had little to offer.

No university would be that daft today, especially after the decolonisation moment, but at that time the so-called canon wars inflamed conservatives, leading to publications such as Allan Bloom's *The Closing of the American Mind*. I loved the debate and was attracted to the notion of a common core curriculum which gave students the foundations of learning about the classics from the past and the great literature of the present through the medium of a much more inclusive canon. The idea stuck.

As a postgraduate student, I observed and enjoyed the intellectual culture of the American university. When I emerged from morning classes around noon, I would go to noticeboards to choose from any number of public lectures I could attend with my 'brown bag' lunch. Should I go to a lecture by the great German philosopher Jürgen Habermas? Or the talk by the Indian-British literary theorist Homi Bhabha?

It was those observations that made me realise a university is not constituted by routines of administration such as registration, classes and graduation. The lifeblood of a university is to be found in its intellectual life and culture that streams through the organisational veins giving a bright red colour to its complexion and, in the process, showing up the distinction with colourless institutions like religious bodies, private clubs or political parties.

I had learnt what I could in America and was now ready to return to South Africa and pay back the gifts of education from which I had so richly benefited.

7
University leader

'We want great leaders ... unbought, unbound, unafraid, and untimidated to tell the truth.'
Cornel West

Given a ten-hour time difference, it was around 4 am in California when I sneaked into the offices of Stanford's African Studies building to take a telephone call from an interviewing panel at the University of Durban-Westville (UDW) on the east coast of South Africa. There were no mobile phones at the time and I did not want to wake the family at that hour in our small apartment.

The post was advertised as a chair in curriculum studies. I had successfully defended my doctoral thesis and was on a short return visit to my old university. That job had my name on it, I thought. I felt confident with a PhD, a reasonable stack of publications and evidence of service in and beyond the academy.

The chairman of the selection committee was vice-chancellor Jairam Reddy, whom I recognised as the genteel professor of dentistry at UWC who once gave me lifts home as an undergraduate student.

I became aware that panel members were tossing me softball questions and I concluded that they had already made up their minds that I was the preferred candidate if, indeed, there was anybody else in contention. Barely 20 minutes into the interview, Jairam stopped the process and asked me when I could start. This was odd, of course. Typically, you interview the candidate for about an hour then let them go so the committee can deliberate. Weeks later, there is a letter of invitation or regret. Except here, in the middle of the meeting, I was given the job without further discussion.

The question of where to work in South Africa had occupied my mind for some time. I knew I could not go back to high school biology teaching, but I also knew I wanted to teach more than anything else. A university appointment was the most logical next step. I started to ask around and was excited when a professor of education from UWC asked to visit me on the Stanford campus. He was Muslim so we arranged for a wonderful halaal dinner prepared by Cape Town friends also studying at Stanford.

What followed was a wonderful and warm conversation about South African politics and, with confidences assured, a healthy round of gossip on academic friends and foes back home. As dessert was served, I asked the visiting professor whether there might be any jobs in his faculty or department that I might apply for. His response knocked me off my feet: 'Over my dead body.' What? I was not demanding a job, simply querying whether there might be opportunities I could compete for. I was stunned and drove him back to his hotel without more than a word or two exchanged between us.

I can deal with any problem, but when I don't understand it I tend to fret. What was this all about? I had no negative record at UWC or its education faculty. Was this perhaps the green-eyed monster at work, a resentment that I had a Stanford degree when most did all their qualifications at UWC? Or was I a threat, coming in with overseas qualifications to a fairly average education outfit even by South African standards?

'Over my dead body.' A few weeks later he dropped dead and his dean offered me his job.

By this time, I had already signed a contract for a permanent appointment at UDW as a full professor. As I would not have appointed myself as a full professor, this was a surprise, and I later found that it had caused concern among UDW colleagues. After all, they had to spend years working themselves up the academic staircase from junior lecturer to lecturer, senior lecturer, associate professor then full professor, and few ever achieved professorial status.

Before I was offered the post, I had spent two years working with a US Agency for International Development-funded company which supported education non-government organisations (NGOs) in South Africa during the final years of apartheid. USAID could not legally fund the apartheid government, so it spent its resources on non-state entities in fields like early childhood education, adult literacy, and science and mathematics education. They were regarded as anti-apartheid NGOs but in reality these groups, led largely by liberal whites, were simply redressing the neglect that apartheid education left in its wake.

This was a wonderful opportunity to learn from the non-state sector and my task was to lead a small team offering NGOs technical assistance and training, in USAID terminology. The early 1990s was a difficult and challenging time in South Africa, a period of transition captured in that beautiful phrase of Antonio Gramsci: 'The old is dying, the new is not yet born.' For example, on a visit to a stunning early childhood initiative in the rural Free State we were warned that the right-wing radical group, the Afrikaner Weerstandsbeweging, had earlier cordoned off Viljoenskroon and prevented traffic from entering the town and the township where the centre we funded was located.

I marvelled at how a white farmer and his wife, the Evanses, had created on their farm in Viljoenskroon a large early childhood facility that trained the wives of farmworkers in the literacy and management skills needed to lead such a centre. Its services later expanded throughout the country. Jane and Anthony Evans became close friends until death robbed us of this generous man, a farmer who was also an Oxford graduate. Jane eventually handed over the leadership reins to one of the farmworkers' wives, Maria Mohlahleli. The last time I met Maria was in an airport, where she was on her way overseas to present the work of Ntataise (a Sesotho word meaning to lead a young child by the hand) to international funders.

It was during these visits to education NGOs up and down the country that I realised one thing: without them, the dire situation in apartheid education would have been infinitely worse. Today, that assessment has scarcely changed. The desperate situation in post-apartheid education would be dire indeed if not for these entities that bring help and hope in forgotten places.

Through these engagements with education bodies, I learnt a range of technical skills, such as how to do advanced monitoring and evaluation in the non-government sector; how to write non-academic reports useful to aid agencies and policy workers; and, perhaps most importantly, how to access and work with communities in a respectful way.

But my heart was in university teaching and research, so off I went to UDW where they were waiting patiently for me to make the transition. I got to the office a few days early to get a sense of the physical space and start carrying in my books. Arriving in jeans and an off-colour T-shirt, I asked for the keys to the corner office. The secretary was miffed as she reached for the key chain. 'You people from Rentokil are always late.' I enjoyed the misrecognition and waited for the horrified colleague to discover the mistake when she came dashing into the office to find out why it was taking so long to deal with the cockroaches.

I was intrigued to be at a university designed for South Africans of Indian origin, a space where I was different and had to learn about a community of mainly Hindus and Muslims whom I knew little about. I was surprised at the number of Indians who were Christians. The only Indians I knew about in Cape Town were banded together in a small area called Rylands Estate; they drove fancy sedans and worked as doctors and pharmacists. There were no poor Indians in Rylands. At least that was the stereotype.

I had a crash course in the origins of the university on Salisbury Island in the Port of Durban. The old hands revelled in telling the story of isolation and protest on 'the island'. I was embarrassed to admit I had never heard of the place. Before UDW was established as another bush university, Indians had to attend Fort Hare University in the Eastern Cape while smaller numbers got into the University of Natal on a permit system.

What had happened in the transition to UDW, now in the leafy suburb of Westville, is that a strong culture of activism and protest developed on the campus which, like its bush counterparts, was initially led by white conservative Afrikaner vice-chancellors. All strains of activist ideologies permeated the university, from the congress politics of the ANC to the Black Consciousness movement, each having their respective heroes. After the first democratic elections in 1994 – the year I arrived – the university transformed rapidly as non-Indian admissions grew. It was wonderful to see the apartheid barriers to access fall so quickly, at least in the student body, which also included a small number of white students.

Then chaos followed. An anarchist union, the Combined Staff Association (Comsa), decided to wreck the university through a campaign that centred largely on dramatically increasing the wages of Indian working-class staff. Hardly a day went by without a mass meeting or a protest, but then things really got ugly. The union mercilessly attacked the office of the vice-chancellor, sometimes even breaking into and destroying the administration offices. Huge amounts of money were transferred from university accounts, causing alarm in the leadership. Everything was contested, from simple things like the minutes of stakeholder meetings to who had the right to participate in council meetings.

I watched this horror show and could not believe a university could fall apart in such a dramatic way. Anyone who stood in the way of the union was heavily criticised, followed home, abused in the local press and, in the case of an international professor, hounded until he took shelter on a small yacht in the harbour. When his little boy was threatened in the campus kindergarten, the professor upped and left the country with his family.

Meanwhile, management had its own problems. Like all bush universities, UDW opened admission to all students, regardless of racial classification, and many came from poor homes. They could not afford the fees and the management spent liberally from the ample reserves to cover their costs on what turned out to be a fatally wrong assumption: that the democratic government would bail out historically disadvantaged universities with a massive grant that would begin to equalise the resources of white and black institutions. That did not happen and universities like UDW descended into financial crisis at the very point that the union was demanding more resources to close the salary gap between academics and workers.

Students were protesting, workers were up in arms and management was on a hiding to nothing. The police came onto campus, followed by private security, both of which inflamed the situation. A law student was shot and killed and it felt as if the university's very future was in question. A seemingly radical left had outmanoeuvred the ANC's academic and student leaders. Before long, President Nelson Mandela inaugurated the first commission of inquiry into a South African university. It was that bad. The commission, under heavy fire from Comsa, completed its work and allowed the university to reboot as anarchists were removed from campus.

While being active in a progressive union of academics (the Academic Staff Association) to offset the reign of terror led by Comsa, I put my head down to transform the faculty of education where I became dean. In that position I encountered what I would also face at my next two university appointments.

First, an older group of professors who were not scholars by any definition; they were hardworking lecturers who thrived on the minutiae of administration rather than the production of research and publications. They were good men for college teaching but it was clear to me that they needed to be loved and replaced. Many of them became professors because of long service rather than new discoveries in educational research, and with my arrival they knew their time was up.

Second, a younger group of lecturers and senior lecturers were chomping at the bit to become serious researchers and scholars. I chose the best and made serious investments in their development. First, they were required to register for and complete doctoral degrees. With a small team of like-minded people, we launched a series of research and development activities: training workshops, weekly seminars, invited guests, joint publications. We sent the group to present at top education research conferences around the world. Things were on the move and some colleagues from the white University of Natal joined the lively research activities of UDW's education faculty.

I had to learn some serious transition management skills for the older academics. It was not their fault that they came into UDW when a bush university was not expected to raise serious scholars. Betty, a dear friend ever since, asked me with some emotion: 'Where were you when I was a young lecturer?' The men, on the other hand, were struggling and some resisted outright the new energy and direction of the faculty of education.

One of the first things I did was to raise the standard for doctoral examinations. Students would have to do an oral defence and external examiners had to include reputable researchers, including at least one from an international university. The problem was that those doctoral students already in the final stages of their degrees were now to be examined according to new standards. Many failed because of the low quality of their work. This also reflected on the supervisor, and I had to be cautious in managing the transition to new standards.

One supervisor lost his cool with me: 'We had our own standards and now you come here with all these American ideas.' It stung but I asked him whether he was happy for us to reproduce Bantu education on our campus. There is no reason, I insisted, that Africa should not also produce leading researchers. In the case of his student, though, I knew that I had to allow the pass even though I shuddered at the young man's lack of readiness for academic or professional work beyond his PhD. That was the last compromise I made to accommodate the old regime.

I was surprised by the energy and enthusiasm of the young academics for this push to transform the faculty into a place of excellence. I was mentor to many and supervisor to a few. What was particularly pleasing was that junior staff, including a lab assistant and an admin assistant, registered for higher degrees, and I am delighted to say that today some of them are well-established professors.

In the Indian caste system, academic appointment was not the pre-destined career of many younger staff. This was something I never quite understood. My young colleagues were sophisticated academics from middle-class families. Surely caste thinking was something they ignored or discarded? Intellectually, yes. But emotionally, I could sense at least some regard for those traditions.

Colleagues would, for example, speak reverently about the Bharuthram brothers, two accomplished physicists who I was constantly told came from the priestly class of Brahmins. Another colleague, brilliant in her field, told me she was from a lowly caste of laundry washers. She went on to become a full professor and a leader in higher education institutions.

Despite the chaos caused by the union, it was also at UDW where I started to learn important lessons that would serve me well in future leadership. I learnt from Mala Singh, a professor of philosophy, how to make engaging intellectual arguments in a university senate. She was brilliant in arguing for and against the Indian Documentation Centre, a structure that at once essentialised Indian culture from the apartheid years yet at the same time contained perhaps the only university-based collection of artefacts from early Indian settlements. How do you transform something without denying it?

I learnt from the erudite vice-chancellor, Jairam Reddy, how to chair a senate meeting in ways that capture the inputs of everyone present then synthesise diverse views on the spot before re-presenting them to the assembly as two or three options on which to decide. His leadership of the senate, an academic body of mainly professors, was simply brilliant. But he was far too decent and thoughtful to survive the physical and emotional onslaught by a renegade union and left shortly after I arrived. It was a sad moment and I felt robbed of a leader from whom I was learning so much.

I also learnt negative lessons at UDW, like how not to manage a meeting. The operations of the council, a university's highest governance authority, were difficult to digest. I was always, for my sins, chosen as one of the two senate representatives to council. It was not unusual for a council meeting to start late on a Friday afternoon and end on a Saturday evening or Sunday morning.

The first few hours, unbelievably, were often taken up by a debate about who should be in the meeting in the first place. The union would send disruptors or those who did not qualify to attend these meetings. Then long debates would ensue about the validity of the previous meeting's minutes. As I wrote in my 2023 book, *Corrupted* (a study of dysfunctional universities), if you can control the minutes of a meeting, you control the institution.

Whether or not somebody said something pertinent that was recorded from a previous meeting was constantly up for grabs. I sat there stunned by what I saw and made a decision: whenever I would one day chair an academic meeting under my authority, it would be short, to the point, and done.

At home, things were buzzing along well. Mikhail and Sara were in primary school and excelling under the loving but firm parent leadership of their mother. They brought, and bring, so much joy into our lives. Sara struggled with a slight hearing disability ('grommets' was new to my vocabulary) which affected her learning and speech, but she soldiered on and always had a small group of friends to whom she was attached.

Enrolled at Westville Junior Primary, there were chilling moments. Like a little girl from Cowies Hill who told Sara she could come to her house once she had washed the brown off her skin. This kind of prejudice had little to do with the girl, of course, but told a sad story about the racism of Durban's white middle-class parents. While she mentioned the incident, it did nothing to Sara's confidence as a child in recently desegregated schools.

I was always apprehensive about how Mikhail would fare back home since he had a wit and smartness about him that could be quite challenging for a South African school. I was horrified when he brought home his teacher's notes from a history lesson at Berea West Primary. They contained a full-on attack on the murderous King Shaka (there are other views on the great Zulu leader) and choice insults about other historical figures, including Mahatma Gandhi. As a parent, I found myself constantly swinging between laughing (how ridiculous) and crying (how sad).

The teacher's notes read something like this: 'Gandhi was thrown off a train in Pietermaritzburg, but this was good for him because it helped to build his character.' What a wonderful riposte to white racism in the city of flowers. Before long I was called in because Mikhail had found short cuts for solving maths problems which infuriated the teacher. I had some choice words for the principal and the maths teacher, though I was careful not to play the professorial hand.

These were the early days of our democracy, the mid-1990s, so it was perhaps not difficult to understand that former white schools were struggling with the growing number of black middle-class students (and parents). Yet I could not be silent, and at the first meeting of parents at Mikhail's school I complimented the principal on progress made with respect to integrating the student body.

However, I continued, I would also like my child to be taught by some black teachers. Oh, my word. It was as if I had asked Osama bin Laden to take over the life orientation class. The daggers in the eyes of the mainly

Indian parents were sharp. I understood then and in the many years later that what black parents wanted more than anything was for their children to be taught by whites. The assumption that competence was wrapped inside a white skin is something South Africans have still not shaken.

Grace was starting university studies for the first time, since she had had to go and work after high school. Her dream of becoming a teacher, like her favourite and highly competent Aunt Jessie, did not come true, but she did exceptionally well studying psychology through Unisa and now holds a master's degree in executive coaching from Stellenbosch University. Every year, wherever we worked, she gradually built her academic accomplishments, with regular distinctions along the way.

She was also active in the local Baptist church and kept the children on the straight and narrow through Sunday school and holiday camps, where they developed a strong and open faith as young Christians. She was the tough cop and I was the easy one, always conscious that the children were constantly reminded that their father was a professor with a public persona and that they should live up to his reputation. I desperately wanted to tell the school and the teachers not to put that pressure on our children and let them thrive as independent individuals.

After several years as dean, I was appointed acting deputy vice-chancellor for academic affairs by a rather strange vice-chancellor. Having lived in the US for many years – I am not sure it was officially 'exile' – Mapule Ramashala ruled the turbulent university with the imperiousness of an American university president that paid little attention to the broad stakeholder politics characterising South African higher education.

She also had nasty racial and ethnic politics expressed as bitterness towards those who were not 'African' and very little on the curriculum vitae in terms of high-level scholarly accomplishment. Most of all, she had no effective strategy for dealing with the political turbulence on campus or the dire financial situation, except to do what corporate universities do so well in the US: cut budgets.

Within a short period, the senate presented a vote of no-confidence in the vice-chancellor and she left. The next time I saw Ramashala was when the minister appointed me as administrator at a different Durban university and there she sat, a sorry figure who simply did not know how to lead with the confidence of campus citizens. Shortly thereafter, she passed away.

Easily the most devastating moment in my relationship with Ramashala was when I approached her for support for a colleague in the faculty who was on the verge of retirement. Ramashala had made positive noises during various campus talks about recognising and advancing women, who were sorely under-represented in South African universities at all levels of employment. I was excited about her position and therefore thought Catherine McCarthy's case would be an easy one to resolve.

Catherine was one of those women who came into university employment when the act of marriage immediately disqualified you from benefits such as medical aid and pension. It is hard to believe such blatant discrimination this side of the millennium but it routinely happened to women working in the state sector. Now Catherine faced a crisis: she was due to retire at the end of the year and did not have enough funds to be able to continue supporting her invalid husband. I wrote letter after letter to Ramashala, pleading for some relief to Catherine to prevent the couple from hitting skid row in their retirement years.

The answer was a cold 'no' from the presumed feminist vice-chancellor. I was deeply disappointed and Catherine was distraught as the year rolled to an end. I had left the Durban campus for a family holiday in Cape Town. Just after midnight in the early hours of 1 January, the phone rang. I collapsed on the floor crying. Catherine McCarthy had gone into her art education workshop and slit her wrists. In her calculation, the insurance payout that would follow was the only way she could support her husband. More than that, it was the ultimate sacrifice of love. As I lay there on the floor I remembered the words from scripture: *Greater love hath no man than this, that he lay down his life for his friends.* That friend was her beloved husband.

Back in Durban, it was time to leave, so I started wrapping up my business as dean then acting deputy vice-chancellor, pleased with the strength of the faculty of education. Several junior staff now had PhDs and growing publication records. We had together invented a cross-field course-based master's degree in education called Coordinated Masters' in Education and Training alongside a full research dissertation.

We had also established networks with leading universities in the world and, most importantly, there were half a dozen academics who were now ready to lead the new vision for the faculty. By the time the government-mandated mergers came along in the 2000s and the UDW education faculty had to merge with their counterparts at the white Natal university, it was clear to all that the intellectual and strategic capacity for change leadership lay firmly with the Westville campus.

Offers started to come in. Colin Bundy was the vice-chancellor at one of the country's top two research universities and asked whether I would consider moving to Wits as one of his deputies. It was tempting but I wanted more of a challenge, a university where the problem of change would be much more difficult to pursue. The English universities like Wits already had a head start on transformation, so it would be easier to develop a consensus on the way forward. Around this time, I also got a call from the University of Pretoria (UP), where I later discovered that the former director-general of education in the first democratic government, Chabani Manganyi, had bent the ear of an entrepreneurial young vice-chancellor called Johan van Zyl, an agricultural economist, to reach out to the dean at UDW.

I flew up for the interview in Pretoria and recognised two or three other candidates from the faculty of education also hovering in the waiting area. A strange arrangement to have all of us visible to each other, I thought, but I greeted them and was called into the council chamber. There was an unexpectedly large number of mainly white men around the table and at that point I knew this university was light years away from UDW in every sense. Everyone was polite and the questions in English and Afrikaans were no accident: could I speak Afrikaans at a level of competence that would make me acceptable to the faculty, the university and the community? The education of young white Afrikaans students for the teaching profession was something this community took very seriously.

Once again, I was thrown softball questions which suggested, as in my UDW interview seven years earlier, that I probably had the job already.

But, if so, why were the other candidates outside the chamber? One of the interviewers was an older white man who launched into a long presentation on education without any discernible question. He was the head of the Afrikaans college of education associated with UP. Before long, I learnt that I was to lead the incorporation of the college into the faculty of education at the university. Then I knew why he was so nervous. A black man deciding on the future of dozens of white college lecturers must have caused the poor man some anxiety. How could this even happen?

Anyway, the interview was over and the vice-chancellor, as is customary, led me out of the council chamber. But then, and this is not custom, he asked me to accompany him to his office. Behind me, the next candidate went inside.

I could not believe what happened next. While the interviews were continuing, the VC was discussing the terms of my contract. I accepted and went back to Durban to inform the family and plan the next stop in our journey: Pretoria. I was excited but a little apprehensive as well. Yet this was what I wanted – to be in a university where once again I was the odd one out, the minority coming in. I looked forward to that discomfort.

On arrival at the gates of UP off Lynnwood Road, I was approached by one of the two black security guards. 'Good evening,' I said, 'I am the new dean of education and I was told you will give me the key to my office.' The guard looked amused and I could see the two of them having a good laugh. Strange, I thought. Then they both came back to the car. 'Who did you say are you again?' 'The dean of education,' I responded. 'Well,' said the guard, stretching out his hand, 'I'm Bishop Tutu!' It took a few seconds to register that at this solidly white university in 2000, six years since the end of apartheid, a black dean made no sense at all to my brothers.

Dressed casually, the next day I decided to take a walk through the education and law building which housed these two faculties on the main campus. Going down one of the long passages on the ground floor, I saw an open door and stepped inside. The young blonde woman sitting behind the desk look startled.

'Yeeeeeeeeessss?' she asked.

'Excuse me ma'am,' I said. 'I would like to have a chance to study at this place. How do I go about that? What must I do?' The woman looked mildly irritated by the interruption even as she managed an awkward smile. 'This. Is. A. University,' she said, drawing out the words in case I needed slow, monosyllabic announcements to aid understanding. I could choose Unisa, she suggested, where adult learners go, but 'This. Is. A. University.' 'Th-thank you,' I said, and continued down the passage.

Then I saw the sign for the head of educational psychology. I popped in there too and recognised the sad-looking white man with the thinning hair because he had been a member of my interview panel. Panicking at seeing his incoming dean, he leapt out of his chair and jumped around as if his hair was on fire. In that moment, something told me that being a dean at UP was a serious position. 'Show me around,' I asked him in Afrikaans, and he led me back down the passage I had just come along. At about the same time, the young white woman I had approached earlier was coming the other way. The expression on her face was priceless. Wide-eyed, and having noticed the deferential attitude of the head of department, she knew something was wrong and nervously said, 'Prof Louis …?' 'Oh,' he said to her, 'meet our new dean.' She muttered something and made for the toilet. This job is going to be fun, I said to myself.

On my first day, I entered the dean's suite and my secretary also leapt out of her seat, extending a hand to *'meneer die dekaan'*. I tried to calm her down and asked that she call me by my first name. Something told me that was not going to happen. It is nothing now, 30 years into our democracy, but at the time I settled into my seat and could not help reflecting on how unlikely my appointment was. One of the oldest education faculties in the country and its first black dean.

Black Dean was the title of an extended reflection I later published in the *Harvard Educational Review* on my experiences at UP. 'Dean' meant I had enormous authority over the people I led, much more than I could have imagined in the same position at UDW. 'Black' meant I was simply another racially defined employee who probably got the job because of my race. 'Black dean' meant many of my colleagues had to carefully navigate these two identities in their relationship with me and be careful not to let the wrong one express itself in the wrong place at the wrong time. It did not always work.

The 'dean' part was interesting because of the amount of power the title conferred in a historically white Afrikaans university. As I have done with every new academic leadership appointment, I met all my staff individually to ask how I could best serve them, what was important to them and what I should change. I will never forget one of the most common responses from my new colleagues: 'You don't have to ask us what to do. You're the dean. You decide for us.'

It soon became clear that this unfettered authority applied to all levels of leadership at Afrikaans universities, meaning the vice-chancellor, more commonly called rector at these institutions, was a close relative of the almighty. This kind of power was a double-edged sword because you could change things quickly but also undermine the practice of democracy.

The 'black' part was equally interesting because I experienced a level of unconsciousness among my colleagues that was simply unbelievable. Two examples must suffice.

A senior colleague, one of the only white Afrikaans woman professors, asked me to do a guest lecture to her class of honours students in education. I really looked forward to my first teaching assignment at UP and spent hours preparing, as I normally do whether teaching at a school or a university. I was excited and bounced into the lecture room with my colleague. Then she introduced me with an unintended sideswipe that took the wind out of my pedagogical sails.

'This', she told the all-white Afrikaans class, 'is Professor Jansen. He is our new dean.' So far, so good. Then, without warning, she let rip with this beauty: 'Well, you might think that he is here because he is black, but I can assure you that he knows what he is talking about. He got his PhD from Stanford University.' With that, she handed me over to the class. Moments earlier, I had been energised, ready to deliver a super-duper lecture, but now I felt stranded. Had I heard correctly or had my second-language ears failed me? Nope, I assured myself, that is what she said. I had not thought about being black in the moment before I was about to teach. Now I was self-consciously black as I delivered a lecture on my comparative research on curriculum change in Zimbabwe and South Africa. It happened again and again. You do your job and you're reminded that you're black.

The second memorable moment was during listening sessions where I insisted on meeting the ground staff, all black workers who maintained the beautiful Groenkloof campus which the faculty of education moved to after the incorporation of the teachers college. The male labourers were seated around the long table outside the dean's suite with their white manager standing alongside me, beckoning stereotype with his khaki shorts and long socks.

I asked the group how they experienced the campus and what I could do for them. Instead, their boss, the white man, spoke on their behalf and turned his body towards me with the response in Afrikaans. 'Well, as you know, professor, these blacks are quite lazy.' My mouth hung open. My mind raced. Was he separating me from fellow blacks on grounds that I was coloured, in his estimation? Or was I dean and therefore colourless, so the remark should make sense to me? That he was abominably racist was, however, crystal clear and I warned the older man in front of everyone that if he ever used that kind of language again, he would be in deep trouble.

These were moments that offered me startling insights into the lives of my white brothers and sisters. What if, in their words and actions, they had no idea they were racists? That their behaviour was racially offensive? I knew as a leader that merely rushing in after an incident and calling the perpetrator racist would resolve little. This stuff ran deep in contexts where an everyday act of racism was its own common sense. I knew as a teacher that changing ingrained beliefs and behaviours that racialised others would require much more than the necessary condemnation.

One way of dealing with racist beliefs among my colleagues was by challenging stereotypes simply by doing what we were supposed to do in the first place: deliver world-class scholarship. As at UDW, I set the academic bar high. Again, I started with the standard for academic appointment and promotion. At UP it was very low, and over time my colleagues had convinced themselves that what they did was excellent when it was not.

Decades of academic isolation had taken their toll on white universities, especially the Afrikaans institutions.

Whereas before it was relatively easy to become a professor, now it was near impossible. My white male colleagues in their late 50s and 60s were the first to bear the brunt of the new standards. They knew they had become professors because they were white, male and – with singular exceptions – members of the Broederbond, later the Afrikanerbond, the secret society of Afrikaners that took care of the interests of this white ethnic group. I worked through their CVs and could not believe my eyes. There was nothing there in terms of intellectual substance, let alone scholarly distinction. They published, if at all, in low-level journals, and the odd book was a didactic text rather than one of groundbreaking scholarship.

Others had forgotten to clean up their CVs or, perhaps, did not even recognise dangerous entries this side of 1994: a few had been colonels and captains in some of the most murderous units of the South African military. I read in horror about what must have been completely normal for my colleagues just the other day when apartheid met its ignominious end. I remember lying awake at night in Pretoria and trying to process these horrors. Just like that, people who were one moment killing 'terrorists' on the border were now my subordinates. Where, asked my mentor Chabani Manganyi, a clinical psychologist advising the UP rector, do you think all those people went after 1994? It was a profound question for us, the firsts, entering these forebidding institutions after apartheid.

I called together these older colleagues and told them they were unlikely to match the new standards, let alone the trajectory of the new faculty of education. I then approached the rector for permission to buy out their time through retirement so that they would not have to struggle through the closing years of their academic careers with the new direction we were pursuing.

I had seldom seen such relief in the faces of colleagues who had just been told they would not make it in the new environment. A few didn't even bother to greet; they simply took off. One, who had had a senior role in the apartheid military, committed suicide for reasons probably more complex than this release alone.

There was no triumphalism here for anyone and the more I thought about the mutual decision that released my colleagues, the more a sadness gripped me about how the one life you have could end on such a low note because of a change of regime and, in the case of this faculty, a change of dean.

What should I do with the rest of my colleagues?

I called a meeting with the younger academics, those with master's degrees or doing doctoral studies. After reviewing everyone's CV, I told the group they were in serious trouble. Most had attained all their degrees from UP and were indoctrinated in the meaninglessness of fundamental pedagogics. 'Your career is over,' I told them, 'unless we do something quickly.' In the middle of one of my motivational talks with the group, I joked with one of them, 'take your PhD certificate back to the registrar and tell him it was a mistake.' That turned out to be the one colleague who excelled in her subsequent academic career.

The next step was to take about 12 of these promising young scholars out of the country and attach them to a world leader in their respective fields, which ranged from educational psychology and education law to curriculum studies and teacher education. Off they went, first as a group to several universities in the US, then as individuals to their mentors, who were mainly in America but also in other parts of the world. When they heard they were being sent abroad, they simply did not believe it; at that time, just to get money for conference attendance in another province turned out to be a challenge in our faculty of education.

The transformation of most of these academics was fulfilling to me as a leader. For example, two of my young colleagues from the 'ed psych' department were attached to an eminent psychologist at Yale University who later became its president. They thrived with Peter Salovey as mentor and went on to become full professors with their own books, rewards and eminent international appointments. Many others lifted their academic careers as a result of this immersion abroad combined with an intensive series of seminars within the faculty to prepare them for advanced scholarship.

Two colleagues simply could not take off despite these opportunities. My sense was that they did not have the capacity for advanced scholarship in education; one of them told me she came to teach at university and that was it. Another was too attached emotionally and intellectually to the apron strings of his older supervisor, also in the faculty, and could not make the separation – perhaps because of the added fear of being seen as disloyal. A senior colleague from the previous regime who became my biggest supporter for the transformation of the faculty offered light relief. Aware of my evangelical roots, he offered this consolation: 'Relax, man, even Jesus had a dropout and there were only 12 of them to work with.'

With Education Minister Kader Asmal having announced mergers and incorporations, UP's faculty of education was required to incorporate the Afrikaans Normaal Kollege Pretoria. The faculty would move to the old college campus in Groenkloof, which also housed a smaller building used for teacher education by Unisa next door. I was to lead the incorporation of the college, which included decisions about which staff to retain and which to let go. There was incredible stress and anxiety among the lecturers, especially the older ones, since they could lose their jobs.

I knew I had to keep the best of the college lecturers since universities then and now have no idea how to train primary school teachers. For decades, universities trained secondary school teachers and they did that reasonably well. I set up a committee to assist me and the interviews began. At the back of my mind, two things were important: keep the best; and use the savings from the inevitable retrenchments to bring in new academics with fresh thinking from outside the ideological orbit of Afrikaans universities.

In those early years of democracy, I was aware of my duty to be fair and inclusive throughout the process. The mass retrenchment of white colleagues was not part of my politics or humanity. In addition, I had to be conscious of not being seen as mean-spirited, since any sign of retribution would make it difficult to rebuild the place.

I searched in those interviews for white Afrikaans colleagues who had some open-mindedness towards change in their demeanour and for whom our academic transformation project was something they found worthwhile. To be sure, there were several such college staff who presented themselves for future employment not as college lecturers but as university academics. I am sure we made some mistakes in the selections but mostly we got it right. We ended with a mix of experience and youth as well as open-minded colleagues and settled but solid primary school teacher educators.

One of the more senior college lecturers who thought she should not have been excluded from selection came to my office with her husband. It was the weirdest encounter. Here was this accomplished senior lecturer sitting back while her husband, a lawyer, led the charge. The way he addressed me was arrogant and on the margins of talking down to the black man in the dean's office, and I decided to await my chance. Let him clear his throat. As soon as he was done I told him to leave my office. The poor chap almost fell of his chair; this clearly had not happened to him before in either the old or the new South Africa. 'This is about your wife,' I said to him in Afrikaans, 'and she works for me. She can speak for herself. Should I need you to add anything, I will call you back in.'

It was one of those eye-opening things that I witnessed at this conservative university. White women were treated as appendages, the secretaries of the academy. They were to know their place, even the odd one who became dean or more. One day in a senior management meeting that included the deans and members of senior management (the rectorate), I had to do one of those ear-checking things when a white male dean, irritated with one of the senior female women from his tribe, addressed her with the diminutive *'mevroutjie'* (little woman). I obviously had something to say about that.

But nothing troubled me as much as what I saw on a visit to one of Stellenbosch University's faculties during my time at UP. I was doing a study for the national department of health on the subject of nutrition policy and practice in schools. With a Kenyan consultant, the nutrition expert, we visited universities around the country, with my role being that of curriculum specialist. On arriving at Stellenbosch, we were to wait for a professor for our scheduled interview. What I saw that day should have required therapy since the images remain stuck in my mind.

In his office and all around the suite he occupied were some of the most beautiful women I had ever seen. All white, all blonde, all young, and all dressed to a T. It was as if Charlie's Angels were tiptoeing around the prof's office while two amused black men looked at the glittering performance while sipping from dainty teacups.

Suddenly, the large doors of the boardroom swung open and walking slowly, almost like in the movies, out came professor X (I am so tempted to name him), also dressed to a T in pink and white. Around him fluttered the flattering women and I could not help thinking of the seraphims and cherubims of Isaiah 6 flying around the divine with their faces and feet covered in the presence of glory.

'What the hell is this?' I asked myself. The powdered one glided past us into his office and we were summoned for an audience. My stomach turned. 'You know what,' I said to the only other black dean at UP at the time, 'white women are black.'

Dealing with everyday prejudices like race and gender put a strain on my emotions as a leader in difficult places, but no challenge was more visceral and in-your-face than the question of Afrikaans. It started when I went into a shop to buy cakes shortly after arriving in the administrative capital of South Africa.

An old Afrikaans woman was having it out with the baker in the Pretoria city centre. She told him that if the displayed names of the cakes were still in English on her next visit, she would no longer support him. I was confused: wait, you want cakes to eat but the labels must be in Afrikaans? Yikes, where was I?

Since the moment I stepped onto the UP campus I was aware of the pressure to demonstrate your capacity and/or willingness to speak Afrikaans. Growing up, Afrikaans was a second language you had to learn at school or a voluntary language in which you could express yourself, but at UP it was high politics. I started to adjust but it was difficult because you have to speak a language every day to be fluent and I had been in Durban for half a dozen years.

So, I bought the Afrikaans daily in that part of the country, *Beeld*, and on Sundays *Rapport*. I listened to Radio Sonder Grense (cynics who bemoaned the decline of Afrikaans in public called it Radio Sonder Mense) and spoke Afrikaans to my first-language colleagues. I attended and was often asked to speak at Afrikaans cultural festivals, including a large annual event in the ostrich town of Oudtshoorn.

I must get good at this, I told myself, since people listened and attached to me differently when I addressed them in their own language. Nelson Mandela was onto this as well, probably from nearly three decades communicating with Afrikaner wardens in the prison system: 'If you talk to a man in a language he understands, it goes to his head. If you talk to him in his own language, it goes to his heart.'

That was especially true in the case of my white, Afrikaans colleagues. What did irritate me was the expectation that I could speak Afrikaans because I was assumed to be coloured. *They* all speak Afrikaans. These people's views were shaped by rurality, the agricultural world they were familiar with where coloured people spoke Afrikaans as their first language, partly out of necessity – the farms. Few had any sense of the diversity of languages in the suburbs of the Cape, for example, where many families, like my own, were English speakers.

As eager as I was to learn and speak Afrikaans 'properly', I was constantly made aware of the fact that this was not about language at all. The fierce emotions around Afrikaans at UP and in non-English white society in general were about three other things.

One, the bitter war with the British at the turn of the 20th century and the ignominy that followed for Dutch/Afrikaans speakers in English-dominated culture and institutions. Afrikaans was humiliated.

Two, the outspoken pride at how the Afrikaner nationalists invested in Afrikaans as *'n broodsaak*, as the historian Hermann Giliomee so movingly put it; a matter of survival, in other words. Afrikaans triumphed.

Three, the loss of status for Afrikaans in the post-apartheid period as institutions of state became anglicised. Afrikaans was defeated.

My irritation with the Afrikaans *taalstryders* (language warriors) started to show. When a right-wing student movement at UP put up posters saying '*Praat Afrikaans of hou jou bek*', I was infuriated since this happened at the very moment we were bringing more and more black students onto a campus dominated by whites and Afrikaans. None of the newcomers could speak Afrikaans, especially the cohort of Indian students. Imagine such a welcome. Nonetheless, the pressure was real on me as a dean to demonstrate my bona fides with respect to Afrikaans.

I did what was necessary. Because mine was a faculty of education, I visited all the traditional feeder schools of UP, such as Affies (the affectionate name for two prominent Afrikaans schools, one for boys and the other girls) and the co-ed Menlo Park High. Going to Affies boys was an experience all its own.

As I walked up the long path from the street to the admin section, it was break time and several white boys were standing outside. As I passed them, I heard the odd insult and race-baiting. I was not angry but intrigued that these kids could say such things under their breath to a complete stranger. When I got to the secretarial pool to the left of the main entrance, there was no movement and I had to announce that I was there to see the principal. There was little enthusiasm, as would happen in so many of my visits to black and white schools.

I sat and waited, trying to absorb as much as I could from this strange setup. Then the principal's door opened and a very tall man, a former Springbok rugby fullback, looked at me and said, '*Is jy Professor Jansen?*' I confirmed the same. Then this memorable response also in Afrikaans: 'I like you black people. It's the damn English who drive me nuts.' I bent over in laughter over the fact that he could even say this to someone he had never met before.

With him and all the other white Afrikaans principals, the discussion in their offices turned around one topic: what was I going to do as the new dean at their university to promote Afrikaans? It got tiring after a while but I was beginning to sense that Afrikaans on campus was a serious affair. Writing to principals in all Pretoria high schools to introduce myself, one of my staff mixed up the English and Afrikaans letters and the wrong one went to the Affies principal. He bypassed me and called the rector in a fury because he had received correspondence in English.

On reflection, I have identified three kinds of Afrikaans in my life story.

There was the second-language Afrikaans that we spoke on occasion to tell a story that English did not convey that well. It was mostly a humorous Afrikaans or, in the case of my mother, a reprimanding Afrikaans. In my father's usage it was the language you switched with English while preaching to a dual language audience on the Cape Flats; in the middle-class assemblies of Wynberg or Athlone, code-switching in gospel preaching was not necessary. In other words, Afrikaans was brought in on a need-to-use basis only. It was unforced, easygoing Afrikaans in which the more versatile among us flourished.

Then there was the formal Afrikaans of Pretoria. Words were formed differently in your mouth. It was an elite, sophisticated, *volmondige* (rounded) Afrikaans that sounded as if you were speaking with a hardboiled egg in your mouth. When I heard this Afrikaans spoken at UP, I was in awe and tried to learn from the speaker. I remember the dean of medicine in his farewell speech citing these incredible words from the Psalms (the 16th) that could not possibly carry the same cadences of beauty in the English language: '*Die meetsnoere het vir my in lieflike plekke geval; ja, my erfenis is mooi.*' I had goosebumps since I recognised the more familiar English version of the sixth verse. I needed to invoke that kind of Afrikaans from time to time in meetings with the executive or on marketing days with parents; proper Afrikaans, in other words.

There was also official Afrikaans, the Afrikaans of command and control. The Afrikaans that insulted and humiliated you. The Afrikaans that knocked on our council house door in the early hours looking for an activist brother. The Afrikaans that reddened in the face with anger if you answered in English; an unforgiving Afrikaans. '*So dronk soos 'n kleurling onderwyser,*' an idiomatic expression that once found its way into textbooks, was not communicating an objective fact; it was using the language to degrade a whole class of teachers they called coloured. No other language could express the subjective intent of that idiom as well as Afrikaans.

These lines crossed and sometimes confused me during my first radio interview with a white Afrikaans radio personality at one of the Afrikaans festivals. I was required there in my capacity as '*die dekaan by Tukkies*'. Carike Keuzenkamp was an impressively fluent, green-eyed interviewer.

She spoke a mix of formal and official Afrikaans that was simultaneously welcoming and open-hearted. I felt drawn in by her warmth of personality and yet – for good reason, it turned out – cautious.

This superficially warm Afrikaans had many layers and as she peppered me with welcoming questions she did something I have never forgotten. She insisted my name was '*Your-naar-taan*' not, the English Jonathan. '*Ek sit hier met Professor Your-na-tan Jan-sin.*' I had never heard both my names Afrikanerised in this way, but she insisted, and I knew what she was doing – subjecting me individually and culturally to what I am supposed to be, an Afrikaanse *kleurling* who needed to be reminded of his place.

It was not the first time: I recall a philosophy professor at the University of the Free State mocking the pronunciation of my name, overemphasising the English pronunciation during the language policy debates I was leading there.

Smiles apart, Carike was in command and control mode, and I could not wait for the interview to be over and go home.

In time, I became more aware of the not-so-hidden prejudices that cropped up in my interactions with white Afrikaans speakers. When someone you did not know addressed you with the word '*jy*' it meant they were being angry, disrespectful or both. When a student used '*jy*' it was especially provocative.

Two boys from another faculty came to the education campus to see me about something and started with '*jy*'. I stopped the conversation, stood up from the office couch and decided to teach them a lesson. 'I am not your mate. I do not play rugby with you. To you I am Professor Jansen. If I were white, you would call me *oom* or professor, never *jy*. But you are such disrespectful louts, you do not even know how to address senior people in this university who look like me. Is this how your parents raised you? Get out of here.'

I had found a way to teach without being angry and I knew this was a lesson they needed to learn for one simple reason: they would keep acting like this on and against black people who did not have the voice to speak back against this kind of abuse. For me this was a teaching moment, harsh as it seemed, and I could only hope that something registered in their minds from that incident. What this act of reprimand also did, of course, was to establish my authority in a public institution steeped in whiteness. It was a lesson I had to teach fellow black colleagues as well.

It is often hard for black academics (and other staff), regardless of their level of accomplishment, to occupy white spaces such as university campuses. My attitude has always been that these are public institutions funded by all of us as taxpayers and therefore I would, to use an Old Testament invocation, occupy the land. But this is easier said than done. I recruited an outstanding science education and leadership expert from Michigan State University – one of many black South Africans whom I headhunted to apply to UP's faculty of education. One morning he came into my office distraught. 'JJ,' he said, 'I just experienced racism on our campus.' 'Tell me about it,' I replied.

When the newcomer prof was parking his car, one of the white admin staff confronted him and told him the parking space was not for him but for senior members of staff. He was outraged and brought that upset into my office. When I heard the story, I told him that what he had experienced was not racism. He was the problem. What? 'Yes, you are the problem. You come into this university as if you are a visitor, as if you have to apologise to white people for being here. If you had taken possession of this public university, you would have told the admin member to take a hike, that this is your institution and that you will park where you want to. She is not the problem. Help me transform the place by acting as if you belong here.'

It was clear to me as a leader that transformation required both correction and conciliation, and that the context would determine when and in what doses the correct medicine would apply. The boys needed to be corrected; the staff needed to be connected.

I was conscious of the enormous authority vested in the dean as a leader at UP and knew this stood in the way of building genuine relationships across lines of race, culture and class. So, I invited three colleagues to the dean's office during my first year. One was the white professor of computer education whose demeanour suggested that butter would not melt in her mouth. Another was a senior member of the administrative staff, also white. The third was one of the black gardeners who worked around the main building. None of them knew why they had been called to see the dean and all of them assumed they had done something wrong.

When the stern professor of computer education arrived, she looked around the big office and saw a basin and towel on the floor. I could see something register in her face, and as she sat down I explained that I wanted to introduce myself as her servant leader; as an expression of that commitment, I wanted to ask if I could have the privilege of washing her feet. 'No,' she said. 'No, this cannot be,' and she covered her face with her hands as emotion overtook her. 'Okay, yes,' she eventually said.

I got down on my knees and washed and dried her feet. A powerful connection was made in that moment and we sat for a while to talk. Then came the next person, and the last, and with the same introduction I washed the feet of my colleagues. From that moment on, our relationships were touched and transformed. Word got out, of course, and there was much discussion.

None of this would have had any meaning in the more secular and diverse institutions, such as UCT or Wits. But here, at that time, it worked because of the Christian ethos of the place. After all, when I got there meetings were still opened with a prayer and a short Bible reading. That is why my colleagues understood the intersecting symbolisms of a black male leader washing a white person's feet in a hierarchical and authority-driven institution. What I also knew in those moments was that the Christian religious character of our formal meetings had to change, and I led the charge for these observances to stop. It was perfectly possible, I argued, to live the values of our collective faith and secular communities without pretending that a public university was a church.

I had the usual seven-year itch which later made it into an entry in one of my popular books, *Letters to my Children*. In this book of tweets, it says that 'If you stay in the same job for longer than seven years, you lack imagination.' It was time to move on, and in the seventh year Minister of Education Naledi Pandor approached me to take over the Durban University of Technology as administrator. An assessor report had found that the governance function had collapsed due to poor council leadership being in cahoots with corrupted Student Representative Council leaders. This laid the groundwork for the appointment of an administrator which, in this case, meant taking over the roles of the council (a one-person council, in effect) and management (the vice-chancellor) and steering the university to normal functionality within 18 months.

I completed that job but then the minister wanted me to administer a second university in the Durban area, Mangosuthu University of Technology (MUT). The UP vice-chancellor was not happy since he needed more than an acting dean in my place. Fair enough, so I resigned, aware of the risk that the administrator assignment was a short-term commitment and that I might well be out of a job after MUT. I have been called to higher duty, I explained to the family. But I was confident that something would come up in terms of university leadership opportunities.

We were settled in Menlo Park, a short drive to UP's main and education campuses. Mikhail and Sara-Jane moved smoothly from primary to high school and, in the case of our son, the first years of university (UP). We noticed something interesting: the children did okay at school but thrived at university. I attributed this to the solid but stifling education of these old English schools.

When we were informed as parents in Sara's first year of high school that the girls would do knitting (as they had done for a century), I raised my hand and asked why. My son at the boys' school next door did not do knitting, I informed the visibly irritated audience. Sara had warned me not to ask difficult questions in the Grade 8 orientation meeting, but my hand shot up before my head remembered that I had promised to stay quiet.

Her school had outdated rules on everything, including how to wear your hair, and I told the friendly principal on a visit to her office that they needed to change in line with the new country. They did not listen and not long afterwards a national scandal broke out at the school when black girls revolted against the hair rules. The protests spread to other schools, including one in Cape Town, causing irreparable damage to institutional reputations.

Mikhail loved Pretoria and met his future wife in friendship circles. The boys' school was also steeped in tradition and at both schools, when asked to speak to the students, I would try to shake them up a little bit. The principal of Boys High asked to me address the students and their families on valediction night. He was and still is a good friend but I could see the terror in his eyes as I started to speak, the teachers behind me on the stage draped in graduation gowns as if they were somewhere in middle England.

'This is a good school,' I told the audience, 'and it has given my son a solid high school education. But don't get too far ahead of yourselves. Your only contribution to national culture has been two hookers.' The boys roared with laughter, remembering John Smit and Chiliboy Ralepelle.

Grace found her mojo in Pretoria. She studied courses that prepared her for leadership in the hospitality industry, including accreditation authority to grade hotels and guesthouses. She managed a superstar guest house called Rozenhof, which welcomed ambassadors, judges and other elites from the administrative capital. Managing demanding guests and an even more demanding owner was hard work but she enjoyed this position of leadership as we found time to explore the beautiful northern parts of the country while raising two decent children who made us proud in the way they lived their lives.

My decision to leave UP for the first time split the family. Mikhail stayed behind for reasons of romance and academics – he was pursuing a master's in educational psychology and things with Kat were getting serious. Sara moved with us to the next university assignment to start a degree in social work.

8
Reconciliation broker

'Forgiveness does not exonerate the perpetrator. Forgiveness liberates the victim. It's a gift you give yourself.'
TD Jakes

My personal transformation started before I accepted the job of rector at the University of the Free State (UFS) in 2009. I remember the moment clearly. A father and his daughter came to see me after dark in the education dean's office at the University of Pretoria. I did not mind late appointments since I tended to work long hours; South African academics tend to scurry for the gate around 4 pm as if there is a bomb scare on campus. This was especially the case for the staff we had incorporated from the college of education; their internal work clock was historically in sync with that of schools.

Sometimes, late-night visitors offered a humorous moment. An *ouma* from Kempton Park near Johannesburg airport called me to say she wanted to see me about her granddaughter; could she come through in the early evening. The elderly but spritely lady arrived supported by a walking stick. Since I was alone, she asked if she could see the dean. 'I am the dean, *ouma*.' She lifted her stick and gently pushed me aside with, *'Ag nee my kind, moet nie my tyd mors nie'* (Oh please my child, do not waste my time), as she wandered into the empty office behind me. The country had just changed a little too fast for *ouma*.

The next visit, however, would change my life.

The knock on the outside door (my secretary was long gone) indicated the arrival of another set of expected guests and I greeted them in Afrikaans. The father was dressed in modest and somewhat odd clothing. A creased white shirt, grey-black pants and shoelaces of different colours.

The daughter was dressed modestly in neatly ironed clothing, hair pulled back and a tentative smile on her face. They were from Pretoria West which, in the class arrangements of the suburbs, meant they were struggling whites in contrast to those of their tribe who lived in the sprawling suburbs of Pretoria East or the expensive housing around the campuses.

Now I understood the possible reason for the father's setting our appointment after sunset. He should not be seen, given his mission to the black dean's office. '*Meneer*,' he began in Afrikaans, 'this child of mine always wanted to become a teacher.' I looked briefly towards the young woman and in the half-smile I saw slightly moist eyes. 'The problem is, if I can be honest with you, I do not have the money to make her dream come true.' With breaking voice, he asked, 'Can you help me?'

I felt the lump in my throat and then it happened. As I looked at the father and daughter less than a metre away from me, I saw my father and myself in conversation when I first expressed my intent to go to university. 'I want you to go but we can't afford it,' my father said. I remember his sadness and my ambition. We had no one to ask for help until I learnt about government bursaries for certain jobs.

What I sensed profoundly in that meeting was the bond that held us together as struggling human beings across the passage of time. In that moment, I did not see him as a white man but as a father like my own. I did not classify the eager student by her race but recognised that she must have felt what I had felt in the moment with my father, a desperation to study if only she could secure the funds. It is hard to explain, but in that binding moment we were humans with a shared problem and a mutual desire stretched over 27 years. It was time to answer the father and encourage the daughter.

'Of course, *meneer*, I will find your daughter a bursary. My child, I don't want you to worry any more. You just work hard to become the best teacher in your subject. *Goeienaand, julle.*'

Until that point I was guarded in my relations with white people. Yes, I reached out to my colleagues and friendships were started, but I was always cautious around whites for fear of getting hurt (again and again) as had happened for most of my life in South Africa. I was, let me be candid, also a little arrogant. I knew I had power and I also knew I could wield it behind the shield of *regstelling* (affirmative action) that pushed forward black people at the expense of white people without further thought.

In that transformative moment, my caution fell away and I was never able to see white staff and students as anything other than my brothers and my sisters caught up with me in the struggle to be decent, kind, generous and human. This was without doubt an inflection point in my journey of racial reconciliation.

It was around this time that a vice-chancellor in the Eastern Cape, now deceased, recommended an inspiring book by Jim Collins, *Good to Great*. What Collins found common in his study of great leaders was two things: a clear moral vision and deep sense of personal humility. I desired that for my own leadership.

I was ready, therefore, when a call came from the chancellor of UFS badgering me to apply for the senior leadership position at this higher education institution in central South Africa. The university was in the middle of its most serious crisis in a century after four white male students racially abused five black workers (four of them women) and the video of one of the incidents went viral across the world. One of the white students appeared to be urinating into food which was then given to the workers to ingest. It was an unbelievably egregious act of racism perpetrated against people whom the white boys knew – the workers who cleaned their male residence called Reitz, the name of a former president of the Boer Republic. The situation demanded racial justice.

I had been to the main campus of this old university only once and that was in the early 1990s during the dying days of apartheid. At that time, I was presenting a report on a study commissioned by an education activist group aligned with the ANC called the National Education Coordinating Committee (NECC), a group of students, parents and teachers. The first 'C' in its new name (coordinating) reflected its change in mission from the 1980s when the first 'C' stood for crisis and its goal was to manage school uprisings. The report explored options for the NECC now that

Mandela was free and negotiations suggested a new democratic state was about to become a reality.

In that year, I think 1992, the gathering was somewhat improbable: a black liberation organisation having its conference on the grounds of a white Afrikaans university in a largely rural province. As memorable was the image of an ANC stalwart, a white woman breastfeeding her baby in front of a sea of black mainly male faces, on this conservative campus. Even more unlikely at the time was that as one of the speakers I would return to the same university 17 years later to be its rector.

Yet here I was in 2009 landing right in the middle of a devastating racial crisis. The council leadership at the time had announced that the next rector would be, in the clumsy words of its chairperson, a black or brown person. I bristled when I heard the word brown but understood that the enormity of this racial crisis required, among other actions, that the university leadership break the pattern of serial white rector appointments and, as a sop to the growing number of black students (if not staff) and a furious governing party in the province, offer them a not-white academic leader.

There were three finalists and the outcome was anything but foregone. The internal favourite of the white academics, especially those from the faculty of science, was its white dean. He impressed in his presentation with a fluid mastery of the local African language, Sesotho. It was obvious that he was the heir apparent regardless of the content and weight of our respective curricula vitae, a wonderful example of racial entitlement.

The other external person was a friend, a black woman with a chemistry background who had also held senior academic leadership positions in different universities. Apparently, her short, offhand comments on Afrikaans during the question-and-answer session did not endear her to the university audience.

I got the job and decided to spend the first few months trying to understand the place and its people, and deciphering how on earth these young men could have committed such an atrocity when they had been children when apartheid ended. I had some insights into the last problem which are laid out in my book, *Knowledge in the Blood*, released in the year of my appointment at UFS. It is an account of my white students at UP and how they came to make sense of a past they were not part of yet behaved as if they were.

I had not seen this level of depravity among my UP students, so I decided to dig deep. I knew from my research and leadership experiences that you cannot presume to change anything unless you understand it well. I visited every residence, male and female, and did two things. One, I told them in no uncertain terms that racism had no place at the university under my leadership. Two, I wanted to know what they thought I should do to make UFS a more peaceful and just campus.

I met the academic staff in their faculties to gauge their concerns and hear of their dreams for the university. The same discussions happened with the administration staff and the workers of the university. I met leaders of the religious organisations around town, all of whom saw students as recruits for their respective missions. I lost count of how many pastors and dominees came to pray for me.

On one occasion a group of five energetic Pentecostals came to lay hands on me and pray for improved race relations on campus. I must have opened my eyes at the wrong moment because, for a split second, only four of them were on terra firma. The other one was somewhere between the roof and the ground.

Teacher unions, political parties, leaders of farmers' associations, rugby coaches ... everybody was consulted on what they thought was wrong on campus and what I should do to fix it.

Three months later and sitting on large heaps of data, I began to get a clear idea about how Reitz had happened. The university management had rightly terminated the studies of the four boys as part of their punishment and the case was handed over for criminal and civil investigation. But something bothered me about the university's actions. There was hardly any institutional inquiry as to how this atrocity could have happened on UFS grounds in the first place. After many interviews and hours of hard thinking, I came to some conclusions.

The five boys were the product of a racist institution. Not only did UFS not challenge and interrupt the fraught knowledge of blacks that they brought into the university; it actively encouraged race-based and indeed racist thinking at every stop along their way to the final years of study.

To begin with, the *koshuise* (student residences) were all racially segregated to varying degrees, none more than the infamous Reitz residence. In other words, despite timid attempts to encourage residential integration, for most of their student lives the boys lived in what they assumed to be normative conditions for residence life on a campus, in other words white life.

Then, to my surprise, I found that the video capturing the abuse of black workers had won a prize awarded by the university. In essence, the video was a protest action against residential integration in which the black workers were props being treated as first-year students during the annual initiation of newcomers. The dean of students at the time was apparently angry about something else when the video leaked: 'How could you allow yourself to be caught?' as opposed to, 'How could you produce such a racist video?'

In other words, had the video not leaked, it is possible that nobody in the institution would have batted an eyelid. As I continued with 'the listening campaign', as it was dubbed, staff and students brought to my attention other racist incidents from the past and I knew that if any of this leaked UFS would for all intents and purposes be shut down. None of those incidents haunted me more than one from a department in the science faculty where two white academics (one a Dutchman) had depicted a black lab assistant as an ape in a hand-drawn sketch. It was shown to me on condition I did not pursue the matter, but this was something no leader could set aside even with the trauma of Reitz hanging over our heads. When I discovered that both the culprits had left the university, I abandoned the investigation.

Alone in the office late one night, I realised the Reitz scandal would be the most difficult leadership challenge I had faced. I also knew there was no way I could take this bull by the horns without building an exceptionally strong team that combined expertise in the hard science of management (working with systems) and wisdom in the soft science of leadership (working with people).

Soon I had a solid team of advisers and confidants who would meet me at 5 pm or 6 pm after everybody had left. This group included members of my senior management team like Nicky Morgan, who had led protests during my undergraduate days at UWC; John Samuel, who was the head of the ANC education desk during the early 1990s; André Keet, a critical theorist and human rights activist; and Choice Makhetha, who had the heart of a student adviser and who had lived through the earlier traumas of UFS.

The advisory team included Lis Lange, who still is the best academic manager and administrator available to a South African university; and JC van der Merwe and Rudi Buys, young white Afrikaans men who were leading the transformation of residences. In composing the advisory team, I knew I had to include white UFS colleagues not only because of their human value but because in this 100-year-old university they knew where the bodies were buried.

I tested my ideas with this group before formally presenting my position on transformation to the university community; and I insisted on them telling me where I was going wrong and how I could refine my strategy for change. Without this team of close allies, I would have made many more errors of leadership, but they gave me confidence and direction. Their criticism was especially important in an Afrikaans university, where deference to the rector meant the leader could make major blunders without being warned. This group flipped the script, and while the feedback sometimes hurt, I knew they had my back.

When I presented my thoughts on what to do with the Reitz boys, there were those who said no, it was too risky given the expected public response. Others said that if the strategy worked, it could have major spin-offs for transformation. I took the consultation wider – to senior members of council, alumni, student leaders and wise men and women on and off campus whom I trusted.

My inauguration as the 13th rector and vice-chancellor of UFS provided an ideal platform to present our vision for the university and the plan for Reitz. In my speech in October 2009, I began by apologising to the university community and to South Africa for the horrific acts of the four students. The fact that I was not appointed at the time of the incident was irrelevant. The fact that I was the first black head of UFS was also coincidental. As the head of the institution, I was liable and spoke for my university.

I said I would invite the students back to UFS on conditions that I outlined in the days after the inauguration: that there was a genuine apology, that the workers accepted the apology, that there was compensation to the victims for what happened, and that a process of reconciliation was embarked on by all parties. It took more than a year for all those conditions to be agreed to and met.

My justification for pursuing this road was, in the first instance, that there was a blind spot in the official response to the Reitz four. While the boys were rightly expelled, the university was let off the hook. The argument made by some of my senior colleagues – that these were four bad apples in an otherwise normal university – was, quite simply, disingenuous. The institution aided and abetted their white supremacist beliefs and actions. At the very least, the university would have to share the responsibility for Reitz. There was little resistance to this argument on or off campus.

Disciplinary action for one incident was not enough. A whole series of things at the institution would have to change radically. There would be new institutional symbols, from the coat of arms to the motto of the university and its insignia. There would be an end to Christian Bible readings and prayers at the start of official meetings for the simple reason that those were actions continuous with what was done under apartheid. Ours was, after all, a secular institution in which we hoped to register more students from different faith communities, including those who did not believe.

Drinking bars in the residences would be shut immediately since there was more than enough evidence that drunk male students were often emboldened to commit racist and sexist acts. It was clear to me that students did not commit racist acts because they were drunk; it was the state of drunkenness that loosened the inhibitions which kept racism barely concealed behind a façade of decency.

Residences would be racially integrated on a 50/50 basis and students who did not want to be at UFS could leave for elsewhere. It was time to end management prevarication over whether the residences were to be fully integrated or not.

Parenthetically, around this time not a few of my UFS colleagues warned me that integrating the residences meant white students would flee towards our competitor in the Afrikaans world of higher education, North-West University, still known by its pre-merger nickname of 'Potch', the Potchefstroom University for Christian Higher Education.

In short, it was not enough to ban four racist students from campus. It was equally important to change the rules of the game so it would be more difficult for students to get away with racism as a way of life on campus. I knew in my heart of hearts that future acts of racism were inevitable. Racism does not retreat into its shell because of new policies, programmes or regulations. We would have to brace for more retaliatory acts of racism because of the university's new direction. However, at least now we had clear policies and equally clear disciplinary consequences that would over time reduce these hateful incidents.

There would also have to be powerful gestures to demonstrate not only discipline but embrace, and this required taking the risk of offering reconciliation as one instrument for restoring the relationship between the students and the workers and, at the same time, showing the campus (and the country) a different way of bridging the chasm between black and white South Africans despite our bitter past.

None of this was novel. Nelson Mandela, through the power of his example, had forgiven those who put him in prison for 27 years despite the incalculable losses he suffered in relation to his family. The prison wardens, prosecutors and a long list of political enemies were not punished in the democratic transition. Instead, our national leadership offered the path of a Truth and Reconciliation Commission rather than Nuremberg-type trials for the perpetrators of apartheid.

In churches and homes, white South Africans who sought forgiveness would, with few exceptions, receive such grace. Around the country, civil society organisations were working to bring white and black citizens together to deliberate and own up to wrongdoing through painstaking and heartbreaking processes of reconciliation and restitution. I participated in many of these events. What I was about to announce was not new.

A Johannesburg newspaper had asked for a copy of my inaugural address and we shared the document, which was embargoed until after the speech was delivered. The speech lay out in some detail the path to, and meaning of, the withdrawal of the university's charges and the offer to the students to return to their studies. Such details of fact and the nuance of argument were lost in the headlines that followed: racist students forgiven, could return to campus. All hell broke loose and our media department was thrown into crisis as every newspaper and television station in the country, and some from abroad, descended on the main campus of UFS.

Whatever I said in countless interviews hardly mattered. Like the fact that this was a long-term process with conditions. That the court and civil processes were still under way. That all parties had to agree to reconciliation and restitution before the announcement could become reality. All the public heard was that the racists had been given a new lease on their student lives.

I already knew that most of the four students were not really in need of continued studies; they were ready for graduation, if not on campus. It was the symbolism of the act that mattered more: that the doors were open to completion of outstanding modules for one or two of them, or for postgraduate studies. I also realised that none of those students would risk the physical danger of being discovered on campus.

As the dust started to settle, there were two distinct responses in broader society. One was that I was the devil himself, to put it mildly, and had to be dealt with. The racists must rot in jail, nothing less. The anger was palpable among black students and activist leaders from the governing party.

At this point in the first months of my appointment in Bloemfontein, Grace was still in Pretoria with the children as they finished school (Sara) and university (Mikhail). When a leader of the ANC Youth League announced that 'The rector must die', my family saw these words on *Pretoria News* lamppost posters. They were anxious, especially because of their distance from Bloemfontein and being unable to assess the situation for themselves.

But there was another response that I sensed across communities in South Africa, black and white. I felt that strength of support to be very strong throughout Cape Town where I grew up; that love, support and encouragement I will not forget.

In the minds of many other South Africans, I did the right thing and much of this came through on radio talk shows and in many presentations on the decision that I was giving in all the provinces. What were they saying? That this is a nation being built on the foundations of forgiveness, not retaliation. That groundwork for that understanding was laid by other political leaders during the bumpy transition from apartheid to democracy.

An open letter by Archbishop Desmond Tutu in the national newspapers made a major impact on public opinion. In a letter of support for what I had done, Tutu declared that 'forgiveness is not for sissies'. I felt a weight fall off my shoulders.

The Arch invited me to see him in his modest Milnerton home. I flew to Cape Town and was a little anxious about what he would say to me. After a short wait, the great man appeared, hugged me and led me into his office. 'Please sit down,' he said. 'Let us pray.' As he thanked God for me and petitioned for strength in my leadership, I broke down in tears. I do not deserve this, I told the gracious old man.

The process of reconciliation unfolded slowly because of an egotistical cast of characters who all 'wanted in' on this opportunity. The South African Human Rights Commission (SAHRC) assigned a team to ensure it could control the process and claim success, which it duly did. The lawyer representing the five workers wanted to know during the process if I could arrange a job for him at the university. Any number of politicians came through my office offering to help and be helped. It was a sorry sight.

In the meantime, my team continued the hard work which began with bringing representatives of the two parties into long meetings to seek agreement on the reconciliation process. After more than a year of 'talks about talks', to use a strange phrase from the constitutional negotiations for a new South Africa, everybody was on the same page with respect to key issues: acknowledgement, reconciliation, compensation and empowerment.

On acknowledgement, the four boys had to recognise and own their misdeeds. Since theirs was a public act of humiliation, the acknowledgement of human wrongs also had to be a public event. On reconciliation, both parties agreed to enter a process that *could* lead to the coming together of the boys and the workers (nothing was assured). On compensation, it was agreed that a significant amount of money would be paid to the workers with the accompanying statement that no amount of material payback could make up for what happened on that fateful day. On empowerment, the university agreed to train and develop the workers so they could establish and manage their own company and contract with UFS as service providers with their own workers. In addition, we would offer scholarship support for any worker or their children who wanted to pursue studies at UFS.

On a Friday night, the four students and five workers finally met in one of the boardrooms down the corridor from my office with a facilitator present. We waited and waited for an outcome from this final phase in the reconciliation process. In the smaller meeting room off my office, several senior colleagues had their heads bowed in prayer. We reminded each other that deliberations could go either way, perhaps to cushion the shock of possible disappointment.

Suddenly, the doors of the boardroom opened and we were told a decision had been reached to engage in the final step of the process and we could enter the meeting for that purpose. On one side of the table sat the workers with their supportive families; on the other side sat the students without their families. An Afrikaans word ran through my head as I observed the boys: *stoksielalleen* (transliterated, alone in your soul like a stick on its own).

What happened next is something I will never forget. One of the boys, the spokesman, started with a heartfelt apology to the workers. He began in English and then, as the emotion hit, reverted to Afrikaans and said this:

'*Sal julle ons asseblief vergewe?*'
Will you please forgive us?

I became aware of a slight trembling in my hands as my eyes turned towards the workers. Before the student could even continue, one of the women responded – not in her home language, Sesotho, but in the language of the perpetrators:

'*Maar natuurlik! Julle is ons kinders.*'

But of course! You are our children.

We all sat there stunned then rapturous applause broke out as the students and the workers made their way around the long table to embrace each other and the moment. Shortly afterwards a formal ceremony was held on campus to confirm in public what had happened behind closed doors. I was left off the agenda for the evening and I was happy about that. However, the politicians and the SAHRC members went around the table congratulating each other.

I was relieved that all of this was finally over and that the workers could get on with their lives as bosses of their own company. Not that this outcome was at all assured. More than once my senior colleagues warned that the decision to bring back the boys and seek reconciliation might unravel.

The firebrand leader of the ANC Youth League, Julius Malema, declared in public that he was going to pay me a visit on the UFS main campus. I do not know how the word got out but that early morning there was no place on the Red Square, the beautifully paved red stone area in front of the main building and my outward-facing office. Lifting the wooden blinds slightly, I saw a massive crowd of people that included international media with cameras trained on the entrance to the building. Then it struck me, the announcement by Malema was interpreted by those who opposed my decision as, 'Julius is coming to sort out the rector.' You could feel the excitement in the air outside, the smell of blood. This was high noon at Kovsies, the affectionate name for the university.

Julius was late but was received with an overwhelming amount of noise as he entered the main building with cameras flashing for the coming news cycle.

Early that morning as I pondered the day in my office, my trusted secretary Ilse came through the door separating our workspaces. '*Prof, hier het 'n Boer vroeg vanoggend uit die platteland gebel.*' A farmer had called early that morning from somewhere in the rural areas? This was strange. Why would he do that? 'He wanted you to know', continued Ilse, 'that they heard about the visit by Julius Malema. He then gathered his family and workers together in the barn and they prayed for you throughout the night. This morning he wanted you to know that everything will work out. Don't worry about Malema. It will be okay.'

Wait. A white farmer called his people together to pray for a black vice-chancellor he had never met to petition for his well-being. I sat down to let the message sink in. Ilse turned around towards her office as if this was the most ordinary message to deliver in a typical workday. I believed in prayer, but this was a bit too much.

I had met Malema before so as he strode into the little boardroom adjoining my office we greeted each other warmly. When I was an administrator at Mangosuthu University of Technology he came with the same entourage and helped calm the fires between the two main youth political organisations, the ANC's South African Students Congress (Sasco) and the rival Inkatha Freedom Party's South African Democratic Students Movement (Sadesmo). Given the bloody history of tension between these two parties, especially in KwaZulu-Natal, I feared the worst. But with incredible charm and authority, Malema came and left without incident. I liked the young man, and even in this testing moment there was a good deal of mutual respect.

'Prof, can you explain to us why you forgave those boys?' I thought this was a good start. He did not dive into the fray but wanted to know more before taking a position. 'Sure', I said, and started to explain the actions taken against the students and the hypocrisy of the university in not owning up to its complicity in the sordid affair. Simply blaming the students meant transformation was going nowhere at UFS since the conditions that made their behaviour possible were not addressed. The students paid a heavy price in the court of public opinion and still had to appear in court. But for the UFS, inviting them back meant requiring the four students to take responsibility in the place where they had committed the racist act.

I was halfway through my planned 20-minute explanation when Malema stopped me. 'Prof, that's enough. You made the right decision. It is better to have them here and re-educate them than to send them back into the community where they would be a danger to other black people.'

At that point Floyd Shivambu, his deputy, leapt out of his seat in horror. No, I could not be let off that easily. 'Sit down,' responded Julius. 'The Prof has spoken.' Around the table, my senior team, whom I had asked to attend the session, were surprised and affected by the unexpected response.

Malema left the room to address the excitable crowd outside. Suddenly, everything went quiet. One of my colleagues rushed into my office and said, 'he told them you were right, that "he (the rector) is one of us".' It was as if someone had released the holding paddles behind my eyes as I shut my office door and let the emotions flow.

No number had been left for me to call the white farmer who had predicted the outcome. In that moment, if I had not already believed in God, I would have done so. The spiritual impact of what had happened is hard to describe. The sense that there was something much bigger than me going on in that boardroom was crystal clear. As I subsequently travelled around the country on speaking commitments and marketing efforts on behalf of the university, I was stunned by how many people, black and white, told me they had prayed for me on the day Malema visited the campus.

It was now time to institutionalise this commitment to reconciliation within the broader ethos and branding of the university. We built and inaugurated an Institute for Reconciliation and Social Justice. It was first led by John Samuel, the former adviser to Nelson Mandela, who understood the spirit of the initiative and brought black and white students into community in this safe space for deliberation and activism. Giants of reconciliation came through the institute, including Desmond Tutu and a remarkable doctor from Gaza who wrote the bestselling book *I Shall Not Hate* after Israeli tanks killed his three daughters and a niece in their home. When asked whether he hated the Jews, Izzeldin Abuelaish responded, 'Which Jews should I hate? The ones I heal in surgery? Which ones?'

The institute was later taken over by André Keet, one of the finest intellects in South Africa, who brought deep thinking into this space that combined outreach to activist students with academic rigour in research and publications. Under John and André, students found a space where they could share their ideas, frustrations and aspirations on a campus in the throes of change.

We needed a crisp, powerful statement of mission to carry the university forward after Reitz and reconciliation. I was surprised by how the typical vision and mission statements of universities around the world were so *nikseggend* (saying nothing). More than that, they all said the same – something about world-class, which simply begged the question in the African context: what is that exactly? Something about producing leaders, which you automatically do in a sea of poverty even if not quite intended. Something about being African or Afropolitan, which reminded me so much of Léopold Senghor's famous rebuke: a tiger does not declare its tigritude.

We needed something different, so the team settled on two goals: the human project and the academic project. In every speech on or off campus I repeated the mantra, human project, academic project. It carried for me the transformative motto of Cornell stripped of all pretensions: any student, any study. Nothing more needs to be added.

The human project captured our commitment to reconciliation. There was a humanity that preceded our politics. There was something deeply human about all of us that existed outside the constricting thought of racial categorisation. If we saw each other as human first, then other solutions to our dilemmas might follow. This is not colour blindness. It is human sightedness, a different way of seeing each other that enabled us to deal differently with race as a human construct and its all too real consequences.

The academic project enabled us to address the low academic standards of the UFS. If we failed to deal with this problem, reconciliation would fall flat on its face as a quasi-spiritual project rather than a profound human as well as intellectual pursuit. When I joined the university, it had one of the lowest pass rates in the country. Before my time, it had opened up access to students as a matter of transformation but also as a financial imperative.

As I arrived, I was informed that the university had passed through a financial crisis that led to many staff being laid off. One way to deal with that trauma was to increase the number of students to optimise subsidy income from the government. However, this often meant that students with poor matric marks gained access, which not only lowered the academic standard but also led to UFS being penalised in the same subsidy for low output or graduation rates. That had to change, and fortunately my senior colleagues had started to establish a campus in the south of Bloemfontein where students with poor but promising results could spend a year or two on an effective bridging course before embarking on full-scale degree programmes on the main campus. It worked like a charm.

However, the academic standards were also low for appointment and especially promotion. It was again important to do what I did at UDW and UP: ensure that the new class of professors could hold their own anywhere in the world. There was a lot of anger among white academics on campus, especially women. 'You are moving the goalposts,' they rightly argued. Many men had made it to professorship on earlier standards and now the quality and depth of scholarship counted much more in deciding who became a prof and who did not.

Unsurprisingly, the number of applications for promotion dropped sharply. Over time, the message got through: only the best in the academic community would be considered for associate and full professorship at the UFS. I could not help musing to myself: when I came, there were racialised whispers that standards would drop under the new black rector. Now they were complaining that the standards were too high.

It was perfectly possible, I argued, that a university concerned about humanity as its overriding commitment could simultaneously be concerned about the quality of education it was dishing out in the name of transformation. In fact, reconciliation needed a solid academic base to give it the intellectual weight and direction required. At the same time, academic ambition needed a human face rather than the mindless pursuit of 'research outputs' for individual reward or institutional ranking.

Our commitment to reconciliation was tested repeatedly. I only realised later that with such a radical act of forgiveness, pushback was inevitable. A theologian friend captured this reality beautifully. 'Grace is always scandalous,' he would remind me from incidents in biblical history. To forgive is to unleash the worst in us, that very human instinct for retribution.

One of the first tests of reconciliation came from the student residences. As more black students moved into the desegregating residences, white male students in particular found ways to register their disgust. I was informed in a call one night that in a male residence, a drunk white student had urinated on the bedsheets of a black student. I was down there in a flash and the white student leaders pleaded for mercy; after all, we had forgiven the four white boys. This, I knew, was a test.

He was just drunk, professor, give him another chance. I repeated my mantra that alcohol does not make students racist; it brings out their racism. That night, the pissing student was ejected from the residence and subjected to the university's disciplinary procedures. Reconciliation, I reminded the students, is not the opposite of social justice. It is the other side of the same coin and right now justice was required.

Reconciliation was also tested by some of the black student leaders. There was political mileage to be gained among African nationalists if you could show that you were against any *toenadering* (rapprochement) with white students. Show the finger, in other words, to the management's attempts at bringing black and white together. It was from this group that you would hear that Mandela's legacy was tainted because he had been soft by not dealing with the hard issues of land redistribution and the dispensing of justice for whites. There was no middle ground in this kind of retributive politics.

That strain among elements of black student politics was there throughout my time at UFS. It insisted that the Reitz decision not be forgotten and that whites pay for what they did to the country. Nowhere was this more evident than in a strange creature on campus called the student parliament.

Like several other universities, UFS organised the students based on external party politics. What this meant was that on campus there was an ANC party (Sasco), a DA party (DA Students' Organisation), an EFF party, a Freedom Front Plus party, and on our Qwaqwa campus bordering KwaZulu-Natal an IFP party (Sadesmo). In a normal world, this mirror image of national party politics expressed through campus politics could work well.

But this was South Africa and it soon became clear that the students in the majority parties, which were black, were mimicking the politics of aggression, insult, provocation and sometimes outright attacks on those in the smaller parties, which were white. The muscular politics of the time meant that when the student parliament convened, the campus would be in disarray and parents started to come to my office to complain about the emotional and psychological toll this was taking on their children.

Parliament became a serious concern for the university management and council. Despite the hard work on building the human project and growing national and international regard for the reconciliation project, student leaders from the majority parties were hellbent on revenge against the white students. When a group of black students decided to disrupt a netball match between UFS and another university, council decided the enormous damage being done to the institution's reputation and human relationships on campus meant it was time for a different kind of student politics.

It was decided that while we wanted active student politics, it could no longer be organised on a party-political basis. What further motivated the decision was the discovery that external political parties were investing significant sums in their campus-based organisations to sustain this kind of aggression. The prize for the most disruptive among the student leaders was guaranteed employment in government or party, which were often indistinguishable. It was astonishing to see how many student leaders from the ANC graduated from campus to cosy employment in the provincial and, on occasion, national governments.

All this ambition came at a heavy cost to the university, and once the party-political basis for student organisation was terminated the campus became a much more manageable and pleasant place for student life and activism. But I knew there was a brooding resentment about this decision that never really went away, even years later.

There was a final test of our commitment to finding another path towards a shared humanity on campus. Towards the end of my time at UFS, an aggrieved student led a march on a rugby match, against the wishes of his own student council. There was no reason for the march, as most of the demands from students and workers had been resolved, including a tendentious decision to insource contract workers. There was no money in the coffers for such a huge commitment but we agreed to a phasing in of the insourcing agreement.

Halfway there, the renegade leader called the acting dean to say he would turn around the small march, ostensibly about fees and insourcing, if I allowed the reregistration of students who had fallen foul of the 'n+2' rule (any student who failed a module or course more than once could not continue but had to complete the outstanding credits through Unisa or another university). The individuals he was speaking about were a few of the party-political students, his buddies, who believed they had more rights than other students. I had no choice but to say no to such a transaction on the basis of fairness towards all our students and consistency in the application of rules.

The student leader and his group then stormed the rugby pitch and were set on by parents and students for interrupting the match. The younger, agile students fled, leaving behind the older, less mobile workers to be attacked. The then premier of the province added his voice to this tragedy: the same thing would have happened if they had interrupted a soccer match; black sports supporters would have attacked the disruptors. But this was UFS and the racial optics of the moment carried the news headlines for weeks.

This event reinforced my position that we needed a different kind of student politics on university campuses that included party-political interests but went beyond them. Put differently, the campus needed a new generation of activist leaders in the student body.

We proceeded to invest significant amounts of money in identifying and nurturing the future leadership of the campus and the country. We started with first-years, recognising that we could rebuild the student culture around these emergent leaders who would still be with us for three (the typical bachelor's degree) or more years (for example, the typical medical or law degrees).

If reconciliation was going to be embedded in the culture of the newly envisaged UFS, it would have to be built via these student leaders. Led by an exceptionally talented dean of students, Rudi Buys, and his team, we set to work. We identified through nomination and interviews the most promising leaders in residence life, in clubs and societies, in student leadership. These young leaders went through a series of training workshops, with some of them selected for placement in leading universities around the world. In Japan, the Netherlands, the US and other countries, these student leaders were exposed to new ideas, new cultures and new ways of doing activism and development in campus life.

The students from rural South Africa learnt about race, gender and sexual identity in ways that were quite intimidating for many of them They were encouraged to share rooms not only with friends but with those supposedly different from them. Groups were deliberately organised to prevent students settling back into comfortable racial affiliations; our leaders needed to be different.

We took the entire student leadership to Germany and Poland to study how the Germans and the Jews dealt with history and memory after the Shoah. Some students visited Rwanda in the aftermath of the genocide of the Tutsis and their Hutu friends. These structured visits were designed to generate from the bottom up a new kind of UFS student leader.

We introduced a compulsory core curriculum for all first-year students in which they learnt about race, identity and history but also astronomy, economics and the law. The idea was to educate them before they were trained, to broaden their knowledge about themselves, others and a larger world. After initial resistance to anything but what they had come to study – such as urban planning or medicine – many students found the broader education and the accompanying skills valuable for their learning across the disciplines.

To lead these students, I had to change the exemplar of leadership on display to 40 000 students every day. I opened my doors to first-years without appointment and held regular sessions under trees on all three campuses where students could raise any issue with their rector. I developed the habit of greeting every student and talking to them during daily walks across the campus.

'Did you pray for your rector this morning?' I asked two students who looked Afrikaans (no, seriously, I could detect language preference most times). 'Yes, rector,' they responded in Afrikaans. 'And what did you pray for?' I asked. 'That you might lose weight.' I had a good laugh. 'You know I can change your marks?' They laughed this time.

In every appointment we made, I remembered the wisdom conveyed in the title of the riveting book *The Students are Watching* by Nancy Faust Sizer and Theodore Sizer. We probably had the most diverse senior management team of all universities in South Africa: black and white, Afrikaans, English and Sesotho speakers, foreign and local, gay and straight, men and women. And all of them were superbly talented. When the students observed this team in public gatherings, from graduations to other assemblies, they would hopefully see that we practised what we preached. What I also wanted them to witness was the power of our leadership choices that signalled without words our commitment to conciliation.

I remember a group of ANC activists from the province coming to see me about the lack of transformation at UFS. On their side of the table sat about six young African men, on our side a highly diverse group of senior managers. After their lament about transformation, I asked them to be serious for a moment. Look at you: you come here with a team of all African men and you dare to talk to us about transformation? Clearly embarrassed by preset talking points about the only thing they knew – race – the poor visitors left shortly afterwards.

The dramatic challenges apart, it was clear to most people inside and outside UFS that the university had transformed significantly since the Reitz incident. My core advisory team shared the view that the direction of the university based on the dual commitments of the human and academic projects would always be challenged precisely because of its transformative ends. And it was not the lack of transformation but its relative success that brought out the occasional and sometimes intense resistance against the deeper changes at the university.

If some black student leaders saw it as their role to resist the transformative drive of the university, the local Afrikaans newspaper, *Volksblad*, believed its role was also to resist the new direction of its beloved Kovsies. The onslaught was relentless, day after day, and any number of issues would lead the front page of a newspaper whose parent company kept threatening to close it because of declining subscriptions and the cost of print.

The ultimate test of reconciliation at UFS was the future of Afrikaans on campus. For most of my time as rector I had discouraged any move to lessen the place and influence of Afrikaans, whether in teaching, administration or residence life. When students first approached me about being an all-English campus, I made lengthy arguments that Afrikaans was not 'a white man's language' but one developed and renewed over time with inputs from other languages. I used common examples from Malay and slave cultures in the Cape and argued with conviction that it was also my mother's language from her roots in the Boland area of the rural Western Cape.

Regardless, stories came through from lecture venues that white Afrikaans students had an advantage over black students, most of whom spoke other African languages, and for purposes of their university education, English. This made me uneasy but so many of these stories sounded anecdotal rather than proven accounts of systematic discrimination. I allowed for the debate but was not yet convinced. If anything, I thought, demographic changes on the main campus would over time probably change the language policy anyway.

From a change-management point of view, I was also aware that we were pushing change on too many fronts to take on this major emotional and political issue, Afrikaans. This is a major consideration when trying to change a place, large or small – taking on the right issues and the right number of issues so that you do not collapse the organisation. Overreach, and you're gone. For leaders this is an issue of judgement in which wisdom is required: when to change what and why. You need to know your organisation from the inside out, and it was my judgement that Afrikaans would enjoy its place at UFS even if through an evolutionary process it eventually made space for English. But not right now, I calculated.

Then something happened to change my mind. During one of my student lunches, most of those around the table were Dutch students spending a semester at the university. After delightful conversations, they asked to see me as a group. I was delighted to welcome them to campus from one of my favourite places to visit, the Netherlands, and in that happy moment I was not expecting this bombshell.

'We have been attending classes on your campus,' they said, 'and we could follow what was being taught in the Afrikaans classes and the English classes. We need to tell you about racism in the teaching of more than one subject. The Afrikaans lecturer gives lecture notes and exam tips in the mainly white Afrikaans classes but not in the mainly black English classes. This is discrimination, and we saw it in more than one class.'

These visitors had no issues with Afrikaans, as so many of us have because of the Soweto uprising of 1976 when the language was forced down the throats of black students. They were just reporting what they had seen and heard after a semester at UFS.

I shared this with my management team and said we had no choice but to launch a systematic investigation into the problem. Is it true and, if so, what needs to be done? What helped us activate this important decision was that students were protesting across the country about the high costs of higher education and the colonial legacies harboured in former white universities. When one of the student leaders brought the issue of Afrikaans to a campus-wide town hall meeting, I could say confidently that we were moving forward with an investigation which would inform our decision on Afrikaans.

The *Volksblad* went apoplectic, and in its favourite space for attacks on the university, the letters to the editor, intense and toxic entries appeared. This was the first time I started to get hate mail and a few death threats. Outside my house, for sale signs went up announcing my departure. The university placed round-the-clock guards on the property, just in case. An investigation into Afrikaans was, for some, a call to arms. For others, this was the ultimate loss, their treasured language long held as an ethnic property, not simply as a means of communication. Some colleagues who would otherwise be *beleefd* (super polite) suddenly turned ugly. We had touched a nerve.

In all my life in higher education management, I had seldom devoted as much time to a single issue as in the case of Afrikaans. I was conflicted. I loved the language because I had discovered its humour, its literary wealth, its coarseness of rebuke, its subtleties of communication and, most of all, its facility for access to fellow citizens who would otherwise hear me differently.

It was in Afrikaans that I could rush off in the early morning to pray with a principal in Ugie whose wife was murdered during a break-in at their home. It was in Afrikaans that my team and I could console the community in a southern Free State town after a farm murder. It was in Afrikaans that a white student would ask if she could pray for me after waiting outside my office early one morning. I had experienced another Afrikaans in the Free State that endeared me to the hearts of the people I served.

But as a leader I had a responsibility to all my students and all their languages. And if it was true that there was systematic rather than incidental discrimination against black students in teaching, then that was the Afrikaans we needed to deal with. We had countless meetings with anyone who had a view on Afrikaans, black and white, staff and students, those on and off campus. I visited each of the faculties to listen to their concerns and felt the sense of impending loss among some of my Afrikaans-committed academics.

We were lucky to have a language investigation panel led by Dionne van Reenen, a supersmart thinker of Afrikaner stock who led the many deliberations with openness, candidness and relentless focus. My vice-rector for academic matters, Lis Lange, brought academic rigour to the investigatory process and was able to synthesise the substantial volumes of data into an accessible form for all stakeholders, including students, the senate and the council.

After lengthy debates and exhaustive consultations, management took a position to council: English would be the primary language of instruction in an otherwise multilingual university. Students in theology, teaching or some of the other professions would continue to have their courses in Afrikaans simply because their career destinations put them in Afrikaans contexts, such as teaching foundation phase in an Afrikaans primary school. But in all other disciplines, teaching would be in English.

Council accepted and approved the new language policy and immediately there was a challenge from conservative organisations off campus. We were prepared for the matter to go all the way to the highest court on appeal after appeal. Eventually, the matter was decided in the university's favour and other historically Afrikaans universities followed suit with their own court battles that followed.

It was a sad day when the finely tuned implementation process started but the UFS decision was a necessary and inevitable transition towards English. The Afrikaans *taalstryders* were distraught; many had hoped that an earlier language proposal by Jakes Gerwel, an Afrikaans literature expert, would hold: that in an act of conciliation, there would be a dedicated Afrikaans university in the north (presumably Potchefstroom, now North-West University) and one in the south (presumably Stellenbosch). After all, this was Mandela's director-general and a prominent academic with activist credentials; surely his voice would carry weight?

I was never sure whether Jakes really meant what he proposed; he was too smart not to foresee the inevitable. At the same time, he was emotionally Afrikaans. Many years ago, as he passed me in my seated row in a plane, he made a snide comment under his breath that I was reading an English newspaper rather than an Afrikaans title. I thought that to be an odd, if not silly, comment but I remember that incident to this day. Regardless, even if Jakes had made a serious proposal for language accommodation, it was out of touch with the politics of country and campus and would simply not be defensible the further we moved away from the heady days of reconciliation under the Tutus and the Mandelas.

In the larger language community, there was a gradual acceptance of the Afrikaans decision and I found acceptance among Afrikaans speakers of all stripes for another interesting reason: most young Afrikaans students wanted to strengthen their abilities in English.

Many had their short-term sights set on au pair jobs in Europe and North America and English-teaching positions in Asia; and a growing awareness that their generation would be required to work across the world meant, quite simply, that added proficiency in English would help their cause. In addition, many of these students no longer held onto those deep emotional attachments to the Boer War and anti-English sentiment carried over from more than a century ago. They had moved on from their grandparents' and parents' inherited traumas. They were looking forward to immersion in an English world that would serve their families well as jobseekers and/or emigrants.

Where it all started was with that inaugural speech that introduced me to the campus and the country as well as the radical idea of reconciliation that would steer my vision for leadership in the years ahead. Shortly after the speech, a professor from the theology faculty came to my office for an urgent meeting. Dolf Britz was shaking his head back and forth as he repeated a single line from the speech: 'I can forgive because I have been forgiven.' He understood better than most that there was a deep spiritual dimension to this risky commitment. He knew that apart from the university leadership's commitment to reconciliation, there were personal motivations that informed my thinking on the matter.

As I prepared the inaugural address, I remembered how often I had failed people and failed myself; that despite my best intentions, I sometimes hurt other people and disappointed those closest to me. I knew deep down that I was imperfect, somebody constantly struggling to be a better person than I was before. And every time I got up, again and again, I was forgiven and released to continue this very human journey. Dolf also knew that in my faltering faith I had experienced the splendour of forgiveness.

Another man who came to see me after the inaugural speech was a famous Free State unionist with an even more famous national surname, Makhathini. He was respectful in parts but could not restrain his anger about our decision to bring back the Reitz students and embark on the path of reconciliation. I let him speak his mind and felt his pain; on that I dared not judge him. But I was curious, so I asked, 'Mr Makhathini, have you ever been forgiven for wrongdoing?'

Since so much of our management time, energy and resources were invested in reconciliation through residence life, it is fair to ask whether this project was successful in achieving that end. At the time, it was. We inched forward in residence-wide desegregation. The influx of massive infrastructural funding also allowed us to build new student accommodation unencumbered by the history and traditions of the much older residences, where initiation and humiliation were inseparable experiences for incoming first-years. While those rituals were welcomed by white students based on shared memories from their parents, they were often processed as racism by black students.

Students gradually accepted the co-living spaces as black and white Kovsies shared the *koshuis* (student residence) building, if seldom the same rooms. The male residence Vishuis, named after Abraham Fischer, father of the struggle stalwart Braam Fischer (derivate, fish or Vis-), enjoyed semi-private status with the university, which meant hard-core resistance to integration was especially evident there. It was therefore not surprising that when the invasion of the rugby pitch happened, the protesting students singled out Vishuis residents as having joined the parents and other visitors to campus during the on-field assault.

Overall, the transformation of the residences proceeded according to plan. In the process, I quickly learnt the difference between desegregation and integration. In the UFS context, the former referred to the removal of race as the organising principle for residence placement; the latter has to do with the establishment of meaningful and productive interactions between black and white students within these living spaces. One other thing I noticed was that it was much easier for women students to embrace normal living and interactions in residences than men, an observation requiring further sociological enquiry.

Outside the residences, race relations on campus seemed to be normalising. Black and white students entered romantic relationships and, in some cases, married. I was fascinated by the open and visible demonstrations of affection that should have been normal in other spaces. Here in the Free State and on the UFS campus, however, they were near impossible around the time of the Reitz incident and certainly in its aftermath. I wrote a book about these developments, *Making Love in a War Zone*.

When I returned for meetings and a friend's graduation in Bloemfontein in December 2023, I discovered a very different campus. There were hardly any white students in the residences and only a few hundred in the incoming first-year class. I do not think the project of racial reconciliation was a priority for the new management and this was a costly mistake. Where did all the white students go? Probably to those universities with concentrated numbers of whites in the student population like the Potchefstroom campus of North-West University.

As indicated earlier, 'Potch' was always thrown in my face as the option for white students if we did not do more to keep them at UFS. What the parents and their allies were really saying is that a transforming UFS, with all the changes going on, was pushing away students into normalised white spaces. I remember around that time a furore at Potch around a Nazi salute by white students during orientation, and wondered what kind of parent would want to enrol their child in that kind of situation.

By December 2023, UFS was for all intents and purposes a black campus as far as student enrolments were concerned. It was heartbreaking to witness because you cannot do racial reconciliation with yourself. You need the racial other in the same space for this important national project. But I had left seven years earlier and recognised that the new UFS leadership might have had other priorities.

Still, the writing was on the wall, and I had to do some deep thinking about why South African universities *as institutions* find racial integration so difficult. One reason is that other institutions are still deeply segregated. All the churches in Bloemfontein, for example, were either all white, like the Dutch Reformed Church, or all black, like the many township churches. There was one exception, though, and that was Pastor At Boshoff's Christian Revival Church on the outskirts of the city. I was invited there a couple of times and intrigued by the number of white and black worshippers filling up this mega-church every Sunday morning. It was certainly a desegrated space worth thinking about; but I had my doubts about the extent of genuine integration among parishioners. The weight of apartheid hung heavily over all institutions and that was certainly true of UFS despite the enormous efforts to reconcile divided peoples.

Our two children always seemed to find the race question ridiculous. That is because, since their birth, they had woken up in a home where there were black and white, foreigners and South Africans, gay and straight, Jews, Muslims and Christians. That was the case while we lived in the US and in all the provinces where we lived and worked.

Not once did we refer to our children as a 'race', even though they were alert to the fact that the society in which they were growing up was organised on the basis of racial distinction. Their friends coming through our homes were therefore not predictable by race. Mikhail dated a white girl and Sara for a long time only dated black African guys, if one cared to notice such meaningless categories in human relationships.

It is relatively easy to raise your own children to embrace the full humanity of others. But by the time other people's children arrive on a university campus at 17 or 18 years old, it is much more difficult to deal with their settled views on who they are and who other people are. That is what makes education and development such an interesting challenge.

9
Development activist

'In South Africa there are very few ways out of poverty, and education is one of them'.
Jennie Glennie

When Sinoxolo Gcilitshana marched across the graduation stage at the University of the Free State with a degree in the teaching of history, his was one of the most unlikely South African success stories.

I was still at UFS when I received a call from a teacher at an elite Cape Town high school. She was a sub-examiner in matric history and had witnessed something remarkable. A student from Oscar Mpetha High in Nyanga, Cape Town, had achieved the highest marks in the subject. I told her this was not possible since I had done some work at Oscar Mpetha and the school was thoroughly dysfunctional. The principal at the time was a South African Democratic Teachers Union bigwig and nobody would touch the incompetent leader.

On one of my visits the teachers all sat in the staffroom doing nothing while children waited in vain for instruction in their hot classrooms. It was the anniversary of Steve Biko's death, so I took over one of the classes and taught them about the stalwart's life and his teachings on Black Consciousness. As I left the school, one of the teachers came running out and asked if I could get her a job, any job, somewhere else. She had a degree in the commercial subjects. 'No ma'am,' I told her. 'I will not get you a job unless you first demonstrate that you can do your current job. Please go and teach the children. They are waiting for you.' She was not amused.

Any other school, but not Oscar Mpetha, I told the matric sub-examiner on the phone. I checked with the authorities, who confirmed Sinoxolo's almost perfect score in history, better than any candidate from the elite schools of the Cape. Why? The reason I eventually found did not surprise me. Sinoxolo's teacher was Zimbabwean, and at that point everything fell into place.

I needed to find the young man. I tracked him down via social media and obtained a cellphone number. 'Good morning, Sinoxolo, you may not know me but I was told about your amazing achievement in history.'

'No, prof, I know you from social media; happy to meet you.'

'Sinoxolo, what are your plans going forward?'

'Thank you for asking,' replied the history whizz. 'I am on my way to Golden Arrow to become a bus driver.'

Nothing wrong with being a bus driver, I said, but would you not like to study further? It turned out that Sinoxolo had been turned down at UCT and had no money for university studies. 'Listen, Sinoxolo, please turn around, go back home, and tell your mother that you are going to study in Bloemfontein at UFS. Pack your bags for there is a ticket on the way to you right now. You will be travelling with a young man from Delft [another tough neighbourhood on the outskirts of Cape Town not far from the airport].' The Delft student was recommended to me for university studies by one of his teachers whom I had taught at Trafs years before.

Early the next morning, the two young men arrived at the bus station in Bloemfontein. They looked scared, like any Capetonian who ventures over the Du Toitskloof pass for the first time. Grace served them a hearty breakfast, then we left to register them as UFS students.

Even before completing his first semester, Sinoxolo was in my office: he wanted to go home. His father had abandoned the family and he felt his mother and sister needed protection from the elements outside their shack. 'I am not in favour of you throwing away this opportunity,' I told him. 'But call your mother, and if she agrees I will get you a bus ticket back home.' The mother told me clearly that he was to finish his degree and only come home during the university holidays.

Before long Sinoxolo was thriving in his studies and became head of his Kyalami men's residence, where he established a library so students coming back from classes could read interesting books as part of their broader education. Sinoxolo spoke to all who cared to listen about his dreams to become the vice-chancellor of Wits University. I teased him about his lack of ambition: why not UFS? I asked.

A few years later, I got a call from the accomplished professor of literature, Njabulo Ndebele. He wanted me to know about a remarkable young history teacher whom his foundation had just selected to be a Mandela Rhodes Fellow.

Not long afterwards I received another call, this time with the devastating news that Sinoxolo had been murdered in his flat near the Pretoria school where he was teaching.

I tell the story of Sinoxolo to demonstrate the trajectory of development work in South Africa. The discovery of great talent that emerges against the odds. The struggle of such talent to succeed despite the weight of the past and threats in the present. The sheer joy of individual attainment inspiring hope among the unseen talented. And the denial of life and learning when so much has been invested in a promising student. In the turbulence of South Africa, development and disappointment walk hand in hand.

Throughout my career I have always pursued two commitments at the same time. One, to become a leading scholar in educational research anywhere in the world. Two, to leverage the benefits of educational research for improving the human condition.

Between the UFS job as vice-chancellor and an upcoming appointment at Stellenbosch University as distinguished professor of education, I was fortunate to be awarded a year-long fellowship at the Center for Advanced Study in the Behavioral Sciences at Stanford University. It was a time to reflect on leadership in crisis situations and to present this research as guidance to other university leaders. I completed the book *As by Fire* then accepted a job back in the Western Cape where my journey had started.

The Stellenbosch offer was something I had always wanted after a career at the coalface of higher education leadership – simply to be an ordinary professor doing research and development. I made it clear to my senior colleagues that I did not want to attend a management or senate meeting again. I was happy to advise and mentor senior colleagues when approached, but the humdrum of administration and executive meetings was something I had done all my life; now I just wanted to be a professor doing research and development work around the country and in other parts of the world.

It took a while for my colleagues in the faculty of education and the senior executive to understand this decision but eventually they left me alone. I started by building a strong research team and a focused programme of development for schools and talented scholars in the academy.

Because I love teaching, I took on a postgraduate teachers course but stopped doing that during the pandemic because I simply could not teach through a screen. It was then that I became aware that so much of my teaching on critical issues in education policy (such as racial integration in schools) depended on being able to see the students 'live'. I modulated my teaching based on information drawn from their body language, how they cringed almost imperceptibly when a difficult issue was raised or how they queried with their faces when they did not understand. I used such incoming data to slow down or accelerate, pause, simplify or invite questions, depending on what was available to the mind. Without such connection, there was a poverty to my pedagogy.

I did, however, continue master's and doctoral supervision since this mostly involved one-on-one sessions and I could also learn and grow through interactions with outstanding minds.

I could not believe how lucky I was to be living my best life as a scholar. Now I could put in 18 hours of work a day doing little else than research and writing, speaking and consulting, mentoring and advising. 'How are you?' people would ask. 'Oh, they pay me too much,' I would respond. Grace and I spent much of what we earned by giving back to communities, whether it was for the support of high school girls, which she led, or financial assistance for university students, which I managed.

In every university where I had the privilege of leading, the focus on schools became a major focus of my work. It is the one thing I knew something about: how to leverage research to spur development in schools. In Durban, our focus was on explaining why some schools in the most disadvantaged areas of KwaZulu-Natal consistently produced effective examination results. We were particularly interested in an area called Umlazi and our research teams descended on a few extraordinary schools.

One factor stood out: principal leadership. Where there was strong principal leadership, schools flourished. It was not resources, though we were careful not to downplay the importance of enabling funds for reasons that went beyond the causal link between leadership and results – social justice. There was a danger in fetishising the lack of material resources in order to play up academic scores when gross inequalities between privileged (white) and poor (black) schools disfigured the education landscape in all nine provinces.

With time, our research showed that it was more than the singular hero version of change that predicted effective schools. Change was 'stretched over' several leaders in the school, as the literature on distributed leadership would explain. The great man theory of leadership was not sufficient to explain change in schools.

Moving from Durban to Pretoria, my research slowly shifted from schools to higher education as our teams started to investigate topics such as institutional mergers and curriculum change in universities. With respect to the latter, I had developed a strong interest in institutional theories of curriculum change – that is, how universities as institutions enable or constrain the content and delivery of curriculum.

When I took the position at UFS there were now two tracks to my research – understanding universities and how they worked, and school improvement studies. After a request from the premier and his education MEC, UFS put at the disposal of the province our best ideas and resources, such that this rural part of central South Africa became the top-performing region in the matric results.

There was another factor that explained the success of highly effective schools – the quality of the teachers and, therefore, the quality of teacher support. I had first seen this years before in northern Namibia through the Ibis Life Science Project funded by a Danish NGO. This highly successful venture combined centre-based training with in-school support: an expert teacher worked alongside a local teacher, observing and being observed in the teaching of the subject.

Here was a solution to the political problem of school inspectors in South Africa. Our model brought mentors into the school who were not there to judge the struggling teacher but who worked alongside them as fellow professionals. Such interventions were small and expensive by definition and would take a long time and a lot of money to go to scale. But the mentorship model was effective if not spectacular in terms of reach.

In the meantime, I was determined to develop my own research and research profile as a scholar. I wanted both: to do groundbreaking research and to lead universities. It was not easy. The demands of pursuing two vocations were exhausting, yet I absolutely loved doing both.

My scholarly identity mattered. I wanted to get up in a senate and speak with authority and credibility about the importance of research in the life of an academic. Whatever its shortcomings, one of the best available measures of scholarly worth is the National Research Foundation's (NRF) rating system. I knew it was important not only to be productive (the volume of research outputs) but generative (the stimulation of new thinking) in respect of research. Behind this commitment was a memorable line from a respected leader in the NRF when I once asked him about quantity versus quality as a young academic. Gerhard von Gruenewaldt's wisdom still rings in my years: 'At the NRF we not only count, we weigh.'

Publishing a lot helps but publishing in the right places makes the difference. These were hard lessons learnt and I followed the script systematically until my B became an A. That I got the A rating on the job as vice-chancellor was a source of some satisfaction but also held strategic value: I could lead by example.

My long and determined research journey made me realise there was no reason why every young academic who came after me had to learn by knocking their heads along the way, taking unnecessary detours and, quite frankly, wasting time. How I wish that in 1991 at the age of 35, when I returned from PhD studies, someone had taken me aside as a young professor and given me scholarly guidance.

Guidance on which journals to publish in and which to avoid. On why chapters in books are a waste of time unless you are invited by a guru in your field. How the third book you produce must be different from the second and that, in turn, different from the first. Why academic duty (administration, meetings, examiner tasks) could sink you unless you learn how to manage it well. And why good teaching is, at its best, scholarly, and not simply the delivery of information.

In short, nobody taught me how to be a professor.

It was time to act. What I had experimented with at UDW and UP with emerging scholars became a fully fledged design for the UFS 'future professors programme'. When I presented the concept for Mellon Foundation funding to its South African agent in Cape Town, Dr Stuart Saunders, he felt the name 'future professors' was presumptuous. Either he was so English, I thought, that he balked at this proposal from a historically Afrikaans university; or he was still stewing from our heated interaction at the Yale Club years ago when I was a student representative and he was UCT's vice-chancellor looking to Americans to fund bursaries for black students. He might have given a small amount for the programme, I can't recall, but I was going ahead regardless of external support.

I recruited a team of top scholars from UFS and we designed a programme that had an immediate effect on the institution. What was its grounding logic?

First, I knew that setting higher standards for promotion was not enough; it was also important to demonstrate to the next generation of scholars and scientists *how* to get there.

Second, I knew that in the absence of a radical intervention to build the class of professors, UFS and many other universities were likely to take short cuts because of political pressure from the government to produce more black professors.

Third, I knew that more and more senior professors were retiring and that they would need to be replaced by top young academics coming through the system more quickly than would be the case otherwise.

Fourth, I knew the future of the South African academy would depend almost exclusively on the quality of the next generation of professors.

During my time at Stanford and Cornell I was fascinated by the fact that the university's reputation rested on a few world-beating academics like Sagan and McClintock at Cornell or Linus Pauling and Philip Zimbardo at Stanford. If South Africa's 20-plus public universities could raise some stars of the academy, then Africa too would be in a position to build strong higher education institutions.

I was, however, deeply aware of South Africa's troubled history with the professoriate. When Afrikaners seized state power in the 20th century they emerged from a position of social weakness and political defeat. This was visible within all their institutions, including higher education.

Afrikaner academics had an inferiority complex in relation to the more established English universities like Wits and UCT, with their primordial connections to institutions in the mother country like Oxford and Cambridge. It would become a badge of honour for the English, if not a form of initiation, to do PPE (politics, philosophy and economics) at Oxford and come back and parade their academic Englishness.

While many young Afrikaner academics spread their wings throughout the world, especially among cultural cousins in universities of the Netherlands and Belgium, they were the poorer relatives to those coming through the Oxbridge system. Moreover, their local universities were relatively new and underperforming in the research stakes.

For all intents and purposes, the Afrikaans universities functioned like teaching colleges without the clout in research and ratings that placed the English universities at the top of the pile. An Afrikaner scientist at UCT, Jack de Wet, had the courage to inform the Stellenbosch rector that his university would remain a junior partner in the scientific enterprise unless it took research seriously.

When the Afrikaner National Party seized political power in 1948, one of its goals was to build competing Afrikaans universities in areas close to the more established English institutions. Rand Afrikaans University was built across the freeway from Wits. The University of Port Elizabeth was the antidote to the English Rhodes University, 132 km inland along the N2. And so on.

There was a problem, though. You can build a physical university relatively quickly but you cannot populate it with professors at the same speed. Professors are generated patiently over time from junior lecturer status upwards. Such a career would be marked by high levels of quality publications, the supervision of master's and doctoral students and the capacity to profess something that sets you apart from other scholars in your discipline. You cannot flick a switch and produce a professor.

The problem for nationalists, white or black, is the relentless politics that bears down on the slow logics of professorial development. So, the Afrikaans universities decided to fast-track the process and make white men professors despite their alarmingly weak curricula vitae. You needed only to be male, white, Afrikaans and a member of the Broederbond and a professorship was waiting for you. How did I know this? Because as dean at UP and rector at UFS I saw first-hand the enormous damage done to the academic standards of higher education by the dumbing down of the academy through the dilution of the professoriate.

It should not have been surprising, therefore, that black nationalists would do in the 21st century exactly what Afrikaner nationalists did a few generations before: accelerate the racial allocation of professorships to their respective tribes in order to overcome inferiority complexes, on the one hand, and satisfy nationalistic desires for showing progress in 'transformation' regardless of merit.

I was distraught when I saw universities like Unisa openly declare through their promotion criteria that you could become a professor with the skimpiest of CVs, in other words without a substantive record of high-level research publications in the top international journals in your discipline, alongside the production of quality doctoral students who themselves developed records of achievement in their respective professions.

My biggest concern was the damage this would do to the South African university system. I saw young black academics at UP in whom we had invested significant resources go from lecturer level in my faculty to full professor at a historically disadvantaged university somewhere in the north of the country.

I was sympathetic as far as the reasons for this internal migration were concerned. A promotion means more money, enhanced status and greater mobility – things all humans desire in their professions. But the costs would be high in terms of the credibility of our universities, the integrity of our training programmes and, ultimately, the value of the degree.

As black universities proceeded along this route of cheapening the professorship, I noticed the inevitable gap that opened up even further between the class of professors in the former white universities and those in the still disadvantaged universities. In many cases, the equality of personnel across the higher education sector in terms of the professorship existed on paper only.

In reality, there were still two distinct university systems, one populated by leading professors in the country and, for a few of them, in the world. And one populated by professors who would not stand a snowball's chance in hell of gaining appointment, let alone promotion, in competitive universities anywhere. We wanted to rush things and we paid the price for the dilution of the one currency universities have at their proposal: the class of professors.

This does not mean there were not mediocre professors in the former white universities; there are lots there too. Or that there are not singular brilliant professors in the black universities. I am talking about concentrated sets of top professors that keep Wits, Stellenbosch and UCT in the upper tiers of almost any university world ranking system; and a deadweight of so-called 'professors' at Vaal University of Technology or Unisa who have never had an original idea in their lives or made any major breakthroughs in their disciplines.

In this regard, there is something we are reluctant to talk about, and that is black conservatism in the South African academy. Somehow we walk around with this idea that if someone is pigmentally black they are progressive in their thinking or in the content of their research. Yes, academics might cloak themselves in the language of progressivism by putting the words decolonisation or decoloniality in the titles of articles that have nothing to do with these profound concepts; but, in reality, their social and epistemological worlds as academics can be quite conservative. In the same way, the assumption that white professors are inherently conservative is refuted by the history of academic activism in South Africa. In the heat of development battles, those lines of distinction between white (conservative) and black (progressive) academics are drawn firmly, especially when it comes to the professoriate.

For all these reasons and more, there was an urgency to the intervention dubbed the Future Professors Programme (FPP). We advertised on the UFS campus for senior lecturer equivalents who were already showing signs of life in their academic capacity and productivity. In other words, we were looking for those more likely to become professors in a relatively short time.

Ideologically, this focus on accomplished academics is a hard sell in a place like South Africa. Our flat politics of egalitarianism means that when you talk about developing high-achieving scholars, the default position of university managements is academic development. In colloquial terms, the poorest of the poor. Most of our intervention programmes, such as the government-funded New Generation of Academics Programme for new entrants to the academy, are indeed about the lowest tier of academic appointment, to raise up young people for lecturing positions, not to advance high-performing individuals for professorships. Academic development that we routinely do for first-year students coming into university from poor school backgrounds is a way of thinking that has transferred into how we think of professional development for junior lecturers.

To be sure, I have also been involved in academic development for lower-tier lecturers all my life. When, for example, we incorporated the Afrikaans college of education into the faculty of education at the University of Pretoria, most of the selected lecturers did not have doctorates and some did not even have a master's degree. That was when I launched compulsory daily research training programmes for all staff after lecturing hours. If they were going to be part of a university, they would have to be trained in the habits of the scholar as well as the concepts and methods of research and how to publish. Our first publication as a joint endeavour included a study of the college incorporation process itself. We shocked the journal editors when more than 20 names of each of the trainee lecturers appeared at the top of the manuscript.

This whole experience was hard for my incorporated colleagues. They had little to no experience of advanced research. They had to work after lecturing for hours every day. I did most of the training myself, which meant taking up to three hours a day out of my usual decanal commitments. It was, in retrospect, a wonderful way of getting to know my new college colleagues at close quarters, and they were mostly good sports even when tested late on a Friday afternoon by staying for research training.

It was tough. One early evening, a science education lecturer came to see me in my office. This young lecturer was an excellent undergraduate teacher and I selected her because she was one of the few with a doctorate from the incoming college group. Her faced looked bleak and I sensed the meeting was going to be difficult.

'Well,' she said, 'I was praying last night and God told me that I should stop coming to your training sessions because my husband and family come first.' I tried to steady myself on the leathery chair that suddenly felt slippery. Wait, I thought to myself, God had something to say about academic development sessions to advance the career of a promising academic?

In my mind, what I had here was a woman who knew her place in a conservative domestic setting and probably had a husband who expected the baby to have been bathed and the supper and slippers to be ready when he came home from work. That the man's wife was a professional in her own right was secondary to his needs, as determined over generations from one patriarchal family setup to the next. Privately I was stewing, not so much because she wanted to opt out of the training sessions but because of the potential loss of a talented lecturer to the academic world of research and development.

When she had finished announcing the divine revelation, I told my colleague it so happened that I had also been on my knees the previous night. However, I got a different message from on high – that she had been given enormous talents and that she would show up the next day in my office and come up with a concocted story about her husband's needs. I can still see her solemn face with just a hint of a smile, for she knew I was making this up.

That was academic development. The FPP was an entirely different kettle of fish.

The UFS version of the FPP had only two broad components – a series of training and development activities about how to produce high-level scholarship and an international placement in a laboratory or seminar setting that the fellow deemed appropriate; where the person did not know where to go, we had specialists to assist them. It worked like a charm and slowly UFS was able to build a new cadre of young professors who were becoming leaders in their respective fields.

By the time I got to Stellenbosch, I had moved on. I was organising a long-term research programme and building a team of postdoctoral students and a small postgraduate community of master's and doctoral students in part to make a contribution to the faculty of education in which I had a nominal appointment; in reality, I was establishing an independent unit for higher education research.

While setting up the unit, I received a call from the then Minister of Higher Education and Training, Dr Naledi Pandor. She is one of the more competent ministers of state and the only one who has reached out to me since 1994 to assist in solving one or other problem in the higher education sector, such as the two administrator appointments in Durban. She had had to disinvite me from one request to serve because fellow ministers in 'the social cluster' could not stomach me offering my expertise. As she grew in seniority in the successive cabinets of government, though, she could ignore the petty and small-minded among her colleagues.

Pandor's request was simple: could you do for the country what you did in the Free State with the preparation of a new class of professors for the South African university system? Of course. I now had to reorganise my entire plan for research and development at Stellenbosch, but this was national service and I wanted to honour her request. I would do this task without remuneration. Fortunately, I had built a team of outstanding administrators and academics at UFS whom I hired to help me establish the national programme, with Stellenbosch as its base.

The new FPP had several components enabled in part by significant funding from the higher education department. First, there would be a highly selective process in which we chose the best young scholars on the cusp of becoming professors. I had an excellent team of selectors, all accomplished academics. Some of the top universities had miniature versions of the FPP and did not send us their top scholars, feeling they were already doing what we were setting out to do; that was not true, and I assumed it to be a case of a little bit of sour grapes.

Second, there would be a comprehensive assessment of each individual fellow's weight of scholarship. The instrument for such assessment was the rating system of the NRF. Every year, hundreds of scientists and scholars apply to see whether they are rateable and, if so, whether they would gain a Y or a P rating, in the case of younger researchers (currently, under 35 years of age), or a senior grade, which could be a C, a B or an A rating. Since most of the selected fellows were likely to apply for a rating, the FPP's comprehensive evaluation would tell them where they stood in relation to the categories described and, importantly, what to do to achieve an optimal rating. These rating assessments were done mainly by A-rated scholars from South African universities.

Third, each annual cohort of fellows would participate in a rich variety of online and face-to-face activities to build their scholarship. These included structured seminars on a range of topics, from academic duty to publishing a scholarly book. In fact, I coedited with one of our selectors, Danie Visser (A in law), a series of important topics for this level of researcher that appear in a book, *On Becoming a Scholar*. The fellows were also exposed to advanced writing workshops, Nobel laureate lectures and targeted visits to national experts in their fields.

Fourth, the fellows were provided with an intensive wraparound programme to take care of their emotional and psychological needs before and after but especially during the Covid years. The psychologists and coaches proved to be enormously helpful to stressed fellows, and as one fellow told me during a one-on-one interview, 'Without the FPP I am not sure I would be here today.' The young woman scientist had gone through a serious and stressful time in her academic career.

Fifth, the fellows would on application be placed in a major university somewhere in the world, working with a leading scientist or scholar in their field. Fortunately, some of the selected fellows had already built an impressive network of partners around the globe so the FPP's role was to provide funding for such short to medium-term visits and/or replacement costs for lectureships in their absence.

The model of development for promising scholars worked well and soon other universities asked to adopt the approach and sought advice on setting up their own 'FPPs'. Oversensitive to my leadership of the FPP and the fact that its initial residency was Stellenbosch University, the minister who replaced Pandor rushed to secure a different institution for what they called phase two of the programme.

When we started the FPP, I was shocked to find we were under pressure from the government to limit, if not avoid altogether, the selection of African academics from other African countries. This was infuriating and I made it clear to the authorities that it was not going to happen. These foreign nationals, some of whom had worked in the South African universities for many years, were academics subject to the values of the international academy. Your national origins are irrelevant because, as an acting vice-chancellor friend so aptly put it, a university is not a country.

It was an academic mean-spiritedness I had not expected from a government whose officials were accommodated abroad when many of them were in exile from apartheid. An earlier president of the republic, Thabo Mbeki, launched an African Renaissance initiative whose intent was to celebrate the achievements of and relationships between Africans across the continent. This was, in fact, a Pan African understanding of the world and that message helped bring young and established Africans from elsewhere on the continent to help rebuild South African science and society. Those were exciting times for universities long isolated from the rest of the world because of apartheid.

Gradually, the tide changed. Successive home affairs ministers, from the disgraced Malusi Gigaba to Aaron Motsoaledi, started to attack immigrants aggressively through stricter policies, laws and regulations which our progressive courts kept rolling back. This was good scapegoating politics for black nationalists reeling under the pressure of corruption, crime, joblessness and the lack of 'service delivery'. In response, the president of the country, no less, in 2024 ventured to announce in the annual January 8th statement of his party: 'We are now enforcing strict immigration law.'

The inhumanity of the politicians was matched only by retaliation on the streets, where struggling South Africans openly attacked foreign nationals for 'taking their jobs'. One was set alight and others murdered. Spaza shops in the townships were razed. And, as our research showed, those hateful behaviours showed up with more subtlety in the corridors of universities when it came to appointments, promotions and opportunities for development – such as the FPP.

Apart from the inhumanity, something else bothered me about the strident actions of some South African universities against other Africans who taught our students, supervised our postgraduates, mentored our young academics and boosted the research profiles and reputations of our institutions. Even if you were heartless in your attitudes to brothers and sisters from other African countries, you were shooting yourself in both feet by denying opportunities to these colleagues. In fact, in our interviews with these academics not one of them said they would readily recommend South Africa to other Africans as a place to serve and grow as an academic researcher and teacher. This was a serious finding for a country desperate to raise the academic stakes in its top universities.

Beyond an appeal to our shared humanity as Africans and as human beings, I came to understand the strategic value of international scholars in building the academic reputation of universities. Cornell, Stanford and every other major research university in the US benefited liberally from European scientists fleeing Nazi Germany and affected states in the 1930s and 1940s.

I waited for the annual announcements of Nobel laureates and regularly saw the name of an immigrant to America. In fact, since 2000, about 40 per cent of Nobel prizes in chemistry, medicine and physics have been awarded to immigrants.

Cornell's Hans Bethe (Nobel in physics, 1967) arrived in the US as a refugee from Germany in 1935 while Roald Hoffmann (Nobel in chemistry, 1981), who lost his father in a Nazi labour camp, moved to America and eventually settled in Ithaca, New York.

A 2013 report revealed that 25 per cent of Stanford's Nobel laureates were foreign-born. In fact, Stanford's first Nobel was Felix Bloch, who left Germany when Hitler came to power in the early 1930s and shortly afterwards joined the physics department on 'the Farm'.

In my mind, the connection was clear. If South African universities could actively recruit the best scholars and scientists from across the continent, we could build a formidable higher education sector that would, in turn, serve development in and beyond Africa. It was inconceivable to me that this rich vein of talent could be ignored, shamed and belittled in the South African academy.

The evidence on the impact of other Africans on South African science was overwhelming. Without Kelly Chibale (Zambia) at the University of Cape Town, generations of South African students would be denied access to his groundbreaking work in medicinal drug research and malaria treatments. Achille Mbembe (Cameroon) at Wits University is the foremost African intellectual in politics and philosophy on the world stage, and his influence on the South African academy has been incomparable in the humanities and social sciences. Tebello Nyokong (Lesotho) has trained generations of chemists in South Africa and without her award-winning research the world would not have access to her remarkable work on alternative cancer treatments. The list of accomplished African scientists from elsewhere on the continent is long and often invisible, given our obsession with national origins.

There was another reason for recruiting African, South African and indeed any leading scholars from around the world to rebuild our universities. You cannot do this with the natives alone. And so I travelled around the world with a target list of top scholars whom I wanted to recruit as dean at UP then as vice-chancellor at UFS.

At UP we hired, among others, Catherine Odora Hoppers (Uganda) and Gilbert Onwu (Nigeria) to teach and research in the faculty of education. Not only did these two colleagues, and others, bring fresh thinking in research in African epistemologies (Catherine) and chemistry education (Gilbert), they helped create new academic cultures within the education sphere. I desperately needed to shift the intellectual tramlines laid down by fundamental pedagogics for decades into completely new theoretical imaginations about education, society and the problem of change.

At the University of the Free State, I jumped on a plane and headed for the UK. A good friend, an accomplished historian, had told me of a South African academic couple who were thinking of returning home. They were among the best of our scholars abroad, so off I went. At the back of my mind, I had that question that every recruiter of staff and students ponders: Why would anyone come to the rural Free State? Even the Free Staters had a joke about incomers: 'you cry when you come,' followed by a word of self-congratulation about the people and the landscape, and 'you cry when you leave'.

I could not read Ian Phimister, the accomplished historian of mining in southern Africa. He gave nothing away but listened carefully to my invitation to leave Sheffield University and move to central South Africa. On that visit, he roped me into teaching one of his classes. That night his partner, Melanie Walker, travelled from Nottingham University to join us. I explained the academic project of UFS and how they could help transform the intellectual landscape of this important university.

Not long afterwards they packed for Bloemfontein, and I could not have foreseen how great an impact these two scholars would make through their sheer intellectual prowess and productivity. Melanie, who has done world-class research on applying and extending the work of the Nobel economist, Amartya Sen, to the field of education, generated an incredible body of scholarship that propelled her to an A1 rating with the NRF. She was the first A1 scholar on campus and the first in the field of education and development.

Ian had little interest in the ratings, for he was building one of the most successful social sciences and humanities research centres I had seen anywhere in the world. I watched him in action. In a large working seminar room, he would have hyper-smart doctoral and postdoctoral students from around Africa and Europe. He would teach from the front of the room but also move from one study desk to another to advise and consult his students.

Each of them would produce a dissertation, which in the case of the PhDs often became a first book, while the postdocs contracted with him to produce a significant book. The quarterly and annual reports from his little research group contained long lists of journal, book and conference outputs that outweighed those of any of the departments in the faculty of humanities.

Then something truly remarkable happened: Phimister's small unit produced the first P-rated history scholar in the history (sorry) of South Africa and, wait for it, a second P shortly after that. In other words, there was high-quality research going on here, and as a result the funding started to come in by the millions – rare for any humanities field.

Such was the quality and impact of the Phimister group's research that senior postgraduate students were sent from European universities to work in his unit. This was important because it signalled in a small way a shift in the flow of ideas and resources between the Global South and the Global North.

It was a phenomenon I wrote about when over-the-top arguments were made by decolonisation activists that Africans were simply handmaidens in the form of research assistants for powerful scholars in the north. Apparently, they took our raw data, processed it in powerful universities in Europe and North America then published great works in their own names. I knew intuitively that this kind of victim play was exaggeration and required much more nuance and accounting for the contribution of African scholars to knowledge in the sciences and humanities.

Ian Phimister in history, Bongani Mayosi in cardiology, and Salim and Quarraisha Karim in infectious diseases were among the examples I used of African academics who were leading in the world from their place in the Global South, rather than simply following trends and ideas from the Global North.

Ian shunned the academic limelight and simply put in the work that completely transformed studies of mining histories in the southern Africa while producing the next generation of professors in his discipline who fanned out across the world for prized appointments at top universities.

Then came the drama which, as I discovered during my career, was not unusual. The first P in history was interested in a position in the history department. This was precisely the kind of young scholar coming out of the

Phimister group that I was desperate to hire at UFS. I was on my way out of UFS for a fellowship at Stanford but I thought this prize appointment was in the bag as I followed the drama from afar.

Not so. The head of department resisted it. It made no sense, and I had the impression that my colleagues in the university leadership could not budge the HoD. Why was this happening? It could not be a lack of resources because council had made strategic funds available for precisely this kind of once-in-a-lifetime appointment. Was it because the P was an Englishman who studied British naval history and the HoD was a passionate student of the Anglo-Boer war? Was the *Engelsman* dead in the water before his CV was even given consideration? The history department had nobody even close to matching this outstanding up-and-coming scholar.

I was to learn this difficult lesson may times over in academic appointments. When you have more than 100 academic departments, it is difficult as a vice-chancellor to direct what happens when it comes to an appointment in one of them. First, you want to respect academic autonomy. Provided they work within the policy frameworks of the university, you really should not tell HoDs what to do in their area of work.

Second, the operational minutiae of a particular department might not be known to you from where you sit in the main administration building. There are calculations any HoD makes with respect to the balance of expertise in various facets of a discipline, the budgets available for appointment and promotion, and the changes in curriculum or teaching under way.

Fine. But this was a P and there were funds available. In this case, had I still been there, I would have called in the HoD and tried to push for the appointment. There are ways for a rector to be persuasive with academic heads if it contributes to the larger vision for the university. I was devastated to hear the outcome and, unsurprisingly, the young P left the country, never to be heard of again.

There was something else going on here that is common to South African higher education and which hampers development in every university. It is a combination of small-mindedness and academic jealousy.

Consider this common experience of aspiring academics. The lecturer wins a prestigious fellowship such as a Fulbright scholarship to the US or a Chevening scholarship to the UK. The excited young academic rushes to the HoD's office and announces the prestigious award. What happens next is something I have yet to understand. There follows a series of managerial questions. Who is going to teach your classes if you disappear for a year? Who is going to pay for the replacement lecturer? How long will you be away? Do you have enough leave credits? And so on.

In workshop after workshop with HoDs and deans, I use the above example for discussion. They all agree this is common practice. Now imagine the absurdity of such a reaction. Here is a young academic who is going to have a chance for development at a top university in the world. The person is likely to come back and their achievements make your department look good. If you are a wise HoD, you might even want to ensure the departing lecturer comes back by promising incentives or, if you're the officious type, bind the person through a contract to come back for at least the number of years they will be away – or pay back the money. If you're narrow-minded, in other words.

I have been an HoD, so I am not unaware of the operational consequences of a departing lecturer. But is this the way to do it? Here is a different possible response, and we do have some academic HoDs in our universities who react more generously.

'Wow, what a wonderful award, let's take you to dinner and celebrate this amazing achievement. Tomorrow we can talk about how to help you make arrangements for your teaching and other duties. I will ask the dean for funding to tide us over in your absence. Please let us know how we can support you as you prepare for the scholarship.'

Henry Kissinger is credited with saying that 'the reason university politics is so vicious is because stakes are so small'. Perhaps. In South Africa our academic cultures are so competitive at the low end of excellence that anyone who dares break out is a threat. Childish questions run through the minds of the petty. But what about me? I never had such opportunities? Or, what about other academics who also work hard but have not had such opportunities?

Wherever I have worked in South African universities, I have been amused at how otherwise close academic friends or collaborators would not send an email or WhatsApp message when a major award or rating was achieved. When we met for our research teams' work, they would pretend nothing had happened. On the other hand, whenever one of them achieved something, I would make a fuss of their accomplishments for the simple reason that when they did well, it was good for all of us.

Some became bitter and ran you down in private meetings with their staff, not thinking that word of their conduct would reach your ears. When I was a young academic this kind of behaviour used to irritate me. Now I genuinely feel sorry for these kinds of colleagues. What a miserable life you must lead when you cannot celebrate the achievements of others.

My advice to young academics, including my postdoctoral fellows, is to focus. Learn to grow a thick skin. And the best payback is to do even better the next time round. If people want to be bitter, that is their downfall. Work even harder, rise even faster, but do not let academic jealousy hold you back.

I have lived that reality in every South African university in which I worked, and that kind of single-mindedness has served me well. In the many hours I worked to develop others, I always paid attention to my own development as well, for a simple reason: my ability to serve others through my scholarship meant I had to develop myself.

Now for the question that so many young academics ask me all the time: How did you run a university and obtain an A1 rating at the same time?

This is how I did it.

Whether I was an HoD, a dean or a vice-chancellor, I arranged with my reporting line (dean, deputy vice-chancellor, chair of council) that I would work my 18-hour days as usual, including weekends when necessary, but I would like to take a short break of two to three months over the dead period (for example, the winter vacation in mid-year and December/early January) for my research and writing. Not once was I turned down and I suspect this had to do with a track record of delivering on the job. You cannot ask for something of this scale without having the credibility of work rate and work outputs to back you up.

Second, I always built around me a team of outstanding co-leaders.

In each of the disciplines of higher education management (finance, human resources, information and communications technology, administration) I had a competent person in charge. This meant that when I was away, any one of those senior people could step up to lead and manage. If you feel threatened by the expertise of your second-tier management, you are dead in the water.

Of course, I had a basic sense of what was required in these disciplines of management so I could ask the right questions to prevent crises. Why were the internal audit results not implemented as required, for example, or what would the balance sheet look like if, hypothetically, every staff member retired on the same day? We prepared for such scenarios. But when most of these disciplines fall outside your primary areas of expertise, you leave it to the experts on your team to lead in your presence and in your absence.

Third, I researched and/or wrote every day within the spaces available to me, such as the early morning or late at night. The habit of researching, reading and writing, once established, meant I did not have to think about what I was doing; it simply happened as part of my daily routine. If I did not write every day, I felt there was something missing, like not eating one of the three meals a day.

Fourth, I used work time efficiently. If somebody was late, I cancelled the meeting. If somebody was too early, I let them wait until the scheduled time. Meetings were focused and efficient; you were assumed to have read the preparatory documents. Lengthy meetings, I long ago concluded, are one sign of a dysfunctional organisation.

Fifth, I did not micromanage people. I trusted them to do the job as agreed. The only time I wanted to hear from them was when there was unexpected trouble. We met weekly as teams and when necessary, but I trusted my colleagues to do their jobs. When I could not trust them to work on their own and at the speed required, we made other plans.

Sixth, I modelled how to work. Whatever someone else did, I probably did more. This worked well, especially when I was a vice-chancellor. I taught first-year students, supervised postgraduate students, always had two or three research programmes in operation, wrote for research outlets but also for the general public through popular books and a weekly column. I spoke in small and large forums on invitation. I worked in schools with reconstruction and development work. Your work ethic as a leader is a powerful message communicated across a large organisation. When some of my professors complained they did not have time for research, my stock response was: let's compare notes. This is perhaps the hardest task for me as a leader of academic and research teams. South Africans are generally a lazy lot, especially those who work in universities. Many of our universities – wait for it – still work according to the timetable set for schools. Years ago, before we had top research institutions, lecturers needed to collect their children at school and when schools closed for the holidays, the university closed for its staff. Our academic work culture is a hangover from the past.

This culture of universities is particularly difficult to change in the Western Cape. I often tease the locals by saying Cape Town is the only city in the country where people make a distinction between getting up and waking up. Perhaps it is the proximity of some of the world's most beautiful beaches and tourist attractions, or maybe the reason lies in a much deeper history at the southern tip of the continent where slaves often slow-walked the master's instructions as a form of resistance. Whatever. What I did find was that it took my postdocs at least a year to learn to work at a pace that kept up with my goals for annual development outcomes. After that, our research hummed and two to four scholarly books made it into the display cabinet in my boardroom every year.

Finally, I always had around me one to three assistants who did some of the laborious work of research. I trained them how to do the routines of research like literature reviews, basic data collection, computer-based data analysis and managing large bibliographic databases online. I could then spend most of my research time thinking, and imagining and composing the research under way. In every grant, I set aside budget for these worker bees of the academy.

At the start, I do everything in the research process myself, in large part to get a sense of the data. But after a few do-it-yourself actions at every stage of the research process, I leave the routine work to skilled assistants.

Then and now, these colleagues save me a lot of time even as they learn, at pace, how to do serious research.

I have, however, never seen my development role as merely producing scholarly books and journal publications. Throughout my academic career I have tried to put out research-informed writing for the broader community. Books such as *We Need to Talk*, followed by *We Need to Act* still await a third volume in the trilogy: *We Need to Run*, as South Africa deteriorates. We can run away from the problem or, like health workers in the middle of a deadly pandemic, run towards it even at risk to our lives.

I thoroughly enjoyed making the link between research, common sense and citizen action through my non-academic books. *Letters to My Children* was a hit with parents and, hopefully, their kids. My goal with that book was to put out a tweet for students every morning for 365 days, having in mind my own two children. Once, I was on an overnight flight and when I landed in another country there were scores of messages on my cellphone 'Where's today's tweet?'

Similarly, these translational works (from research to practice) were focused on schools. There was ample funding for *How to Fix South Africa's Schools*, so we could put out pointed lessons and videos of outstanding schools in poor communities to every high school in the country. I was lucky to have as collaborator the talented young American filmmaker Molly Blank, who translated into video format what I was hoping she could 'see' in the routines and regularities that marked daily life in two schools from each province sampled for track records of high achievement.

I had learnt how to be opportunistic, in a good sense, in my research and development work. One story sticks in the mind. We were living in northern California when the big earthquake struck in 1989. The next day I went to the shops in San Antonio, not far from where we lived in Palo Alto, and there was a guy selling T-shirts with the words 'I survived the 6.9 California earthquake'. Or a week after the Berlin Wall fell, there were chaps selling pieces of rock allegedly from the wall. I found this funny but also a lesson in how to respond in the moment.

When the pandemic struck, therefore, we not only produced high-level research on its effects on academic women (12 publications came out of that, including in top-end journals like *Research Policy*) but I also made sure there were public books that spoke to teachers, such as *Teaching in and Beyond Pandemic Times* (co-edited with a senior teacher), and that gave a voice to students, as in *Learning under Lockdown*. Academic nursing colleagues asked for help with putting together *In Our Own Words*.

Both our children learnt through observation about the gifts of service on the back of master's degrees, which they both attained. Mikhail chose a career in educational psychology serving children with learning challenges in South Africa and where he now works in New Zealand. Sara chose to study social work then transitioned to disaster management as her field of service; shortly afterwards she started her own company, Organized Spaces, while working for an NGO that supports high school girls from difficult circumstances.

Grace's entire life has been one of service, whether taking pensioners from her church on bus trips or working with young women as a development mentor and coach. Her master's thesis was about women who had the triple challenge of simultaneously being mothers, executives and postgraduate students. At UFS, she spearheaded with Carin Buys (psychologist and partner of my dean of students) the impactful No Student Hungry campaign, a novel idea since adopted since by other universities. In the 2020s she works tirelessly with struggling women in her church community and high school girls and their families to ensure they have a combination of good coaching advice and material sustenance in a cruel world.

Our development lives were always linked to learning.

10
Learning lessons

'You could call this selfhood many things. I call it an education.'
Tara Westover, *Educated*

What if?

It's a mind game I have played often in an attempt to explain the extraordinary good fortune that has come my way. What if I hadn't been born into the home of an Abraham and Sarah? What if my parents hadn't possessed such firmness of love and an unyielding faith that kept me on the straight and narrow? What if Mr Galant, my Latin teacher, had not pulled me aside from a soccer game to tell me I had potential? What if I had not met my childhood friend, Archie Dick, who taught me the benefits of studying hard? What if Ernest James had not given me R20 to reregister for studies at UWC? What if Bishop Tutu had not co-invented a scholarship fund that allowed me to study in the US, the single most important event that changed my social and academic fortunes?

None of what I have been blessed with was a foregone conclusion. When I sold fish for Uncle Japie Solomon on the corner of Retreat Road and Prince George Drive and cut down the wrong side (the stomach rather than the back), I thought one could make a decent living selling snoek to white people driving between the suburbs and Muizenberg. Doing the postman's beat as assistant to Sydney Alexander along the Fish Hoek line also looked like a respectable job. My horizons were set by what I could see and what my parents had accomplished. Finishing matric would already be more than their junior certificates.

These 'what if' questions ran through my mind when I entered the majestic graduation hall at the University of Edinburgh to receive an honorary doctorate in education. The glittering chandeliers overhead, the historic artworks lining the walls, the sense of the balconied crowd fitting closely around the floor-level audience, the spectacular interior dome … these all struck me when the doors of McEwan Hall swung open and celebratory organ music welcomed the gowned ceremonial party. I felt the emotion in my breast and thought of my life otherwise.

There is always the useful reminder on such occasions to remain humble, to keep your feet on the ground. Coming through London's Heathrow Airport, I had to clear customs before the onward journey to Edinburgh. I was feeling upbeat and felt something of a connection to the black woman at the customs desk. 'What are you coming to do in the UK?' I piped up: 'I'm getting an honorary degree from the University of Edinburgh.' 'Oh', says the nonplussed customs official, 'is that the one you don't work for?' I laughed so much she had to call me to order.

'What if' questions made the rounds again when I received the call that my book *Knowledge in the Blood* had won the largest cash prize from the British Academy for humanities and social sciences. This was only the second year of the award and because I knew my competition – leading authors from around the world – I was not expecting the honour. The acceptance speech was something I relished but even more so the dinner conversations. The next day I had to offer a seminar to leading scholars in education on a topic different from the subject-matter of my book.

But perhaps the highest honour in my career was an email I received in 2023 inviting me to join the American Academy of Arts and Sciences. This was huge. I knew the American professors who had taught me were not members of this illustrious academy. The international contingent of new members in any year was relatively small, and mainly from Europe at the time. On the day, I sat between the new president of Harvard and the chancellor of City University of New York. The entire experience was surreal and I felt incredibly grateful to be recognised in this way.

Academic and research awards inevitably prompt deep reflection. I was always intrigued by a stunning question someone asked Oprah Winfrey and which she used as a book title: What do you know for sure? Laying out some of the details of my life in the previous chapters, I would like to share ten things I know for sure based on a life, to borrow from the futurist

Alvin Toffler, of constant learning, unlearning and relearning.

Here we go.

1. I am nothing

Everything I am and every gift I have received is a consequence of grace. Nothing is of myself. The journey I have shared makes this amply clear: many people along the way made me possible and shaped the path along which I travelled. I came into this world with nothing, I will leave with nothing, and in between I am nothing. There is indeed nothing to be proud of but a lot to be grateful for.

There was no place for boasting in the world in which Abraham and Sarah reared their children. You received with gratitude what was given to you then gave it back with the same generosity. One of the most moving spiritual songs that remains with me contains these stunning lines:

> Forbid it Lord that I should boast
> Save in the death of Christ my God.

That spiritual commitment offers an anchor in my life and a value frame by which I steer my career. Accept your gifts graciously and keep your feet solidly on the ground.

I was having breakfast with a top economics professor from Stanford whose research was about money and assets. He congratulated me on something and I accepted his kindness but then told him how much I owed others for what I have been able to accomplish. I remember his firm response: 'But you worked hard for what you've done.' 'True,' I replied, 'but everybody else worked hard, none more diligently than my mother, yet she could not rise beyond "staff nurse Jansen" because of the ceiling that society placed on her life.' That is reason enough to remain grounded.

In my business, there is nothing more offputting than a boastful academic who trots about expecting to be revered. Every university has them. I often wonder what they get out of being so arrogant and aware of themselves. Surely the real joy in life is to be able to mix freely with people of all classes and cultures without standing out.

2. You still have to show up

No matter how privileged I was to have parents, teachers, friends and professors who appeared to collude to ensure my success, none of that matters unless you show up. Whenever the door of opportunity opened for me, I sprinted through it.

When the Latin teacher spoke a word of encouragement, I did everything in my power to prove him right. When my professor asked me as a graduate student to teach curriculum policy and practice to senior World Bank officials, I spent months preparing the best possible series of lectures. When I realised I was not going to make it in Charles Drekmeier's doctoral class about Thomas Kuhn and the structure of scientific revolutions, I cut down on sleep and read more than anyone else in that class on the subject.

Showing up implies sacrifice. This I discovered early on by observing my mother Sarah work so hard to give all five children a decent education while accommodating family members circulating through our council home. However, sacrifice does not mean you do not have a life.

This is one of the questions I also get asked, often by young academic mentees: 'What explains your high levels of academic productivity?' The truth is, I escape by reading books that have nothing to do with my field of study. I watch sport and take time off when the Blue Bulls or Tottenham Hotspur play. I love the company of friends and family on weekends and over holidays. I enjoy good orchestral music, theatre and stand-up comedy. I confess to something of an addiction to online games like Wordle and Scrabble. I enjoy Netflix documentaries and good food. I seldom struggle with work–life balance.

However, when I work, I focus. I have taught myself to read fast and I have no idea what writer's block is. I have already shared the importance of using time efficiently; at work, every second counts. And my productivity is underpinned by a life partner who orders the world around us as a family.

But you cannot 'show up' if you do not enjoy what you do. It is a standard question at book launches or book fairs: 'Where you do find the time to write two or more books a year?' The response is well rehearsed. 'Listen, I only love two things in life: eating (as you can see from my circumference) and writing. But nobody has ever asked me where I find the time to eat.' If you love what you do, it is no longer work.

3. If you think for yourself, they're coming for you

South Africa is a tribal society. You are supposed to belong to a group, not to yourself. Ever seen a sole protester with a placard? Hardly, because we fight in a crowd. Thuli Madonsela paid me the best compliment when she said, 'you do not belong in anyone's camp.'

I treasure the freedom to think for myself and hold my own views. As I wrote this memoir and took in the span of my life, it became clear that this was how I always was from the days in which I was disinvited from Friday night Bible studies for asking uncomfortable questions in Ernie de Vries' house to now being disinvited from three universities for having my own voice.

When you are critical of government policy in education, as in my case, you are immediately excluded from your area of expertise, which in my case is anything to do with curriculum. When I wrote an article, 'Ten reasons why OBE [outcomes-based education] will fail', my fate was sealed because I had dared to criticise the new government's ideological touchstone. Years later, when OBE was abandoned after inflicting lasting damage on the school system, not a soul in authority had the humility to acknowledge they were wrong.

My students have been invited onto curriculum commissions but not their mentor and supervisor. It is what happens in an immature and insecure democracy.

4. Choose respect over love

I noticed that my fiercest critics harboured a quiet respect when I stood for something on the basis of principle rather than political affiliation or personal prejudice. Like any human being, I would like to be loved and enjoy the support of crowds. But I love something much more and that is to stand for something I believe in, regardless of the consequences.

Being quiet is not an option, and in dangerous situations it can be read as complicity. I have therefore had no hesitation in speaking out on critical issues in education. I do not enjoy standing out or standing alone when it comes to criticism of government education policy, and yet it was my duty for several reasons.

One, speaking out gives the public affirmation that its own concerns are being heard. Two, speaking up gives prominence to issues of national concern and for that I have been blessed with a weekly newspaper and online column for more than a decade and platforms on radio, television and social media. Three, speaking truth alerts the government of resistance to irresponsible policy proposals or official actions.

Few things are more irritating than when someone introduces me and says 'our speaker is controversial'. Actually, I am not. To speak about inequalities in education or to criticise a minister for dishonest presentations of examination results is not being controversial. So why do people say that? One reason is the fact that almost everybody else in the community of education experts is too scared to say what they know to be true. They fear retribution and being cut off from the largesse that comes with government consultancies. In short, the only reason I stand out is because so many others stand down. I cannot be called controversial because others are afraid to speak.

Students and academics too often want to be loved and admired by adoring crowds rather than asking themselves, 'Where do I stand?' then stringing together a series of arguments in favour of that position. That is a crucial habit of democracy which will gain you respect if not adulation.

5. Everyone can achieve

You're smarter than you think. If I can get this message through to South African youth, I know it will change lives. I have lost count of how many people, students and others, have told me how this simple phrase influenced their life choices and outcomes.

I wish this message had reached me as a child: that I was good, that I could do well and that I had within me the ability to rise beyond my circumstances. It is life-changing, yet our entire education system is rigged to tell us the opposite – that we're useless. It is baked into our understanding not to expect much of ourselves.

Yet the one thing I know for sure is that when unseen talent meets timely opportunity and fierce determination, everything is possible. Time and again I have seen young people thrown away by the system rise to become leading chemists, architects, doctors or teachers, and the reason lies in a study I am leading on P-rated scientists. These are academics under the age of 35 who have done so well in their early research careers that they are given a P (prestigious) rating by the National Research Foundation on grounds that they have the potential to become leading researchers in the world. Through a qualitative study, I tried to pin down the factors that led to only 136 Ps being awarded since the early 1980s. One factor stood out: fierce determination to succeed. In other words, something within the individual allows them to focus on the prize and move everything within their power to get it. It is as simple and as complex as that.

Now an important caveat: we are not all talented in the same things. Gifted teachers will find the one thing you do very well and teach in ways that bring out the best in you.

6. You cannot lead in a racially divided society if you have racial issues

A university leader asked me for advice before taking up a new position. 'Remember that when you lead on a campus you lead all of our people, not only those who look like you,' I said. Well, that advice was ignored and the university came close to collapse.

I know for sure that leaders who are prickly when race comes up (and it will), who point the finger at almost any human action and pounce with the charge of 'racism', or who cannot let a moment pass without talking about whites as racists and/or blacks as victims, will sooner or later burn out as a fading star.

As a black leader on a former white campus, you must have a strong sense of yourself. When you are insecure about your racial identity and wither in the face of the slightest perceived slight by a white colleague, you will not succeed as a leader.

This does not mean, of course, that black leaders in South African society do not carry hurts and disappointments from their racial pasts.

That would be an unreasonable expectation. But when you are a leader you have to learn how to compose yourself in a crisis and how to manage your emotions for the sake of the larger cause.

Some of our black leaders have a deep sense of inferiority and often express that through flamboyance (look at me), aggression (listen to me or else) or paranoia (they're out to get me). This kind of temperament makes leading impossible because the leader is not secure.

Your critics can sense vulnerability, especially when you are insecure in your personal or professional identity and when you are easily rattled by challenges, especially from white colleagues. You cannot lead unless you act with authority rather than through a sense of diminished leadership because of racial woundedness.

7. You are only as good as your second tier of management

The myth of the heroic leader who single-handedly turns around a company's fortunes or a school's demise should have been buried long ago. And yet so many leaders act as if success is vested in their singular personality. What I know for sure is that, as a leader, you are only as good as the members of your senior team. This sense of how to be successful as a leader has an immediate implication. In the memorable words of Jim Collins in *Good to Great*, 'get the right people on the bus.'

In a crowded hall on the UFS campus, students stood in line behind microphones spread throughout the venue and the first question got my attention: 'Ms Winfrey, what is the secret of your success?' Without blinking, Oprah replied: 'I surround myself with people who are smarter than me.' That made intuitive sense to me, but she worded it perfectly.

If you are insecure as a leader, this is not how you choose your senior team. You look for lackeys, people who will suck up to you. You might as well shut down your enterprise, for you will surely fail. The reason is simple: big-headed leadership demands obsequiousness, and when it does not come the leader reacts badly. At one South African university almost every executive meeting was like a circular firing squad in which senior managers were insulted, humiliated and cut down to size. The result was paralysis born of fear.

I had the best possible team as a vice-chancellor, with abundant expertise in finance, auditing, human resources, digitalisation, teaching, research, assessment, security, infrastructure, communications and marketing. As a leader, I needed to know enough about each of those disciplines to be able to ask the right questions of each division leader. When a crisis hits, you allow the relevant expert to lead the response and your role as vice-chancellor is to steer that discussion towards concrete resolutions. For experienced leaders, this becomes routine. For self-obsessed leaders, this becomes a nightmare for the organisation concerned.

To say you rely on the complementary strengths of your senior team means you must recognise their contributions, nurture their talent, support their decisions and, most importantly, encourage them along the way. It also means you trust them wholeheartedly to make good decisions. If a serious breach of trust compromises the organisation, you have to let that person go. These are probably among the toughest decisions for any leader, but unless you make them, you are putting your organisation at continued risk.

8. The most important predictor of your child's racial attitudes is the home in which they were raised

I have run countless workshops for parents asking how they can prepare their children to live in a racially divided country. It is quite simple, actually. What I know for sure is that it depends on how you live your life as parents. What are the direct and indirect messages your children pick up during their first five or six years, even before they get to school?

Young children are remarkably observant about their parents' social attitudes. If the father screams a racial epithet at the television when a black government minister makes a silly claim, that has an enduring effect on what the child learns about how to be among black people. When an overcrowded taxi swerves in front of your car and the parent lets loose about 'them', trust me, the children in the back seat are taking in those messages and having their consciousness shaped about race and racial otherness.

The way you speak to the domestic. The fact that the black woman cleaning the floors has no surname, even to the kids. The scolding for coming late. In a million little ways, you are teaching and the children are learning. Attitudes are being moulded.

Prejudice is not something that afflicts only white people. Now that I have returned to the Cape after decades away, I can see how these prejudices do their work in family homes. The Christians tend to be the worst when it comes to anti-Muslim sentiment in comments like 'they are taking over Rondebosch East; they now call it the Middle East'.

A long time ago I realised that our original sin was not racism but difference. Anything different from the norm – Christian, straight, native-born, dark skin, middle class – is an imagined threat that must be insulted and avoided.

So, parents ask, what do I do? Simple. Make sure that what your children observe in the home is every kind of humanity. Around the braai fire ensure that from time to time there are Muslims, Jews, Christians, Afrikaans and isiZulu speakers, gay and straight people. In other words, give your child a normal upbringing. But you cannot begin with the children, nor can you stage-manage diversity.

This kind of love for difference and diversity starts with you as a parent. It should be something you work on until it becomes part and parcel of who you are, not a premeditated calculation about how to raise your children. It means questioning your own prejudices in a brutally honest way and leading your home away from them.

9. Failure is your friend

In a system that prizes correctness, the importance of failure is neglected in our school system. We punish failure (the stumble) and we look down on failures (the people). It is a signal weakness of the South African education system. Why? Because what I know for sure is that nothing ambitious is achieved without failing first.

On a visit to the Silicon Valley as vice-chancellor, I was eager to meet successful tech people who were South Africans by birth. My aim was to link our emerging tech innovation hub to technology entrepreneurs in places like California.

I took these men to breakfast and asked them why they had become so accomplished in the US but were hardly known in South Africa. One of the things they said stuck with me: 'Here they expect us to fail.' Every one of these entrepreneurs had failed repeatedly before achieving a breakthrough. It makes a huge difference in education when you can study without the fear of failing. This is how it works.

When I recently taught a postgraduate certificate in education class at Stellenbosch University, I set an examination in which you could not prepare using notes or PowerPoint slides distributed in class. You had to be present to follow the contours of an argument and to witness through live teaching what a novel concept looks like in different contexts of application. You had to participate in the classroom debates to capture the essence of a position on a complex subject and to develop your own.

Then came the exam and the students failed because at school and in many other university classes a high premium is placed on recall and reproduction, not thinking for yourself. They were relieved when I gave them thorough feedback on the first attempt and, for those who failed again, another round of feedback, and so on, until they understood the question in ways that brought their own ideas into the responses. Some took five or six attempts but that was not a crisis. As long as they learnt with each attempt, failure was their friend.

Here is the uncomfortable truth about innovators in South Africa: most have to leave the country to advance their work because in other contexts you are allowed to fail. And failure is not failure if you learn from it, stand up and try again. The fear of failure is real and sometimes it requires you to relocate yourself to places where the ability to fail is a valued attribute.

10. Expand your borders

When I emerged from Harare airport in 1989, it was the first time I had set foot on African soil outside home. I was ecstatic to be in a free country which almost ten years earlier had thrown off the shackles of colonialism and white minority rule. In the next few weeks I could hardly contain myself as I went from schools to the ministry of education to the University of Zimbabwe (UZ) and to the home I was sharing with a young Stanford couple.

The reception was awesome, especially from academics at UZ who wanted me over for dinner, to speak in their classes, to advise on one or other project. I did not want to leave, especially after meeting South Africans in exile who were also welcomed and feted by their hosts.

Imagine the horror years later when Zimbabweans and other Africans were targeted in more than one series of violent attacks in South Africa. Our response to foreign nationals reveals a lack of education and humanity. No economic or social calculations can wash away this bare fact. Long before, in meeting students from all over the world, I realised how national borders undermine our humanity. Much of American politics is organised around the supposed crises on the southern border. And more than one commentator has observed how white Ukrainian refugees received a warmer welcome in Europe after Russia invaded their homeland than refugees from Syria or Liberia.

At the heart of these disputes is the question of national borders. What makes the fight over borders particularly strange in South African politics is that they are colonial constructs. And that raises an uncomfortable question: Why did the powerful decolonisation moment on South African campuses in the mid-2010s not raise in its long list of grievances the problem of colonial borders that restrict in grievous ways the flow of African students and scientists into and out of South Africa?

I have a theory: colonial borders and the accompanying xenophobia do not feature in decolonisation politics because the movement itself is nativist at its core and therefore not radical enough when it comes to the political geography of bordered countries that are the visible aftermath of empire. This is why I have decided to stop singing the national anthem; it is national in its conception of political borders.

The same ideological mindset that segregates us within borders is that which separates us from outside our borders. Them and us. And when in a particular historical moment your country has the balance of resources, the reaction of nationalists is to keep others from laying hands on what is presumably yours.

As an internationalist, my work and my heart are borderless. My commitment is to those whose humanity is trampled on anywhere on the planet. Doctors Without Borders and Gift of the Givers are for me the purest expression of what it means to be an activist; the barriers that separate us are meaningless when the goal is to relieve suffering.

What I know for sure is that when you expand the borders of your commitments, your inner life is enriched. A generous spirit perceives in all of humanity not only our unlikeness but our sameness. Apartheid gave us an exaggerated sense of our differences to justify segregation. There is no need to dwell on differences for they are embedded in our minds and hearts. The antidote is to see what we have in common, and that is possible only when your imagination and your politics are not bordered by restrictions that are artificial and meaningless.

Coda

I felt a sense of wonder being in an Anglican church in 2023 because its liturgy was so different from the simple rituals of the Brethren at the breaking of the bread every Sunday morning. Nevertheless, the constant marching back and forth by lines of gowned men and women, young and old, with a huge cross carried by the person in front, was impressive. Was this symbolism, I wondered, carried over from old England to signify 'marching as to war' in times when the state church and armed conquests were tightly bound together?

Here they came again, right past me in the front row of this beautifully built church. Up and down the long aisle. This marching is strange to me as an evangelical, I said a little later from the pulpit. 'Could you guys not find your seats?' Good laughter from the audience. There was decidedly less laughter with the next comment and what I sensed to be nervous laughter from the priest in charge, the man who had invited me to speak about reconciliation, forgiveness and the state of the country.

'My father was in fact an Anglican,' I announced, 'before he found Jesus.' Everybody was awake now. I told the story of my upbringing at the feet of Abraham and Sarah and in the exclusivist practices of the Brethren. Anglicans and Catholics were going to hell, I was taught, because they were not saved from their sins. About 20 minutes into my talk, and with breaking voice, I apologised to the Anglican congregants and asked for their forgiveness for the narrowness and meanness of my starting faith.

The communion followed, then something else unfamiliar happened. Starting from the back, rows of people came to the front of the church, bowed in the direction of the cross, then knelt on cushions to pray and receive communion. The priest and his assistants gave the bread and the wine to to each individual.

I was not going forward.

In my Brethren upbringing, you dare not partake of the bread and wine unless you were perfect in the eyes of God. *For he that eateth and drinketh unworthily eateth and drinketh damnation to himself.* I was definitely not worthy. I did not meet the high standards of Brethren judgment. So I remained seated.

Then something happened that had a deeply emotional impact on me. A young man with Down Syndrome, probably about 16 years old, walked past me to take his turn at the altar. I watched as he received the bread and the wine, then it struck me. Church is for people like him and me. Not for those deemed 'perfect' in the eyes of a fallen humanity, but for those with simple faith. When the young man left to return to his seat, I rushed forward to kneel exactly where he had and the next thing I heard, eyes closed, was the voice of the priest, 'Prof, the body of Christ.' I had seldom felt so blessed, and all because of this courageous young man.

You will have gathered that this patchwork of memories has been put together to tell a bigger story than one about my life. In this regard, I chose the title of the memoir, *Breaking Bread*, to reflect both the exclusivist meaning of my evangelical upbringing and its more generous meaning of human inclusion and togetherness.

Through this memoir, I hope to have invited you into communion as I have reflected on a grateful life. It is a fellowship in which we get to know each other and learn from each other with little else except a simple table with bread and wine. Nothing extravagant, for the goal of communion is our union as human beings. In this communion you do not lose your identity, however you wish to describe yourself. If what matters to you is your faith identity, then breaking bread together with those of other faiths can only strengthen yours. The table implies coming together to share our fears and faith, our fumbles and fortitude, our hurts and our hopes. The meat satisfies our hunger, the wine our thirst.

A different kind of politics and pedagogy emerges when we break bread together, for now we see our troubles through a very different lens, one that starts with mutual recognition, a possibility that offers outcomes other than conflict, war and hopelessness.

Index

50|50 102

Abdea (Trafalgar High School student) 127
Abels, Chris 55
Abrahams, Derek 117
Abrahams, 'Diff' 64
Abrahams, Jolene 117
Abuelaish, Izzeldin 205
Adams, Saleh 122
Adriaan, Lionel 129
Africa (School inspector) 126
Africana Studies and Research Center, Cornell University 144
African National Congress (ANC) 49, 104, 139, 144, 165, 193–194, 197, 200, 203, 208–209, 212
African Renaissance initiative 235
Africa Week (Stanford) 153
Afrikaans 5, 11, 16, 34, 60–61, 69, 75, 78, 81, 83–84, 86, 91, 94–95, 103, 105, 107–109, 115–116, 118–119, 134, 142, 173–178, 180–186, 191–192, 194, 197, 199, 202, 211–216, 228–229, 231, 256
Afrikaans Hoër Meisieskool 184
Afrikaans Hoër Seunskool 184
Afrikanerbond 178
Afrikaner Weerstandsbeweging 164
Akoojee, Mrs (teacher) 68–69, 73
Alexander, Neville 27
Alexander, Sydney 80, 247
'alternative education' 77
American Educational Research Association 151
Amsterdam, Christina 117

ANC Youth League 144, 200, 203
Anderson (Brother) 46
Anderson, Michael ('Spike') 66
Anglican (Church) 5, 35, 67, 141, 261
Anglo-Boer War 216, 240
Angula, Helmut 153–154
apartheid 8, 21, 39, 41–42, 46–47, 51, 62, 69, 75, 77–78, 83, 88–89, 92–93, 97–100, 103–105, 112–116, 121, 123, 126, 132–133, 139–140, 142, 144–145, 149–150, 153–156, 160, 164, 166, 169, 174, 178, 183, 193–194, 198–199, 201, 219, 235, 259
Apple, Mike 143, 148
Archer, I.J.M. 101
Arendse, Mrs (elder's wife) 55
As by Fire 223
Asmal, Kader 100, 180
Atkin, Myron 'Mike' 152
Aurora Associates 141
Ausubel, David 96
Autobiography of Eve 34

Baptist Church 35, 140–141, 171
Barabas 49
Bavasah, Hassan 120
Beamon, Bob 11
Beeld 183
Believers Hymn Book 37
Benjamin family 7
Berea West Primary School 170
Berkeley University 159
Berlin Wall 245
Bethe, Hans 236
Betty (friend of author at University of Durban-Westville) 167
Beyers, Howard 107

Bhabha, Homi 161
Bharuthram brothers 168
Biko, Steve 92, 221
bin Laden, Osama 170
Black Consciousness (BC) 92–93, 165, 221
Black Theology 93
Blank, Molly 245
Bloch, Felix 236–237
Bloom, Allan 160
Bobby (school prefect) 73
Boesak, Allan 52, 92–93
Bo-Kaap Kombuis 128
Bongo, Nat 133
Bonhoeffer, Dietrich 52
Boshoff, At 219
Botha, Dr (lecturer) 83–84, 94, 149
Brethren (Open) 6–7, 11–12, 16–19, 23, 26, 34–37, 39, 41–46, 48–52, 54, 56–57, 80–81, 86, 92, 99, 127, 133, 135, 140, 147, 149, 157–158, 261–262
Brey, Husain 106
Britz, Dolf 217
Broederbond 178, 229
Bronfenbrenner, Urie 144
Brooklyn Chest Hospital 6
Budlender, Steven 131
Bundy, Colin 173
Buys, Carin 246
Buys, Rudi 197, 210, 246
Bynes, Reggie 52–53

Cambridge University 228
Campus Crusade for Christ 44
Canon Collins Trust 142
canon wars 160
Cape Argus 85, 121
Cape Flats 5, 7–8, 11–12, 18, 21, 23, 28, 40–41, 61, 63, 68, 70, 100, 118, 125–126, 150, 185, 270

Cape Flats Distress Association
   (Cafda) 61–62
Cape Herald 85
Cape Peninsula Technikon 104
Cape Teachers Professional
   Association (CTPA) 104,
   115
Cape Technikon (Cape Peninsula
   University of Technology)
   124
Cape Times 17, 85
Cape to Rio yacht race 17
Cape Town City (soccer team)
   60, 63
Carnoy, Martin 149, 152, 159
Carolus, John 117
Castilleja School for Girls, Palo
   Alto 132
Cecil H Green Library 151
Cedar House School 131
Center for Advanced Study
   in the Behavioral Sciences,
   Stanford 223
Chang, Jeff ix
Chapels Brethren 37
Chevening scholarship 240
Chibale, Kelly 237
Christian Revival Church 219
Chung, Fay 155–156
Church of England 36
*Closing of the American Mind,
   The* 160
Cokinis, Mr (teacher) 69
Collins, Jim 193, 254
Coloured Persons Representative
   Council 103
Combined Staff Association
   (Comsa) 166–169
Comparative and International
   Education Society (CIES)
   151–152
constructive engagement policy
   154
Cookson (school athlete) 71
Cooper, Tony 40–42
Cornell, Ezra 143
Cornell University 96, 133–134,
   139, 142–148, 151–152,
   154, 159, 206, 227, 236
Corrupted 169
Cosmos 144
council housing 7–8, 20–22,
   24–25, 30, 47, 56, 62, 68,
   185
Covid pandemic 224, 234,
   245–246

Cressy, Harold 129
Crestway High School 10
Crocker, Chester 153–154
Cry Freedom 92
Cry Rage 76
curriculum studies, theory,
   development 2, 65, 77, 91,
   98, 100–101, 112, 116,
   142–143, 148, 150–153,
   155–156, 158, 160, 162,
   177, 179, 181, 211, 225,
   240, 250–251

David (friend from Congo at
   Cornell) 146
Dawson boys 13–14
Deedat, Ahmed 99
De Gruchy, Steve 52
De Jager, Bill 38
Delpierre, Georges 84–85, 94
Democratic Alliance (DA) 208
Denison University 138–140
Deshler, David 148
De Vries, Ernest (Ernie) 42,
   80–81, 251
De Vries (lecturer on evolution)
   101–102
De Vries, Peter 7, 80–81
De Wet, Jack 228
Diame, Bakary 150, 153
Dick, Archie Lennie 38, 71–72,
   74, 80–82, 133, 247
District Six 119, 123–125, 129
divestment campaigns 145,
   154
Docks Mission 35
Doctors Without Borders 259
Drekmeier, Charles 151, 250
Dreyer, Dr. 21
Dreyer, Neal 41, 79, 86
Drosera capensis 102
Dudley, RO 27
Duncan (Wattle Park camp
   warden) 47–48
Durban University of
   Technology 107, 172, 188
Dutch Reformed Church 6, 29,
   93, 219
Dutch Reformed Mission
   Church 5–6, 29, 35, 93,
   219

ecological systems theory 144
Economic Freedom Fighters
   (EFF) 208
Edmonson, Locksley 143–145

Educational Opportunities
   Council (EOC) 133, 142,
   145
*Education as Cultural
   Imperialism* 149
Education Journal, The 123
Eisner, Elliott 152–153
Elkins, Ansel 34
Emeran, Goosain 130
Emmie (Emelia, Aunt) 31
Epaphras (cousin of author) 36
Escondido Village, Stanford
   150
Esselen Park camp, Worcester
   69
Esterhuyse, Mr (teacher at
   Vredenburg Secondary
   School) 117–118
Evans, Anthony 164
Evans, Jane 164
evolution, theory of 101–102
Exclusive Brethren 36; *see also*
   Brethren; Plymouth Brethren
Extension of University
   Education Act 88

Fatima (student at Trafalgar
   High School) 124
Fischer, Braam 218
Fisher, Cynthia 120
Flanders for Funerals 20
Flanders, Josie 45
forced removals 8, 30, 75,
   123–124; *see also* District Six
Ford family 61
Fredericks, Lilly 37
Freedom Front Plus 208
Fulbright scholarship 240
Fulghum, Robert 5

Gaither Vocal Band 140
Galant, Paul 67–68, 70–71, 82,
   116, 148, 248, 250
Gandhi, Mahatma 170
Gcilitshana, Sinoxolo 221–223
gender studies 95, 143
Georgetown University 153
Gerwel, Jakes 90, 95, 103, 216
Gift of the Givers 259
Gigaba, Malusi 235
Gilloway, Mr (mathematics
   teacher) 74–75, 101
Giroux, Henry 158
Glennie, Jennie 221
Golden Arrow 222
Gonin, A.A. 101

Index

Good to Great 193, 254
Gorbachev, Mikhail 146
Graham, Billy 53
Gramsci, Antonio 164
Group Areas Act 48

Haas (student at Vredenburg Secondary School) 110–111
Habermas, Jürgen 161
Hankey family 127
Harold Cressy High School 71, 76, 129
Harris, Larnelle 140
Harvard Educational Review 175
Harvard University 28, 143, 148–149, 152, 248
Hasbrouck graduate student apartments, Cornell 136, 144, 147
Heimlich, Peter 144
Heineken-Mohamed Groups 95
Hellenic 60, 63
Helm, Hugh 144
Helm, Jill 144
Hendricks family 7, 54
Hendricks, Fred 47, 54–57
Hendricks, Martin 94
Hendricks, Roddy 'Porky' 92
Hewat College 76–77
Hewlett, William 154
Hitler, Adolf 52, 89, 236
HIV/Aids 158
Hoffmann, Roald 236
Hofmeyr (UWC lecturer) 95
Holocaust (Shoah) 28, 211
homophobia 158
Hoppers, Catherine Odora 237
How to Fix South Africa's Schools 245
human rights 13, 197, 201

Ibis Life Science Project, Namibia 225
Ilse (author's secretary at UFS) 203–204
immigration, immigrants 234–236
Immorality Act 56
Indian caste system 168
Indian Documentation Centre 169
inequality 8, 60, 225, 252
Inkatha Freedom Party (IFP) 204, 208

Institute for Reconciliation and Social Justice 205
International Institute of Education (IIE) 141
In Our Own Words 246
Isaacs, Henry 139
I Shall Not Hate 205

Jack (Uncle) 39
Jacobs, Mr (fruit box businessman) 79
Jakes, TD 191
James, Barbara (Babs) 45, 85–87
James, Ernest 87, 247
James, Japie 41–42, 85–87
Jameson, Leander Starr 88
Jansen, Abraham Christian Frederick (father) 2, 5–9, 12–13, 15–20, 22, 25–33, 36, 42, 54, 58, 62, 80, 109, 127–128, 185, 192, 247, 249, 261
Jansen, Alfie (uncle) 20
Jansen, Grace (née Hendricks, wife of author) 3, 39, 44, 54–56, 134–135, 144, 146–147, 157, 170–171, 190, 200, 222, 224, 246, 250
Jansen, David (grandfather) 5, 20, 30–31
Jansen, Denzil (brother) 6, 28–29, 32, 70
Jansen, Doris (aunt) 15, 23
Jansen, Edith (Eddie, aunt) 6, 13, 15, 31, 36
Jansen, Edwin (cousin) 107
Jansen, Hans 31–32
Jansen, Isaac (brother) 6, 10, 70
Jansen, Jonathan David
  18-hour workdays 19, 191, 224, 242–243, 249–250
  on academic jealousy 238–242
  administrator Durban University of Technology 107, 172, 188–189
  administrator Mangosuthu University of Technology (MUT) 189, 204
  on affirmative action 193
  Africana studies, Cornell University 144–145
  on Afrikaans 107–108, 213–216

American Academy of Arts and Sciences member 248
A-rating researcher 226
athletics 70–71, 116–117
birth 29
Black Consciousness influence 92–93
Black Theology influence 92–93
Brethren, breaking relationship with 49–57, 261–262
Castilleja School for Girls guest teacher 132
Center for Advanced Study in the Behavioral Sciences fellowship, Stanford 223, 240
class struggle 19–22
Cornell University master's student 96, 133–154, 159, 206, 227, 236
critical thinker 81, 100, 121, 251
cycling 80
Denison University orientation 138–141
Denzil's death 28–29, 32
Desmond Tutu meeting after Reitz scandal 201
discipline, corporal punishment 11–15, 21–22
on education 3, 28, 43, 55, 59, 62–63, 68–69, 74, 76–77, 81, 83, 90, 97–98, 109–110, 112–113, 115–117, 121, 125, 128, 132–134, 137–138, 140, 142, 144, 149–150, 155, 159–161, 164, 167–168, 171, 173–174, 180, 187, 189–190, 199, 207, 211, 213–214, 220–222, 224–225, 228–231, 233, 237, 240, 242, 247, 251–252, 256–258; *see also* science education
Ernie Steenveld influence 120, 122–125
escapism 250
family & parents' influence 2–3, 19–26, 30–33, 247, 249–250
father's disappearance, relationship 24–26

feet-washing, University of Pretoria 188
on feminism and male chauvinism 44–45
fish-seller 247
Future Professors Programme (FPP) 227, 231–236
gender studies, Cornell University 143
Good Samaritan sermon 50–51
Hewat College political education 76–77
holiday jobs 79–80, 247
internationalist 258–259
James influence 41–42, 85–87
Joey Marks political influence 46
John Novak influence 136–137, 142–143, 148
Julius Malema visit to UFS after Reitz scandal 203–205
Knowledge in the Blood author, award 93, 194, 248
Latin student 68–69, 71–72
lay-preacher, evangelist 34–36, 42–43, 49–50, 54–55, 72
Lennie Dick friendship 38, 71–72, 74, 80–82, 133, 247
matric ball 10–11
mother's cancer, death 28,
Patience Moore relationship 2
Paul Galant influence 67–68
Phoenix High School teacher 149–150
pianist, music teacher 38, 70, 115–116
race, racism, race classification 3, 46–49, 55–57, 60, 78, 88–90, 92, 113, 158, 170, 177, 187, 193, 195–200, 204, 206, 208, 212, 214, 217–218, 253, 256
on reconciliation 50, 193, 198–203, 205–210, 213, 216–219, 261
Reitz residence racist scandal 193, 195–206, 208, 212, 217–218
on religious evangelicalism influence 2–3, 7, 9, 11–13, 19–20, 33–58, 81, 86, 92–94

Retreat years 8–11, 22, 34, 38, 49, 56, 60, 72, 80, 82, 86, 88, 105–106, 127, 247
Savio College teaching 130–131, 133
schooling 2, 13, 21, 28, 59, 62
Soak-and-Slim selling 79
soccer love 12, 23, 26, 36, 60–62, 65, 67–68, 70–72, 247
SPCA confrontation 121
suicide contemplation 25
Sullivan Primary education 59–62
Stanford African Students Association (Sasa) president 150, 153–154
Stanford PhD student, teaching 28, 82, 122, 148–163, 176, 223, 227, 240
Steenberg High years 7, 28, 38, 52, 63–78, 80, 82, 116, 148
Stellenbosch University distinguished professor 223–225, 227, 231–236, 257, 270
St Francis school teacher 132–133
Student Representative Council (SRC) secretary, USA 142, 145
sub-examiner matriculation 119
ten things author knows for sure 248–259
Trafalgar High School teacher 119–135, 222
University of the Free State vice-chancellor 59, 131, 186, 191–223, 225, 227, 229, 231–233, 237–239, 241, 243, 246, 254, 256
Vredenburg Secondary School teacher 74, 109–119, 125, 127–128, 131
Umlazi research 225
Unisa student 112–114
University of Cape Town honorary doctorate 88
University of Durban-Westville (UDW) dean, acting deputy vice-chancellor 162–163, 165–173, 175, 177, 207, 227
University of Edinburgh honorary doctorate 247–248
University of Pretoria dean 91, 173–179, 181–191, 195, 207, 227, 229, 231–232, 237
University of the Western Cape student 2, 24–25, 34, 51–53, 83, 87–96, 98–100, 102–109, 111–112, 128, 149, 160, 162–163, 197, 247
University of the Witwatersrand offer 173
NGO involvement 163–165
on white missionaries 46–49
on writing a memoir 1–3
World Bank seminar 152, 250
Yale Club debate with Stuart Saunders 145–146, 227
Zimbabwe research 155, 177
Jansen, Mikhail (son) 3, 144, 146, 149, 157, 169–170, 189–190, 200, 219–220, 246
Jansen, Naomi (sister) 6, 8, 44, 79
Jansen, Peter (brother) 6, 17, 36, 61, 70
Jansen, Sara-Jane (daughter) 3, 39, 91, 157, 189, 200, 219–220, 246
Jansen, Sarah Susan (née Johnson, mother) 1, 5–16, 18–20, 22–25, 27–31, 33, 36, 54, 58, 62, 65, 72, 77–79, 86, 106, 146–147, 185, 247, 249–250, 261
Jason, David 66
Jessie (Aunt of Grace Jansen) 171
J Henry Meyer Library 151
Jobs, Steve 132
Johnson, Colin 96
Johnson, Grandpa (Sarah's father) 8, 30
Johnson, Gollie (Goliath) 19, 36, 39
Johnson, Johnny 29
Johnson, Kulsum (Sarah's mother) 30
Johnson, Mauritz 143

Index

Jonker, Lewis 89–90, 112
Jonker, Mr (principal) 112, 115
Joorst, Mr (teacher) 69
Joy (Brethern student at UWC) 92

Kadalie, Rhoda 95
Karim, Quarraisha 239
Karim, Salim 239
Kat (Mikhail's partner) 190
Keet, André 197, 205–206
Keuzenkamp, Carike 184–185
Kgosana, Philip 123
Khoi(san) 45, 60
Kies, Bennie 119
Kieswetter, Edward 129
King, Bruce 158
King, Martin Luther 27, 83, 140
Kirkpatrick, Jeane 153
Kissinger, Henry 241
Knowledge and Power in South Africa: Critical perspectives across the disciplines 156
Knowledge in the Blood 93, 194, 248
Knowles, Alan 63
Kuhn, Thomas 151, 250
Kyalami student residence 222

land redistribution 208
Lange, Lis 197, 215
Lather, Patti 158
Learning Lessons 1
Learning Under Lockdown 246
Lennert, Ernie 120
Leonard, Cecil 95–96
Letters to my Children 188, 245
'liberation now, education later' 77
Liberation Theology 93
Lion's Historian, The 80
Livingstone High School 21, 27, 76
Lochner, Mr (school principal) 74
Logan (Brother) 46
Long, Wahbie 80
Luck (Elder) 41

Macozoma, Saki 142
Madonsela, Thuli 251
Maitland conference 48
Makhathini (Free State unionist) 217
Makhetha, Choice 197
Making Love in a War Zone 218
Malema, Julius 203–205
Mandela, Nelson 76, 104, 140, 166, 183, 194, 199, 205, 208, 216, 223
Mangaliso, Mzamo 139
Manganyi, Chabani 173, 178
Mangosuthu University of Technology (MUT) 189, 204
Manuel, Trevor 129
Margie, Aunt 13
Marincowitz, John 125
Marks, Eva (née Jansen) 32
Marks, Joey 46
Marks, Martin 27, 86
Marlene (Trafalgar High School student) 127
Marshall, Alex 125
Martin (school caretaker) 64
Marxist-Leninism 155
Matthews, James 76
Maxwell, John 136
Mayosi, Bongani 239
Mbata, Congress 144
Mbeki, Thabo 235
Mbembe, Achille 237
McLaren, Peter 158
McCarthy, Catherine 172
McClintock, Barbara 144, 228
McConnell, Frank 99
McGinn, Noel 148
Mehl, Merlyn 96
Mellon Foundation 227
Menlo Park High School 184
Meyer, Ivan 117
Millman, Jason 148
Mitchells Plain 123–124, 127
Mohamed, Ismail Jacob (Josef) 95
Mohanty, Chandra 143
Mohlahleli, Maria 164
Mokgoro, Job 140
Montagu 5, 7–8, 27, 30–31, 77–79
Moodie, Gill 1
Moodley, Strini 92
Moore, Ernest 59
Moore, Patience 21
Moore, Rosalind (née Flanders) 6, 21, 51
Moore, Sam 6
Moore, Walter 21
Morag (Wattle Park camp warden) 47–48

Morgan, Nicky 197
Mosidi, Reuben 140
Motsoaledi, Aaron 235
Murray & Roberts 87

Nannucci Dry Cleaners 15
National Education Coordinating Committee (NECC) 193
National Party 228
National Research Foundation (NRF) 226, 234, 238, 252
national socialism 89
Nation on the Couch 80
Nazism, Nazi Germany 28, 51, 219, 236
Ndaba, David 139
Ndebele, Njabulo 223
New Generation of Academics Programme 231
Newkirk, Alan 72
Newkirk, Patrick 66
Nigerian students 154
Nkosi sikelel' iAfrika 139
Non-European Unity Movement 77, 88, 123, 125
Non-Government Organisations (NGOs) 163–164, 225, 246
Noorder Paarl High School 27
Normaal Kollege Pretoria 180, 231
North-West University 199, 216, 219
No Student Hungry campaign 246
Nottingham University 238
Novak, Joseph 134, 136–137, 142–143
Ntataise 164
Nuremberg trials 199
Nyokong, Tebello 237

Ogbu, John 159
Ohio State Fair 140–141
Okkies (school athlete) 66
Oliphant (Brother) 45–46
Oliphant, Joy 45
On Becoming a Scholar 234
Onwu, Gilbert 237
Organized Spaces 246
Oscar Mpetha High School 132, 221
outcomes-based education (OBE) 251
Oxford University 228

Pacaltsdorp 9, 31, 33
Packard, David 154
Pan Africanist Congress (PAC) 139
Pandor, Naledi 188, 233, 235
'paradigm shift' 151
pass laws 123
Patty, Sandi 140
Pauling, Linus 228
Peacock (Elder) 38
Pentecostal church(es) 34–35, 195
Persens, Jan 96–97
Phimister, Ian 238–239
Phoenix High School, Manenberg 149–150
Pieterse, Cosmo 119
Pienaar, Christina 103
Pienaar, Kristo 102–103
Pilate, Pontius 49
Plymouth Brethren 36; *see also* Brethren
Porter Reformatory 70–71
Posner, George 142–143, 148
Potchefstroom University for Christian Higher Education 199
Potgieter, Mr (teacher at Trafalgar High School) 134
Poyo, Mr (science teacher) 73
PPE (politics, philosophy and economics) 228
P-rated science 239, 253
Pretoria Boys High School 190
Pretoria News 200
Princess Bioscope 11
Princeton University 160
Prohibition of Mixed Marriages Act 48, 56
Pythagoras 74

Quibell family 11
Quint, Dr 69–70

race, racism ix, 3, 46–47, 49, 55–57, 60, 75, 78, 88–89, 113, 132, 158, 170, 175, 177, 182, 184, 187, 192–193, 195–196, 198–200, 204, 206, 208, 211–212, 214, 218–219–220, 253–256
Rademeyer, Phoebe 7
Radio Sonder Grense 183
Raglyn (school friend of author) 80

Ralepelle, Chiliboy 190
Ramadan 57–58
Ramashala, Mapule 171–172
Ramirez, Chiqui 156–157
Rand Afrikaans University 228
Rapport 183
Reagan, Ronald 146, 153–154
reconciliation 50, 193, 198–203, 205–210, 213, 216–219, 261
Reddy, Jairam 107, 162, 167
Reitz, FW 193
Reitz residence 193, 195–198, 206, 208, 212, 217–218
research and development 167, 223–224, 232–233, 245
Research Policy 246
Reservation of Separate Amenities Act 48
Rhodes, Cecil John 88, 145
Rhodes, Frank 145
Rhodes Fellowship 223
Rhodes University 144, 228
Rietbron 17–18
Ritchie, Victor 129
Rive, Richard 76
Rodney (church friend of author) 79
Rose (Rosalind, Aunt) 51
Rozenhof Guest House 190
Rwanda genocide 211

Sacred Songs and Solos 37
Sagan, Carl 144, 228
Sakinari (school athlete) 66
Salovey, Peter 179
Samuel, John 197, 205–206
San 60
Saunders, Stuart 145–146, 227
Savio College 130–131, 133
Schaum series (mathematics) 101
Schroeder, Inspector 112, 116
science education 90, 97, 121, 134, 144, 152, 187, 232
Sen, Amartya 238
Senghor, Léopold 206
Senzeni Na? 139
Shaik (Trafalgar High School student) 127
Shaka 170
Shaw, George Bernard 59, 77
Sheffield University 238
Sheldon, Abe 106
Sheldon, Maureen 106
Shivambu, Floyd 205

Shulman, Lee 153
Singh, Mala 168–169
Sizer, Nancy Faust 212
Sizer, Theodore 212
Skinner, Jan 89
Skotaville Publishers 156
Slabber, GP 101
Sledge, Percy 69
Slingers, Apollis 'Polly' 119–120
Smit, John 190
Smock, Bob 145
Smock, David 133, 145
Society for the Prevention of Cruelty to Animals (SPCA) 121
Solomon, Japie 247
Solomon, Jean 73
Song for Sarah 1
South African Council of Churches 142
South African Democratic Students Movement (Sadesmo) 204, 208
South African Democratic Teachers Union 221
South African Human Rights Commission (SAHRC) 201, 203
South African Rugby Union 103
South African Students Congress (Sasco) 204, 208
South West Africa People's Organisation (Swapo) 153
Soweto student uprising 83, 116, 139, 214
Spes Bona High School 90, 130
Stanford African Students Association (Sasa) 150, 153–154
Stanford International Development Education Center (Sidec) 152, 158
Stanford Teacher Education Program 149, 151
Stanford University 28, 122, 148–156, 159–160, 162–163, 176, 223, 227, 236, 240, 249, 258
Stanford Workshops on Political and Social Issues (Swopsi) 153
Steenberg High School 7, 28, 38, 52, 63–78, 80, 82, 116, 148

268

Index

Steenberg Primary School 82
Steenveld, Ernie 'Snoekie' 120, 122–125
Stellenbosch University 58, 80, 84, 100, 103, 105, 171, 181, 223, 235, 257, 270
Stober, Mr (principal) 59–60
Stott, John 52
Strike, Kenneth 148
Structure of Scientific Revolutions, The 151
student protests 1980s 109, 114–115
Student Representative Council (SRC) 141–142, 145
Students are Watching, The 212
South Peninsula High School 71–72
Sullivan Leon 155
Sullivan Primary School 59, 62–63
Sullivan Principles 154–155
Swart, Sandra 80

Tabata, IB 114
Tarzan 140
Teachers' League of South Africa (TLSA) 123
Teaching in and Beyond Pandemic Times 246
Terrence (son of Aunt Doris) 23
Theron, Erika 105
Thomas, Alex 70–71
Thomas, Gladys 76
Toffler, Alvin 248–249
Toweel (boxing family) 61
Trafalgar High School ('Trafs') 76, 119, 121, 123–126, 128–135, 222
tricameral parliament 104
Triegaardt, Dwight 90
Truth and Reconciliation Commission 199
Tutu, Desmond 133, 145, 174, 201, 205, 216, 247

United Democratic Front (UDF) 46, 99, 104
United Nations Educational and Training Programme for Southern Africa 142
University of Cape Town (UCT) 75, 80, 88–89, 91, 103, 123, 129, 145–146, 188, 222, 228, 230, 237
University of Durban-Westville (UDW) 162–163, 165–172, 175, 177, 207
University of Fort Hare 165
University of Natal 165, 167
University of Port Elizabeth 228
University of Pretoria (UP) 91, 173–179, 181–185, 187, 189–191, 195, 207, 227, 229, 231, 237
University of South Africa (Unisa) 112–113, 171, 175, 180, 210, 229–230
University of the Free State (UFS) 59, 131, 186, 191–223, 225, 227, 229, 231–233, 237–238, 240, 246, 254
University of the Western Cape (UWC) 2, 24–25, 34, 51–53, 83, 87–96, 98–100, 102–109, 111–112, 128, 149, 160, 162–163, 197, 247
University of the Witwatersrand 173, 188, 223, 228, 230, 237
University of Wisconsin-Madison 143, 148
University of Zimbabwe 257–258
US Agency for International Development (USAID) 163–164

Vaal University of Technology 230
Van der Merwe, JC 197
Van Gogh, Vincent 109
Van Harte, Edna 139
Van der Ross, Richard 104–105
Van Reenen, Dionne 215
Van Zyl, Johan 173–174
Veldfokus 102
Verwoerd, Hendrik 105
Violet (Aunt) 31–33
Vishuis residence (UFS) 218
Visser, Danie 234
Volksblad 212, 214
Volmink, John 133
Von Gruenewaldt, Gerhard 226
Vredenburg Secondary School 109, 127, 131

Walker, Decker 153
Walker, Melanie 238
Ward, E 64–65
Wattle Park camp 47
Wayne, John 148
We Gon' Be Alright: Notes on Race and Resegregation ix
Weitz, Frans 94
Welcome Estate assembly 54
We Need to Act 245
We Need to Run 245
We Need to Talk 245
West, Cornel 162
Weston High School; *see* Vredenburg Secondary School
Westover, Tara 247
Westerford High School 131
Western Civilisation 160
Westville Junior Primary School 170
Willem, Uncle 25
Williams, Clive 66
Winfrey, Oprah 15, 248, 254
World Alliance of Reformed Churches 93
World Bank 152, 250
Wynberg Conference 47–48

xenophobia 258
Xenopus laevis 97
Yale Club 145–146, 227
Yale University 143, 179

Zimbabwe 155, 177, 222, 258
Zimbardo, Philip 228
Zwaanswyk Primary School 60

About the author

JONATHAN JANSEN is distinguished professor of education at Stellenbosch University. The eldest son of a preacher and a nurse, he grew up on the Cape Flats in a conservative evangelical church which shaped his values for good and bad. He was a biology teacher in the Cape before studies abroad, then returned to leadership in South African universities. Relieved of administration, he now does what professors are supposed to do: think. His family makes him possible and he lives for his two amazing granddaughters.

www.ingramcontent.com/pod-product-compliance
Lightning Source LLC
Chambersburg PA
CBHW062047080426
42734CB00012B/2578